A DREAM ABOUT LIGHTNING BUGS

A DREAM ABOUT

LIGHTNING BUGS

A Life of Music and Cheap Lessons

BEN FOLDS

BALLANTINE BOOKS | NEW YORK

Published in the United States by Ballantine Books, an imprint of
Random House, a division of Penguin Random House LLC, New York.

BALLANTINE and the HOUSE colophon are registered trademarks of
Penguin Random House LLC.

LIBRARY OF CONGRESS CATALOGING-IN-PUBLICATION DATA
Names: Folds, Ben, author.
Title: A dream about lightning bugs : a life of music and
cheap lessons / Ben Folds.
Description: First edition. | New York : Ballantine Books, [2019] | Identifiers: LCCN
2019011730 (print) | LCCN 2019012936 (ebook) | ISBN 9781984817280 (ebook) |
ISBN 9781984817273 (hardcover)
Subjects: LCSH: Folds, Ben. | Rock musicians—United States—Biography.
Classification: LCC ML420.F656 (ebook) | LCC ML420.F656 A3 2019 (print) | DDC
782.42166092 [B]—dc23
LC record available at https://lccn.loc.gov/2019011730

Printed in the United States of America on acid-free paper

randomhousebooks.com

2 4 6 8 9 7 5 3 1

First Edition

Book design by Susan Turner

For Emma

CONTENTS

FILE UNDER "MUSIC"

MUSIC FEELS LIKE THE FRAME ON WHICH I'VE HUNG NEARLY EVERY recollection, giving me access to large files of childhood memories. Each song, each note, has a memory attached to it. Just a few bars of the saxophone intro of "The Girl Can't Help It," by Little Richard, and out of nowhere I can see the towering leg of my father's gray sweatpants passing. I can almost feel the crusty scar of the radiator burn on my forearm and smell the creosote of asphalt shingles. The song "Puff, the Magic Dragon" brings back the texture of the dirty linoleum floor, the spinning of the colorful label of the 45-rpm record, and the window-lit specks of dust on their journey around my room. These memories are from when I was two years old. That's a lot of detail to recall from so far back. Either that or I have a good imagination.

I recently asked my mother if it was accurate to say that I was listening to a couple hours of music a day when I was two years old, and she said no. It was more like eight hours—splayed on the floor at my record player, organizing my records into neat stacks and just listening. And I would become an absolute irate little jackass when interrupted. Eight hours, damn. That's obsessive, but then, some things never change. It's also a lot of input and stimulation for such a young brain.

I happen to believe that all the music I listened to in my toddlerhood has served as a memory tool of sorts. Maybe it's why I can accurately describe the floor plan of our house on Winstead Place in Greensboro, North Carolina. Where all the furniture was placed, where the Christmas tree was, which radiator to avoid ever touching again, the jar of salt I would never ever again mistake for sugar, and the small black-and-white TV playing a rocket launch from Cape Kennedy. We left that house in Greensboro when I was three. In fact, we moved nearly every year of my childhood and I can tell you these sorts of things about each house we lived in.

Neurologists and music therapists are increasingly convinced of the effect of music on the brain. A music therapist friend of mine likes to say that "Music lights up the brain like a Christmas tree." She's referring to the large regions of brain scans that *light up* when stimulated by music. Other important functions, like speech, activate far smaller areas. In fact, there is an observable physical difference between a musician's brain and everyone else's. Here, I googled this for you, so you wouldn't think I was crazy.

Using a voxel-by-voxel morphometric technique, [neuroscientists have] found gray matter volume differences in motor, auditory, and visual-spatial brain regions when comparing professional musicians . . . with a matched group of amateur musicians and non-musicians.
—From "Brain Structures Differ between Musicians and Non-Musicians," Christian Gaser and Gottfried Schlaug, *Journal of Neuroscience,* October 8, 2003

But neuroscience is not my area of expertise, and this is not a book of science or facts. This is a book about what I know. Or what I think I know. It's about music and how it has framed and informed my life, and vice versa. About the stumbles, falls, and other brilliant strokes of luck that brought me here.

A DREAM ABOUT LIGHTNING BUGS

HERE'S A DREAM I HAD WHEN I WAS THREE YEARS OLD. IT'S THE FIRST dream I can remember. It was set in one of those humid Southern dusks I knew as a kid. The kind of night where I'd look forward to the underside of the pillow cooling off, so I could turn it over and get something fresher to rest my head on for a good minute or so. The old folks described this sort of weather as "close." In my dream, a group of kids and I were playing in the backyard of my family's home in Greensboro, North Carolina. Fireflies—"lightnin' bugs," as the same old folks called them—lit up in a dazzling succession and sparkled around the backyard. Somehow, I was the only one who could see these lightnin' bugs, but if I pointed them out, or caught them in a jar, then the others got to see them too. And it made them happy.

This was one of those movie-like dreams and I recall one broad, out-of-body shot panning past a silhouetted herd of children, with me out in front. There was joyous laughter and a burnt sienna sky dotted with flickering insects that no one else could see until I showed them.

And I remember another, tighter shot of children's faces lighting up as I handed them glowing jars with fireflies I'd captured for them. I felt needed and talented at something.

Now, this dream wasn't any kind of revelation. Hell, I was barely three years old. And although it's stuck with me all these years, I've never taken it to be a message from above that I'm a chosen prophet, or Joseph from *Joseph and the Amazing Technicolor Dreamcoat*. However, a half century later, it's obvious to me that the dream reflects the way I see artistry and the role of an artist. At its most basic, making art is about following what's luminous to you and putting it in a jar, to share with others.

Here you go. A melody. See? I found it. It's always been right there. That's why it's so familiar. Maybe it was in the rhythm of the washing machine, the awkward pause in a conversation, or the random collision of two radio stations blasting from two different cars and how it reminded you of your parents trying to be heard over one another. Remove a note, one flicker, and it's the sound of the door closing for the last time and her footsteps fading into the first silence in forever. But wait . . . nope, the silence wasn't really silence after all. You just weren't paying attention. There's always sound beneath the sound you hear. Or something else to see when your eyes adjust. It turns out there was also the sound of children playing outside your window and, below that, the buzz of a ceiling fan. That's a sound you'd overlooked before, but now it's all you can hear. We all see different flickers in a busy sky.

That's where the melodies live. What do *you* notice that glows beneath the silence? Can that glow be bottled, or framed? From time to time, we all catch a split-second glance of a stranger in a storefront window before realizing it's our own reflection. A songwriter's job is to see *that* guy, not the one posing straight on in the bathroom mirror.

As we speed past moments in a day, we want to give form to what we feel, what was obvious but got lost in the shuffle. We want to know that someone else noticed that shape we suspected was hovering just beyond our periphery. And we want that shape, that flicker of shared life experience, captured in a bottle, playing up on a big screen, gracing our living room wall, or singing to us from a speaker. It reminds us where we have been, what we have felt, who we are, and why we are here.

We all see something blinking in the sky at some point, but it's a damn lot of work to put it in the bottle. Maybe that's why only some of us become artists. Because we're obsessive enough, idealistic enough, disciplined enough, or childish enough to wade through whatever is necessary, dedicating life to the search for these elusive flickers, above all else. Who knows where this drive comes from? Some artists, I suppose, were simply cultivated to be artists. Some crave recognition, while others seek relief from pain or an escape from something unbearable. Many just have a knack for making art. But I'd like to think that most artists have had some kind of dream beneath the drive, whether they remember it or not.

I'm amazed when someone sees the sculpture inside a rock while the rest of us just see a rock. I say "hell yes" to the architects who imagine the spaces we will one day live in. And a round of applause for the stylist who sees what hair to cut to make me look respectable for a couple of weeks. I bow low and fast in the direction of those who paint amazing things on the ceilings of chapels, make life-changing movies, or deliver a stand-up routine that recognizes the humor in the mundane. What all those artists have in common is that they point out things that were always there, always dotting the sky. Now we can take it in and live what we missed.

My dream about lightning bugs still fills me with the same pride and sense of purpose as it did when I was three. It reminds me that my job is to see what's blinking out of the darkness and to sharpen the skill required to put it in a jar for others to see. Those long hours of practice, the boring scales, the wading through melodies that are dead behind the eyes in search of the ones with heartbeats. And all that demoralizing failure along the way. The criticism from within, and from others, and all the unglamorous stuff that goes along with the mastering of a craft. It's all for that one moment of seeing a jar light up a face.

And, sure, sometimes someone tells me I'm great or stuffs a dollar into my G-string. I can't say it's not about me sometimes too. I've done well. But that's not really what drives me. That's not what it's really all about. It's not about immortality either. I accept that one day, my music will be gone forever. So will the Sistine Chapel, Bruce Lee movies, and all the silly arts and crafts my aunt ever bought. Gone with the wind. Making songs is something I do here and now. Because light captured is just a moment, a flicker. Like any musical performance, it's not repeatable, but there is always another. As each of my thousands of gigs has let out, the crowds have gone their separate ways. The lid opens, the sun comes up, and the lightning bugs disappear into the light of day. Invisible again. Well after I'm gone, some kid will be chasing the flickering lights through the backyard in his dreams, joy at his heels.

WATCH ME EAT THIS SANDWICH

"Benjamin, how old are you?"
"I'm six! How old are you, Papa?"
"I'm twenty-six. Now, watch me eat this sandwich!"

DEAN FOLDS, MY FATHER, WAS, AND IS, A CHRONIC SMART-ASS. A CAR-penter, contractor, and building inspector a good seventy hours a week, the poor guy just didn't have time to watch me do every little thing under the sun. And I was a persistent and downright obsessive little shit. Anything I did or set my mind to, I wouldn't stop, couldn't stop, and it consumed the entire house. My brother, Chuck, wasn't like this, luckily for my parents. My relentless nature was a problem that neither reason nor punishment was able to solve. Putting the brakes on my focus or interrupting me would come at the expense of that night's sleep, for everyone. I was one of *those* children.

Papa discovered I could be neutralized by absurdity, frozen in my tracks by distraction with something out of left field. Absurdity comes naturally to Dean Folds, who has an endless supply of crazy shit up his sleeve for any

Dean Folds, my father, 1967

occasion. Before I could ask him to watch me stand on my toes, he'd hit me with, "Benjamin! Come here! Watch me take the trash out!" or "Mr. Ben! Mr. Ben! Come in here and watch this! Watch me brush my teeth!"

Who wants to watch anyone doing all that stuff? What a needy bastard! I thought, and just went somewhere else.

One evening I had cut Papa off at the pass in the hall as he was making his daily beeline from the pickup truck to the bedroom, still in his paint-streaked, muddy work clothes.

"Look at this!" I said, extending a sculpture of a face I'd made with Play-Doh, as far into the heavens toward his six-foot-two-ness as I could manage.

He leaned over to study it for a moment. Then he took my creation into his giant hands and stood back up, far away, close to the ceiling where the air was thinner, and began picking bits of it apart. He reconstructed its innocent smile into an evil one, with sharp jagged teeth and beady eyes. He took our frightening collaboration into my bedroom and placed it on a chair in the middle of the room. Then he turned the light out.

"He comes alive in the dark," Papa said, and disappeared into the bathroom.

Satanic Play-Doh man stood between me and the bedroom lamp, so I paced outside of my dark bedroom, trying to figure out how I'd ever get the light back on without being eaten.

Chuck came into the world when I was two but I don't remember my brother's arrival somehow. I was completely lost in my own world, where I remained for most of my childhood. And poor Chuck had no idea what he'd gotten himself into when he joined the family. Our entire youth was marked by *my* obsessions and *my* projects, scattered around the house. From my constant loud record-playing to my incessant piano-pounding later in grade school. Oh, and God help them all when I eventually got some drums. Not just because of the noise, but because I also would take them completely apart in our small house, leaving everyone to step over rims, lugs, and drumheads. Sadly, our parents were too busy to come to Chuck's defense and too tired to deal with me. When Chuck and I shared a room, it wasn't quite what you'd call "shared space." Chuck had to hide in a corner or go outside to get some peace.

My grandmother thought spending eight hours at the record player was pretty odd and sprang for a child psychologist when I was three. After the good doctor sat with me for an hour, he confirmed that I was slow and should be kept behind a year or two in school. But when my grandmother asked about the examination, Mama said, "It went great!" She even went a step further and insisted that the doc said I was *ahead* for my age, which of course left my grandmother scratching her head.

Mama, whose given name is Scotty, decided to ignore the shrink and allowed me to continue my full-time listening. She probably didn't have a choice anyway—I wasn't going to be stopped. She and I both remember nights when she would rush me from my room to the sofa in the living room at one in the morning to try and calm me down. I was quite the night screamer. She'd cover my mouth with her hand and rock me on her lap, whispering loudly, "Shhhh, Papa's been working all day and needs to sleep! Shhhhhh!"

I think that visit to the psychologist is what prompted Mama to start reading to me every night, something she did regularly for a few years. I became just as interested in reading Greek mythology, memorizing and organizing the gods and the mortal characters, as I was in sorting my 45-rpm records. It's like the way some little boys memorize all the Pokémon characters. Soon I loved astronomy and took a shine to all things atomic. The table of elements was catnip for an obsessive little boy who liked lists and numbers. A few years later, Mama doubled down on her objection to the doctor's prognosis, starting me in first grade a year early. I was the youngest one in the class. My hyper-focus and inability to deal with interruption, along with a variety of other odd behaviors, might have easily been seen as a sign of something to worry about. But my parents never made me feel there was anything wrong with me.

Mama herself had an artistic streak, which didn't fit neatly in a world of the Southern working class and the filthy-mouthed construction workers who often featured in our lives. She became a defense attorney of sorts for my creative leanings, exposing me to music, taking me to youth orchestra, and validating artistic interests that might otherwise have been deemed frivolous in a workingman's house. Because in the 1970s, in the blue-collar South, "artsy" things would normally have been written off as being "for queers." She recognized that I had art in my bones and I think that's why she defied the child psychologist. It was in defense of creativity. She saw my flunking of the doctor's test as proof of my imagination. I reminded her of herself.

My mother wasn't a stage mom or anything, though. I don't remember my parents ever telling me to practice. When I began piano and drums in fourth grade, I became my own taskmaster. My parents bent in the wind like reeds as I terrorized the household with painfully long sessions of repeated phrases at the piano or snare drum. And I had horrible temper tantrums when I felt I wasn't getting it right. Breaking of furniture, thrown sticks, shredded music.

I'm not aware of anyone else in my family who played music seriously. Well, there was my aunt Sharon, who I hardly viewed as a

My mother, Scotty Folds, 1967

musician at all. In my young unearned snobbery, I wrote her off. But actually she'd majored in music. I thought she had an awful warble of a voice and a rushing brutish tone on the piano, and I distanced my-self from her as I learned music. The feeling turned out to be mutual. When I began playing piano and making up songs, Aunt Sharon told me my music was noise pollution and that I didn't need to bother writing songs, because "no good music has been made since the nine-teenth century." We had forgotten the art of composition long ago, she said, and a piano-pounding nine-year-old wasn't going to be the one to revive it. Despite all this, I should mention that she *did* show me how to notate one of my songs and she explained what a key center was, and that was certainly something. A big something. She also spent a lot of her life documenting shape-note singing in the Appalachians, so hey there, young Ben—chill about this woman. She's your aunt, for Christ's sake. And she made a difference. And then there was my uncle Jim, who had a knack for music and had learned a few Leon Russell piano riffs by ear. He never had lessons or training, but it was helpful to see an adult enjoying music. He also took great interest in the songs I wrote when I was just a kid, and that went a long way.

Mama was, and is, a talented visual artist but never a lover of the spotlight. Around the time I was in kindergarten, she put some of her stuff in local art contests and won. She began to get a lot of interest in her work, which was very exciting. At least Papa thought so, and he started planning how they could make a business of selling her art. Imagine that! Art putting food on the table! Right up there with honest work! But upon being offered money for her watercolor paintings, she quit making art altogether. She didn't make another piece that I'm aware of for at least three decades. She recently returned to her art, but she sticks to markers on a dry-erase board. Wax on, wax off. She drags an eraser over it when she's done, and it's gone.

Chuck on the left. Me on the right, putting a record on my doggie-themed turntable, 1972.

ERASE AND REWIND

I NEVER MET EITHER ONE OF MY GRANDFATHERS, BUT BOTH MY GRAND-mothers were a strong presence in my life. They were each widowed very young, so Mama and Papa had single working mothers and tragic fathers in common. My grandmother on my father's side was Emma, and to my brother and me, she was Ma-Maw. Ma-Maw looked a lot like Loretta Lynn. She wore a different-color wig each day, piled high like Marge Simpson's. She had a massive boob job in her fifties, took disco lessons, and taught me "the Hustle"—a popular 1970s' disco dance that had its own song. Or maybe it was the other way around. She and her second husband, Rocky, lived in an apartment, and for a few years, in a trailer park. That was my favorite. Their double-wide trailer had mirrors on each interior wall to make it look bigger. It made four people look like sixteen, which is why it was my favorite.

Back in the 1940s, a fifteen-year-old Ma-Maw married my bio-logical grandfather, Glenn Folds. He was, by most accounts, good-looking and extremely charming. Glenn was a traveling John Deere tractor salesman from the metropolis of Martinsville, Virginia, who, at thirty-five years old, swept teenaged Ma-Maw off her hillbilly feet, rescuing her from a life in a poor coal-mining town in West Virginia. And, yes, it all sounds quite romantic, up until the part where Glenn turns out to be a mentally ill child abuser.

When Papa was a young boy, Glenn used to say some scary shit to him at bedtime, like, "Tonight's the night. I'm going to take us all to see Jesus." And then he just sat by the bed with a knife, or a gun, staring. He often told Ma-Maw that after taking the kids to "see Jesus" he would turn the barrel next on her and then himself. It would be awesome. They would all be together in heaven.

I heard these stories straight from Ma-Maw. When I was in college, I decided to drop by her place with a notebook and interview her about Glenn, because his name was never uttered in our house and I wanted to know more about him. She was surprisingly open about it all, recounting some really incredible, funny, and tragic stories. Over the course of our all-day interview, my perception of Ma-Maw, and time itself, shifted. She became a young lady for whom many days and years had passed. I'd always thought grandmothers were born old. It was one of those rare times when the past suddenly seemed present.

Ma-Maw seemed very comfortable with her humble beginnings, her class, and who she'd decided to become. She apologized to no one for her daily wigs or her fake boobs. She didn't try to pretend it was her real hair and her real body. She owned it. She always reminded me of Dolly Parton that way, never making a secret of the "work" she'd had done.

Ma-Maw felt that my father survived the ordeal of his abusive upbringing with his mind intact in part because Glenn mercifully disappeared for months on end, landing in jail in one state or another— once for beating up five cops on the side of a highway. His absence was a respite, a break from the abuse. But it also left Ma-Maw a struggling single working mother. One morning, while Ma-Maw was busy working overtime at a drugstore, my father was accidentally shot with a .22 rifle while camping with friends and nearly died. He was fifteen years old. The local Greensboro newspaper, assuming he would be dead by time of printing, prematurely ran my father's obituary, making Papa one of the few who could quote Mark Twain, "The rumors of my death have been greatly exaggerated," and not be joking.

The doctor, who had come straight from treating wounded soldiers in the jungles of Vietnam, said that three-quarters of Papa's lungs would need to be removed in the morning, barring some kind of miracle. So Ma-Maw, who was quite creative, sat at Papa's hospital bed the whole night, prompting him to visualize little ants crawling into his lungs, taking the infection out piece by piece. All night, Papa dreamed of the ants taking out the bad and bringing in the good. By morning, his condition improved enough to avoid lung removal. Papa believes he was healed by creative visualization, the power of the mind. Ma-Maw, who later converted to Mormonism, changed her story a little, and would later chalk it up to the power of Jesus.

As a teenager, Papa worked to distance himself from his father, who would often drop into his life at school or work and embarrass him somehow. Much later, when I was six, Glenn appeared at our house unannounced. I was asleep, so I missed it, but it seems Glenn made a move on my mother (!) when Papa left them alone for five minutes to go to the bathroom. Papa threw him out and told him that if he came around again, he would kill him. Dean Folds is pretty dry, matter-of-fact, and convincing without ever raising his voice. Not long after that incident, Glenn Folds hanged himself in a motel. Papa didn't attend the funeral, taking us instead to play Putt-Putt across from the mall.

My grandmother on my mother's side was Lois. My brother and I called her Grammy. Her first husband, Charles Kellam, my grandfather, was in the furniture business in High Point, North Carolina. A former North Carolina statewide high school wrestling champion standing five foot five, my grandfather is remembered for performing handstands on two Coke bottles—with his thumbs. I'm happy to remember him this way too, but I'm not sure I believe it. Sadly, Charles was a chronic alcoholic and died of liver complications at forty years old, just before my mother was born, leaving Lois to raise two girls alone.

With her reddish wavy hair and her dark skin tone, Lois claimed to be part Cherokee. Having grown up dirt poor in Missouri, before the Great Depression, Lois, ashamed of her beginnings, always struggled to rewrite her story, even awkwardly affecting the mannerisms of wealth. After Lois's death, my aunt Sharon got heavily into researching our ancestry and confirmed that Lois's father was actually of African descent, with no trace of Cherokee. Lois spent her life covering her redneck past and her mixed racial heritage. She chose to forget that her parents dropped her alone off at an orphanage while her brothers and sisters grew up at home. And she, in turn, did the same to my mother and her sister.

Mama was six years old. I always imagined that this dropping off was meant to be temporary, a way to get some space to restart Lois's life after her husband's death. Only, the months turned into years. Mama always called it a "boarding school," the way her mother had chosen to characterize it, but Papa would always correct that. "It was an *orphanage,* Scotty." It certainly was not a prep school in Connecticut full of rich kids. Photographs of Mama's orphanage, with its shacks on a lawn of trampled brown grass, were stored in a box along with other photos from the same era, of Lois taking flying lessons with a gaggle of wealthy male suitors. Her children safely installed in "boarding school," Lois eventually remarried, and Mama and Aunt Sharon returned to living at home at the end of high school.

Chuck and I were never dropped off at an orphanage. We were never beaten or threatened in bed with a knife, never left in the woods with guns. Those histories weren't mine. They were my parents' and their parents' histories. They might have been mine too if Mama and Papa hadn't each done such an impressive reset. They acknowledged their past, forgave it, perhaps learned from it, but they didn't try and rewrite it. They created a safe space, a clean slate, to bring up two kids.

With this clean slate came a naïveté, a lack of form and formality, and a sort of all-around skepticism of convention that defined my up-

bringing. Rules, routines, and rituals were out the window. A family walk could mean hopping over fences with DO NOT ENTER signs. Mama would often allow me to be late to school if my favorite song was about to play on the radio. On the rare times we all ate together, there was no set dinnertime. I can imagine this sort of upbringing wouldn't work for everyone. Some need borders and conventions more than others. And not everyone is a fan of improvisation.

As a result of my unusual upbringing, I was sent home from school many times for disregarding the rules, and the teachers seemed as frustrated with my parents as they were with me. But my parents did teach me to be a hard worker and to be polite, in a "do unto others" sort of way. My manners are pretty old school sometimes. To this day, I always rise to greet company, open doors for others in public, smile at and acknowledge everyone. "Please," "thank you," and a lot of "yes, ma'am" and "yes, sir" from a bygone Southern era, peppered with lots of "shits" and "fucks." I've always been an odd combination of polite, irreverent, hardworking, and utterly undisciplined.

My parents' era didn't make a high art out of child-raising like we do today. And Mama and Papa were barely twenty when I came along, still children themselves, so they were just winging it.

What the hell is this thing? A boy? Okay, put him in a cardboard box and let's do this!

Mama now seems mildly horrified by the photograph of the cardboard box that served as a cradle when I was an infant. I don't care, though. Why not? Cardboard is light, cheap, and disposable, like a cradle should be. Because babies aren't babies for long, and they don't know the difference anyway. Put a pillow up in that shit and your baby will sleep like . . . well, a baby. Anyway, I've included that photograph in the book for fun.

For equal and fair treatment, I've thrown in a nice shot of my father taking me for a drive when I was four months old. I was placed in catapult position in the front seat of a doorless convertible Jeep, with no seatbelts. Papa, driving, and my uncle Jim in the back seat, as they were off to play tennis. Papa admits there was also a six-pack of

Budweiser beer in the paper bag in the back seat. At least there was a nice hard-plastic baby car seat for me. Still, no straps or seatbelt attachments, no door.

Cardboard boxes were a big part of childhood. We moved so often that we never got around to unpacking all the boxes before moving to the next place. All of this moving was part of my parents' livelihood. Besides their multiple day jobs, they built houses where we would live temporarily until some kind of tax period passed, at which time they could be sold for a profit. And the moves themselves were as informal as the rest of our life. I remember blankets being thrown over a desk, so we could move the desk and all its surface contents at once. Sometimes it's just more efficient to leave everything on top of the furniture and go. When we got to the new house, we removed the blankets and straightened the pencils, stapler, and the coffee cups. If something broke, we threw it away.

My family was constantly in motion, writing our own rules, while the surrounding neighbors, both the new ones and the ones we left behind, seemed permanently fixed. Fixed to their houses, their schedules, their churches, for generations past and to come. At least that was my perception. Their lives were writ on rock tablets, like in the cheesy paintings of Moses on their living room walls. Our life was more like Mama's dry-erase board.

Cardboard cradle

Uncle Jimmy, Ben, Papa, 1966

A WORKING-CLASS TOURIST IS SOMETHING TO BE

WINSTON-SALEM, NORTH CAROLINA, WHERE I SPENT MOST OF MY childhood, boasted as wide a spectrum of social class as anyplace in America in the 1970s. From the lower class right up to the top with everything in between. For a variety of reasons, I experienced them all, living, studying, and working my way through the whole spectrum.

We bounced from working-class to middle-class neighborhoods as we moved to a new house each year. I attended a thoroughly racially integrated school at the peak of Southern desegregation in the 1970s. And my time in youth orchestra and accelerated classes meant mixing with proper wealthy kids. In fact, Winston-Salem had an actual Old Money™ set, the kind that only really exists in select places in the South and cities in the northeast like New York or Boston, the rest of the country being too new for that. Winston-Salem was home to R. J. Reynolds Tobacco, purveyors of *all things nicotine*. That's where Winston cigarettes, Salem cigarettes, and Camels come from. Hanes underwear, Krispy Kreme, and more industry than you could shake a hauserstick at started in Winston-Salem. Back in the 1920s, Winston-Salem was even chosen as the site for the prototype of the Empire State Building, the more diminutive Reynolds Building. All this industry meant that Winston-Salem was also home to a lot of factory workers. "Millionaires and mill rats" living "side by side," as my song "Jackson Cannery" goes (from *Ben Folds Five,* 1995).

Darting around all these social classes, I did a lot of observing. I now think of myself as a social-class tourist—learning a little about each, but never quite at home in any of them. One day I was the nervous poor kid who didn't know which was the salad fork, the next I was worried I'd get beat up for talking too fancy around the country kids. Little habits and words from one class rubbed off on me, giving it away that I didn't belong to the other. I came to see being a part of any class, like any club, as being trapped. And I liked to roam. My family never traveled geographically outside of North Carolina, but I felt like a world traveler. Laugh all you want at their Hawaiian shirts and high black socks, but a tourist gets to appreciate and enjoy all the things the locals take for granted. And it can be a little lonely, but such is the perspective of a songwriter, and this kind of upbringing was excellent training ground.

Yes, my family lived in some redneck neighborhoods, and yes, it's true that there was a gun in every corner of our house. There were houses with yards stacked with old tires and neighbors who threatened to shoot each other because a dog knocked over their trash. Once, a redneck neighbor put a tiny pocket pistol against another redneck neighbor's forehead and actually pulled the trigger. But it didn't penetrate the skull. It just left the poor fellow's face black and blue for six months. I even went to a country dentist whose office was in a cinder-block house on the edge of a pasture. The sounds of mooing cows could be heard outside the window as I looked up at a stained foam-tile ceiling, with country music blasting out of a transistor radio.

This old farmer of a dentist filled fourteen cavities in one week after I got my braces off, one after the other with no novocaine or painkillers. I sensed he thought I looked too soft and *classy*—not quite football player enough.

"Son, you wanna learn how to be a real man?"

"I guess so," I answered.

"You think you can be a real man?" he drawled as he picked up his drill.

"Yes, sir." I shifted in the dentist's chair nervously, sensing I'd just accepted a challenge I wished I hadn't.

I squirmed, and tears streamed down my face, as he kept drilling into what felt like a bare-naked nerve. It was excruciating, and the sound of the drill matched the sensation a little too perfectly.

But I can't claim Springsteen-worthy working-class cred no matter how many anecdotes I might offer. Because unlike the legit working-class types I grew up with, I got to peek at the whole class menu. After my parents finished building a nicer house, we'd leave the working-class neighborhood behind and move to a middle-class development across town, where we'd live for a year until selling and starting the cycle all over again. It was hedgerows and foreign cars one year, and stacks of tires and American pickup trucks the next. I never quite got comfortable with the kids in one neighborhood before it was time to move on. And my parents often didn't get around to learning the names of the neighbors on either side. Papa would give them his own names, like "the Doorslammers" or "that prick across the street."

It turns out the nice neighborhoods had dog and trash-can disputes just like the redneck ones, but with their own middle-class twist, and minus the guns. A Wake Forest professor neighbor once pulled my father aside to show him a Polaroid. It revealed a blurry shadow of a dog in the night with Satan-like red-eye from the flash and two trash cans on their sides, garbage strewn about. It was *definitely* our German shepherd, insisted the professor, and he would have no choice but to use his black-belt karate skills on our dog next time this happened. My father laughed aloud at the man, and so Chuck and I joined in. These were the kinds of surreal middle-class suburban scenes that informed so much of my songwriting, and not just on the album entitled *Rockin' the Suburbs*.

For me, public schools and desegregation were a great gift. But there are many who grew up in my era in the South, black and white alike, who didn't have such a positive experience. I recently heard a radio interview with an African American woman around my age who felt the benefit was to the white kids, who got their little taste of diversity at the expense of the black students. For her it wasn't tourism. She was subject to what she described as a nightmare and felt like a guinea pig. I had never considered that angle, I admit, and it was an eye-opener to hear her speak about it. Just because you've blown through like a tourist, who can always go home when it's no fun anymore, doesn't mean you've experienced the people or the place.

I recall waiting for Papa in a "gun and coin shop" on the outskirts of town, looking at Indian Head pennies, and overhearing actual Klan dudes squinting down barrels and talking about who they'd like to shoot, dropping the N word left and right. But then they'd come over and tell me the history behind the "wheat penny," give me a piece of candy and even a pat on the head. I was only eight years old—I had no idea how to process this stuff. But at school, while showing my black friend Daryl the rare coin I got at such a shop, I certainly knew better than to tell him where I bought it and what had been said.

I didn't love every group I encountered. In fact, I'll be quite happy to never see gun-and-coin dude again. But I learned to stand in other people's shoes, as much as a child can. It's hard to view certain people as anything but monsters, yet there's value in giving it the old college try. By dignifying even the most despicable character as a human being, by offering them what empathy we can manage, we also hold them accountable for their choices. You can't really convincingly condemn a monster for being a monster. He's just being the best monster he can be. Sure, it's easier to make a caricature of someone you don't want to relate to, but the more lines you can step over, the closer you can get to a subject, the better off you'll be—and the more complex and effective your songwriting will be. From the filthy rich to the filthy minded, I learned to meet people one at a time. And for that I'm grateful.

Here's what I take away from facing the folly of class lines, what I learned as a child tourist and later as a songwriter:

Stand in as many pairs of shoes as you can manage, even ones you consider reprehensible or repulsive—even if it's just for a moment. If you're going to be a tourist, be a respectful one. Observe, report, imagine, invent, have fun with, but never write "down" to a character or their point of view, because everyone is the most important person in the world—at least to that one person. And if your tourist photographs suck, maybe it's because you're too far away from your subjects, seeing them only as props dotting the scenery.

Position yourself upon a bedrock of honesty and self-knowledge, so that your writing comes from *your* own unique perspective. Know where *you* stand and what *your* flaws are. Know thyself. Then you can spin all kinds of shit and all the tall tales you like. It's art.

Finally, empathy and perspective are everything, and neither should be taken for granted. After all, there's always someone out there who thinks *you're* the monster. Remember that the ground beneath your feet can always shift and that it should always be questioned.

Even the things that seem still
are still changing
—From "Still," *Over The Hedge* soundtrack, 2004

HALL PASS

WHEN I THINK OF MOORE LABORATORY SCHOOL, THE EXPERIMENTAL public school I attended from first to sixth grade, many smells come to mind. Like this overpowering yeasty bread smell that spilled out from the cafeteria. There was always the lingering of old mop water, and the smell of mimeograph paper, which is something I couldn't quite describe to anyone who didn't live in the 1970s. Let's just say it might be easily confused with the faint essence of barf always present at Moore School.

Many images come to mind too, which I associate with music on the radio at the time, like 10cc's "The Things We Do for Love," which played in my head as I wandered the halls. I see lots of louvered windows through which no breeze would pass and in which no fan would fit. I can see the cinder-block walls, top half painted white, bottom painted sky blue, plastered with kiddie art made of colored construction paper. I don't see chairs and desks, because there were none, aside from the teacher's desk, or the ones in the library. Instead, I see the hairless nasty green carpet on which we sat, usually cross-legged—"Indian style," as it was so crassly called back then. Most of our work was done in dry-erasable books and we made our way through them individually at our own pace, as teachers trolled their beats like geniuses at the Apple Store. We flagged them down when we had a question but were otherwise left alone until we were done, at which time a teacher with bad breath knelt down to check off your work. I usually finished well ahead of time and yearned to get up and move before my ass cheeks got any more numb. I would wander to my cubbyhole where I kept my stuff—my notebooks, pencils, a tube of glue, and tucked away beneath it all my prized stolen yellow laminated hall pass. With this hall pass I could wander with impunity whenever I got bored. I got bored a lot, and I guess I felt entitled to roam where I pleased.

When I first stole my yellow hall pass, the boys' room seemed like as good a place as any to loiter. Until one day when I shuffled in alone and nearly stepped in a pile of human doo-doo, curiously showcased on a paper towel in the middle of the green tiled floor, definitely on purpose.

Well, now, that's different, I thought.

Before I could process this odd bathroom art installation, a very weird child leapt from a dark stall and onto my back, screeching like a wild animal. *Cue seventies' karate-action-movie music.* We struggled from one side of the boys' room floor to the other. His mission was clearly to put my face in his fecal art project. There is a lot to avoid while wrestling a pervert in a filthy, tiled grade school bathroom. It was an awkward dance. But fear of eating shit inspires hidden strength, like in those superhuman feats you see in documentaries, where a 90-pound woman bench-presses a car off her sternum to free herself or her trapped child. I sent the pervert crying with a bloody nose and avoided getting brown on mine.

• • •

From then on, I would spend my stolen-hall-pass time in the safety of a warm library, manned by a bored adult who didn't seem to care that I wasn't in class. The school library had vinyl and headphones in a listening center with stacks of records, even a few rock-and-roll 45s. My favorite was "Ride Captain Ride." There were also lots of horribly politically incorrect joke books with titles like *Nine Hundred and Ninety-Nine Polack Jokes*. I shit you not. I wasn't sure what a Polack was, even though there were kids of Polish descent at our school. These Polacks, whoever they were, sure sounded absurd. There were a good five to ten of those terrible kinds of joke books to choose from. Here's the only joke I still remember:

"Why did the Polacks bring a bucket of dung to their wedding?"

"To keep the flies off the bride." Get it?

The seventies . . . jeez.

And you know what? I'm *still* a public school advocate. Because I would hate to see what kind of boring bastard I'd be now had I not

Self-portrait from sixth grade

been exposed to the rich range of absurdity that was Moore Laboratory School in the 1970s. The insensitive joke books in the school library, the nasty hard carpet, the stealth doo-doo attacks in the bathroom, and a system whose cracks I could slip through with yellow laminated stolen permission.

MEASURE TWICE, CUT ONCE

I WAS IN SECOND GRADE WHEN I REALIZED I WANTED TO PLAY PIANO. While waiting for my ride one day after school, I heard some incredible ragtime piano-playing down the hall. Peeking through the auditorium door, I watched with envy as fellow second-grader Anna Goodman (whom I married years later, and who co-wrote a handful of my songs) was laying down some badassed Scott Joplin, "Maple Leaf Rag."

That, I thought, *is what I want to do. Period.*

A couple of years later, when I was nine years old, my uncle and my father unloaded a piano from his 1950s beat-up Ford pickup one night and plopped it into the hallway. But it was bedtime, and I'd have to wait until the morning to try this piano out. With a small white transistor FM radio hidden beneath my pillow, I took note of all the songs I'd be playing in the morning—some that I heard on the radio, and some that I'd been making up in my head. It was a long, exciting, sleepless night.

When my parents' alarm went off the next morning, I ran straight to the hallway and began playing. Well, it wasn't playing. I just mashed incoherent noise into the keyboard until it was time for the school bus.

But this should be simple! I thought to myself. *The low notes on the left, graduating note by note to the high ones on the right. Easy . . . Right?*

But no. It would be *work* to learn this damn instrument. Fine. I guess I knew that. I had poked around on these pianos before. I supposed I'd just gotten carried away and dreamed a little too big. Oh well. If I had to figure this instrument out one note at a time, that's what I would do. It would suit my obsessive streak anyway. I knew that when I concentrated on something, I clung to it like a pit bull. I could work all day on something that held my interest.

From then on, I would space out through much of the school day, imagining music I wanted to play. Somehow I never went through the stage of learning to play my favorite radio music by ear. I didn't really have the building blocks for that anyway. Playing by ear is about building a vocabulary and connecting dots in a way I was never taught. I just learned through trial and error. When I was finally back at home at the piano, I would hack around in the harmonic darkness, rewarded with just enough discovery to inspire the imagination and more than enough frustration to propel me to improve. It was a cycle of imagining and practicing. The harder I worked at music, the more it sparked the imagination, and the more I imagined, the harder I had to work to keep up with my head. But the frustration of not being able to actually play what I heard in my mind led to terrible tantrums, which continued through high school. In fact, each time our family moved to another house, my main chore was always patching the holes in the walls of my bedroom, where I'd punched, kicked, or thrown things around the room like an idiot. I once punched drywall expecting to put a satisfying hole in it, but I hit a stud instead and broke my hand.

• • •

After a year of playing piano, I had written a good thirty complete instrumental songs, recorded them on a portable cassette recorder, and even placed them on staff paper. I had also learned a few silly songs for my first recital, like "Spinning Song" in my John Thompson book, a few other standard student piano hits of the time, and of course "Maple Leaf Rag" by Scott Joplin. But I only bothered with those because I hoped they would shed some light on how I might find my own ideas on the keyboard. I also knew these were pieces that the babysitter, who was my first teacher, struggled to play. Competition proved to be another motivator.

Much of my time in the summers and the afternoons after school was spent waiting around construction sites as my parents worked. Chuck was someone you could trust with a power tool at a young age, but I was not. Not at any age. Papa would remind me, "Benjamin, measure twice, cut once!" because I would often cut something the wrong length, having measured it too hastily. Realizing my mind wasn't in it, Papa might rethink the whole situation. "Ah. Fuck it, you're going to kill somebody with that goddamn saw, Benjamin!

One of the fancy new houses my parents built. A muddy lot in which to imagine songs.

Give me that. Here's a few bucks. Go to the 7-Eleven and get me a damn Pop-Tart or something." Sure, I was given tools sometimes— a broom, or maybe a rag—just not the kind that would put me or anyone else in danger, in case my mind wandered. And free to roam, my mind *did* wander. I spent those hours on construction sites making up songs in my head.

Of course, I also did kid stuff like everyone else. I liked to play sometimes. I wasn't a total weirdo. I might make a ramp out of plywood and rocks and try some Evel Knievel shit on my bike or find a kid to toss a baseball with. But mostly I walked around in the mud alone, imagining music: naïve, unfettered, unrestrained, and unedited music. When you're making music in your mind, it's okay if it's technically unplayable. It's even okay to hear instruments that don't exist. There's a time and a place for the tools, and the first tool is imagination.

I often think about how grade school art classes are taught. We start out by painting and drawing from our imagination, not by copying a Rembrandt. That comes later. Our earliest artwork is truly original expression, shitty as it may be. We imagine *first*. We often draw something we want to *communicate,* consciously or subconsciously. Play therapists use art as a safe way to let children explain what's going on in their lives and how they feel, because we understand that art is a means of communication.

But in music, for some reason, we begin by copying, by following, by learning to play existing music. That's certainly a good way to learn technique, but in the process it's easy to forget that music is a form of creative expression. In time, we come to believe that music is something that can only be composed by mystical figures we never meet, usually dead ones. But if you've really got something to say, and all of us do, you will want to learn the vocabulary. You will be frustrated and motivated to learn the technique. So why not teach and encourage a little of both, copying and creating?

Just laying here in the bed, half-awake, half-asleep
Thinking about you
I was wondering if you were looking after your most valuable
possession—
Your mind!

That's from a song called "Your Most Valuable Possession" on the Ben Folds Five album *The Unauthorized Biography of Reinhold Messner*. The lyrics are just some ramblings that my father, the same Dean Folds who urged me to measure twice, left on my answering machine as we were recording that album. He was on a lot of cough medicine, he says.

I continued my habit of pacing around and daydreaming about music well into adulthood. In my twenties I paced the front yard with a cereal bowl all morning, wearing only my boxer shorts, for all to see, imagining songs and arrangements.

I still work this way, minus the cereal bowl and boxers in the front yard. Sometimes I find it's best to sit and stare into space, or take a walk, or drop my hands to sit in silence at the piano. And wait.

Sometimes I don't actually hear defined music but just the distant impression of music. The sense that something is coming, like the sky darkening before the rain. I might get a chill, or even want to laugh. At what? I don't yet know. I'm embarrassed to admit this, but I even hear applause sometimes.

Like anyone, when I get impatient, and before I have a solid idea, I might rush straight for an instrument, hoping to stumble upon something that will lead the way. From the piano to an iPad—I can turn my brain off and just play something. That's fun sometimes, but remember that a menu of drum loops is far more limited than your imagination.

Here's my suggestion to musicians: When you're about to reach for whatever musical tools you use, virtual or real, guitar or computer, ask yourself if you're doing so to save time or because you don't feel like straining your brain. Or, more important, ask yourself if you have anything to say yet. If not, keep working (or playing) upstairs, in your brain. Sure, it's okay to react to what happens playing with the tools—the way a chord sounds, a loop, or even an accident. But make sure you express what *you* wanted to say or what you have imagined. Don't let your tools make you their bitch.

Measure twice, cut once. Resist the urge to skip steps. The limitations of the real world will soon impose themselves on your creation. Even the limits of your technique will cut your imagination down to size in time. So imagine wildly first. Or at least try to do so from time to time.

I'm grateful that the piano, the drums, the tape recorder, and the smartphone weren't immediately available to me as a kid. I'm thankful for the boring afternoons spent hanging out with bags of concrete and two-by-fours. I highly recommend enforced boredom as a way to develop your imagination. But don't take my advice; listen to Neil Young. He said it best: "There's a lot to learn for wasting time."

Writing songs while pacing outside—circa 1988

BIG EARS, THIN WALLS

MOST NIGHTS AT OUR HOUSE IT WAS LIGHTS-OUT AT A REASONABLE hour. Lying in bed, I'd hear the muffled tones of my parents' voices from the other side of our bedroom wall. On the odd occasion, the TV would stay on long enough into the night that I could hear local stations signing off with "The Star-Spangled Banner." But sometimes, usually on the weekends, things would get louder. Something fun was happening on the other side of the wall, like the night my father wrestled the morbidly overweight teenager from next door. There was a house-rattling thud and laughter, the sound of breaking furniture, some cursing, and the needle scratching loudly right off the turntable. Then more laughter. Who was winning? My father? Or the oversized kid?

I'd try and guess which adults had dropped over by their voices. Did I know them? How did they all know to come? None of it sounded planned. Maybe it started that afternoon with a few neighbors stopping by to watch a Muhammad Ali fight, with a party spontaneously building from there. They got louder and louder, and the conversations weren't the kind I ever heard in the daytime.

"All right, goddamn, Dean! Bet's on! If the wingspan of a condor isn't twelve feet or more, you'll kiss my ass right out on Glenwood Avenue!"

What? He can't mean that literally, I thought. But, then again, shit was getting crazy, so maybe he did. . . .

"You *know* you're wrong, Dean! You know it!! Right now, let's go outside! I'm gonna pull my britches down out on the goddamn street, so pucker up! Condor's wingspan my assssss!! . . ."

With big ears through thin walls, I listened to every detail as the speech got more slurred, happy, and dangerous. The music got louder, and the needle on the record player would often bounce out of its groove as clumsy feet shook the floor. A kid can begin to gather a lot about how music works, how a song unfolds, by just listening intently and putting the clues together. Dynamics, the loud and soft sounds. Accelerandos, crescendos, indicating excitement. The long mysterious silences, the intonation. Sonic stories.

But it wasn't an official parent party until they broke out the live comedy records. The 1970s were a golden age for comedy and comedy albums. I memorized every word through the bedroom wall. These comedy records are as close to a lullaby as I can recall. Only better. At seven years old I was often serenaded to sleep by George Carlin's routine about farting noises, which he classified as a "bilabial fricative." There were many other gems that my young mind could never un-hear, like, "Get the cross out cho pussy!" which was from Richard Pryor's reimagining of *The Exorcist,* as played by black people.

Laughter roared from the cheap Fisher speakers and from the adults in the living room. The audience on these old comedy records had a distinct and haunting sound. One that carried weight. It meant *something*! That much I could sense. It was the sound of catharsis in crazy times. The comedians seemed to be saying what everyone already knew. The laughter was a sort of "amen." It was a knowing laughter, a drunken and intense laughter. It was post-civil-rights-era laughter, post-Vietnam laughter, post-Watergate laughter. Not always an altogether optimistic sound. But it was the sound of people who proved they could survive and would do so again.

The intensity of these records still gives me chills. I think the comedy of the 1970s tells you as much about what society was going through at that time as the music of the 1960s did. Comedy was already starting to seem like the new rock and roll when I was a kid. And don't get me wrong, I love the music of the 1970s, but it had become big business. Rock music was performed in arenas now, but comedy was still intimate, lean and mean, honest, and the comedians seemed more like the outlaws. Indeed, my idea of rock and roll came in large part from those live comedy records my parents played after bedtime. I mimicked the comedians at school as much as I did the musicians. And I got in a lot of trouble for it. Trying out your own Richard Pryor– or Andy Kaufman–inspired comedy in second grade is not advisable.

It makes sense to me that the first notable entertainers to show up at Ben Folds Five gigs were comedians. I felt right at home with most comedians in a way I haven't always felt with musicians. I don't think the reason I relate to comedians and vice versa is that my music is funny or that I'm funny. Because I'm probably not that damn funny. That's not my job. But I sensed the weight of humor early on. I believe, to my core, that the saddest things are often best illuminated by humor, and I've always felt compelled to express emotion through a comic lens. The type of laughter can indicate the height from which we fear we may fall, the depths to which we could so easily plummet, and the effort required to retain composure in our darkest times. And, of course, sometimes life is just funny.

After a night of comedy, wrestling, and drunken bets, Sunday morning in the Folds household was for sleeping in. No Sunday school for us. I may not be able to recite prayers or sing hymns like many adults I know, who spent their youth at church, but I can reel off George Carlin's "Seven Words You Can Never Say on Television." And I know the wingspan of a condor is not twelve feet. Not even close.

A LINE AND SOME CLUES

ON A FROSTY JANUARY AFTERNOON IN 1977, AN ELEVEN-YEAR-OLD ME trudged his skinny cold ass down Peace Haven Road, squinting directly downward to avoid being stung by the horizontal snow. But I didn't need to look ahead to find my way. I had the recent trail of a bicycle tire to show me roughly where the sidewalk was. Someone else had done the hard work and all I needed to do was follow, head down. And so I fixed my gaze on this thin line in the snow and forged ahead.

Who rides a bike in this weather? I wondered. *For that matter, what kind of monster teacher insists their students wade to piano lessons in this shit?*

Mrs. Dyer, that's who. My new piano teacher, and I wasn't so sure I liked her. The other few teachers I'd had just let me goof off. My mother had fired the last teacher, the fun young guy who played rock, when she heard the lesson from outside the door. I'd spent the half hour showing *him* how to play a cool blues riff I'd made up. In fact, I carried that riff with me into adulthood and used it as a big one bar descending solo run in "Song for the Dumped" by Ben Folds Five, nearly twenty years later.

There would be no blues riffing around Mrs. Dyer. She was old and serious, and I thought she talked funny. It was a European accent, Mama said. Her house smelled strange from some kind of weird food. And she was the only one who had dared to torture me with scales, arpeggios, and all that pesky technique. She was just no fun at all.

Beethoven Sonata in G? I grumbled to myself. *How about "Cantina Band" from* Star Wars *instead? I don't think I like these Europeans. Old people can be so mean.*

The entire walk to Mrs. Dyer's was probably all of a half mile door to door, but the snow made it seem longer. Meanwhile, the thin bike tire began to occupy my imagination.

At first, the line was straight and controlled. Confident. But sometimes it would squiggle a bit and you could see the ghost of its second tire, revealing moments of uncertainty, loss of balance. A story was unfolding, I thought. I wanted to sneak a peek ahead, like glancing at the last page of a book, to see if I could spot the rider or any clues to their whereabouts, but I resisted the urge and kept my head down. This was the kind of entertainment a bored eleven-year-old could get lost in while nearly hypnotized by the sound of crunching snow or the rhythm of his own breathing. It reminded me of the sound at the end of a record before you lift the tonearm. In fact, the tire trail itself, as it passed beneath me, seemed like the groove of a record, and I was the needle. The needle doesn't know what's next. It just follows the groove and plays it as it comes.

The more clues I got about the rider, and where he'd stopped, the more interested I became. Maybe I knew him! Or maybe it wasn't a *him* at all. Maybe I'd find myself awkwardly face-to-face with some *girl*! That would be awful. I never knew exactly what to say to girls. I slowed a bit.

. . .

I want to laugh at how old-fashioned and easily entertained I must sound to a kid today, who has a lot more seductive electronic shit competing for their attention. But a story is a story, in any era. And the best ones, I've always thought, develop from mysteries you want to solve. You just have to take the trip to find out, following a simple line with some clues along the way. I like to think of songs that way. The sequence of the music is like the line in the snow, or the groove in a record. You put your head down, or you put the needle down, and ride it from beginning to end. But something has to propel you forward. A song, like any story, has to hold your interest with clues that are musically paced and poetically ambiguous enough to spark the imagination.

I remember listening intently to "Hotel California" on the radio at about this age. I was sure it was about someone who had died. There were clues. It seemed someone was trapped somewhere, maybe in limbo? The beat, the repetition of the chords, the music itself, was the thread that kept me on the path. And as I followed, listening to the radio in the back seat of the car, I came upon this:

You can check out anytime you like, but you can never leave!

Man! Whoa! That was it! That blew my tiny mind! Of course, there's nothing that special going on here—just some rock-and-roll poetry as interpreted by a child. But it's operating outside the literal in a way that sparked my interest, more than it would have had it been stated clearly. It's a five-minute trail of music with imagery scattered along the way.

I was now certain the singer of this song had passed into the nether world and was trapped in a place he couldn't escape, called— I didn't question why—the Hotel California. There was mention of heaven and hell. A spirit. Being greeted and led somewhere. He was witnessing some kind of ritual or play that demonstrated that evil can never be eradicated.

They stab it with their steely knives, but they just can't kill the beast

(By the way, I've always used "kill the beast" to cue a drummer to play the kind of fill that accompanies this line in "Hotel California." "Right before the last chorus, just go ahead and 'kill the beast'!" I consider that drum fill an institution, equal to the one in "In the Air Tonight" by Phil Collins.)

Who knows what the Eagles meant. The point is that what piqued my interest were the clues I was fed and the rate at which I was fed them. Guided by the line of the song's groove, and interested by well-timed mysteries, I put together the pieces. Then, of course, there are a bunch of guitar solos with no words, which gave me time to chew on it all. All part of the beauty of a song.

Composers like Maurice Ravel have said that they actually composed one painful note at a time. He said, "I did my work slowly, drop by drop. I tore it out of me by pieces." I understand that. Philip Glass says he likes to wait to see the tip of a ship come through the fog, while Bob Dylan said, "My best songs were written very quickly. Just about as much time as it takes to write it down is about as long as it takes to write it." Stephen King puts a few characters in an impossible situation and he follows and reports on them as they find their way out. Whether it's a sprint or a crawl, we're always following something. Something simple. A line and some clues. We don't have to know where it might lead. In fact, your song may end up a question mark, an unsolved mystery.

When I was a couple of blocks from Mrs. Dyer's house, the line in the snow took a wide swerve to the left, then a jerk to the right, increasing in amplitude and desperation, then violently veering out of control, finally surrendering to gravity, and leaving only a big wide mess of snow, at which I now arrived. Ouch! Not such a subtle clue. I paused to take it in. Seeing a wipeout is a gift from God for any young boy! So, sure, I wanted to laugh, but I was also concerned. I'd made a little connection with whoever's bike trail I'd been following. I now looked up through the blizzard—North Carolina's idea of a blizzard—and I saw that the line picked up again, in defeat, I imagined. It was now accompanied by a set of sad footprints, trailing off as far as I could see down the road. Why were they sad? Because I said so.

I wished at that moment that I had a camera to take a picture, to capture it and share it. But would a photograph capture the story? Probably not. It would probably just look like snowy chaos on the ground. But there must be a way of framing this story, I thought. Then again, I didn't actually *know* the story. I only had some clues. Oddly, that was part of the excitement.

I couldn't wait to talk my parents' ears off about it the rest of the afternoon. Maybe I would even add a few slightly fraudulent details,

Practicing piano in the house near Mrs. Dyer's, 1979

like how there was blood in the snow too? Or that I saved the day and helped the kid carry his/her bike home? The literal bare-bones story seemed pretty underwhelming, come to think of it. All I'd really seen was a trail, and the trail had become a mess, big deal. So why was it all so real for me? Why was it so much more interesting than if some-one had said, *Once upon a time there was a bike that went for a while and then fell down?* Could I possibly create a story out of just this bike trail as exciting as the one I had followed in the snow, and what would it take to do so? I wondered.

I had arrived. I trod up Mrs. Dyer's porch stairs and rang the bell. I'd soon be going over boring scales and getting a lecture on how I needed to practice, and I'd have to fake my way through a child's version of Mozart's "Turkish March," which I had neglected to practice. But an eleven-year-old can't yet appreciate what technique is really for. It's for later, when you need the skills to tell a whole story with just a line and some clues.

1979. THE SUMMER OF LOVE

Cultural Latency, Symbols, and Repetition

YEAH, MAN, IT WAS THE SEVENTIES. AND THE TIMES THEY WERE A-
changing, if perhaps a little more slowly in our parts than elsewhere.
The cultural latency of the South often afforded my childhood the
authentic feel and look of the 1960s, even though it was well into the
disco era. The styles, the colors, the language, all felt a few beats
late. That may be why today I sometimes find myself reminiscing
about the sixties as if I actually grew up in them. In fairness, ideas
and trends, especially in music, rarely land everywhere at the same
time. Two towns just thirty miles apart can feel like they exist in different decades, and unless you grew up in New York, L.A., or London, you too probably felt that all the cool stuff happened everywhere
else first.

Music that was too cool for the South often made its way to me
under the radar, by way of a few friends whose families had money
and traveled. They brought home glimpses of the future, like the first

Sony Walkman I ever saw and the punk and new-wave albums that changed my life in high school.

Big-city trends often took a while to traverse the short distance to the surrounding rural areas, what we called "the county" (outside the city limits, but within the county line). When we lived in the county, the bus ride to school felt like time travel. Two worlds, side by side, existing in different decades. I'd board the bus in what looked like an early-sixties' documentary about white Alabama and get off the same bus in the seventies, in full color, filled with post-civil-rights hippies, Afros, and bell-bottoms. Just ten miles away! A few years later, the county people would have the bell-bottoms too, and the city people would decide that school integration was perhaps too idealistic after all, dial it back, and yearn for the 1950s (I, personally, don't understand the romantic appeal of the fifties).

The 1960s that we see in movies, where everyone is on acid and looks like Jim Morrison or Tina Turner, nearly passed us by down South. And what did make its way to us came late and watered down. The "Magic Bus" that the Who sang about never officially stopped in North Carolina. It just lost a wheel eastbound on I-40, which went rolling unnoticed past the WELCOME TO WINSTON-SALEM NORTH CAROLINA sign and hobbled to a halt just inside the newly automated doors of a grocery store called Food Town. And there in the cereal aisle, Chuck and I got an eyeful of our first grown man with long hair. Wide-eyed and suppressing giggles, we followed this poor man like amazed third-world children getting a glimpse of a shiny red sports car for the first time. We referred to him as a "boy girl." Soon, more "boy girls" and their bell-bottom-wearing wives would proliferate, whizzing through Winston-Salem in Volkswagen Bugs and compact Japanese cars. Long-haired hippies had been around for years elsewhere. Had the revolution actually been televised, we would have only seen the reruns.

Clothing with words printed on it and bumper stickers weren't so common until the 1960s and, in our case, of course, the 1970s. And when that trend reached our parts, many went way overboard just to prove we were up on the times. The bumpers and often entire rear panels of the boy girls' vans were plastered with funny stickers that looked as though they'd all been purchased at the same place and applied on the same day. There were some really good ones, like NORTH CAROLINA, FIRST IN PAVEMENT—LAST IN EDUCATION (a play on our state motto on license tags, FIRST IN FLIGHT). VISUALIZE WHIRLED PEAS. And who could forget the classic EAT A BEAVER, SAVE A TREE. I actually didn't know what was meant by that, but I laughed along with my parents anyway.

Soon a natural-food store appeared, which attracted pale, thin, unhealthy-looking ladies with long, braided gray hair, oozing of garlic. It was like a self-conscious Southern theme park version of Haight-Ashbury. I never saw these types outside of this particular shop. Did they change back into their street clothes in the bathroom when they left? There were buckets of oats, roots, and little glass tinctures with handwritten scribble. The word "mucus" was used. A lot. And I once heard a friend's father introduce my friend's mother to someone in the natural-food store as his "lover." Were they *trying* to be gross?

The hippiest of hippies was an art teacher who knew that I was into music. She was kind enough to invite me to a party where she would be singing backup in a *real live rock band*! And so, at twelve years old, I was dropped off into this bizarre scene where teachers I'd known as Ms. or Mr. So-'n'-So by day were transformed into extras on *I Dream of Jeannie* or Warren Beatty in *Shampoo,* stumbling with their drinks through loud music and thick cigarette smoke. The backup-singer chicks for this real live rock band, who all seemed to be Forsyth County public school teachers, were swaying in a sort of lazy belly-dance type movement, staring into space, and singing nasal out-of-tune harmonies into the same mic behind a shirtless man who looked like he'd been rubbed down with baby oil, sporting a massive Afro and bandana. I later found out he was the principal of a neighboring school. A few of the female teachers I knew from school disappeared behind doors and later resurfaced, hair and clothes disheveled and giggling, on the arms of dudes with long hair and leather vests, no shirts beneath. The only male teacher I recognized was a driver's ed teacher in the upper school. The smell of skunk swirled while the band played a song called "Stormy Is Force." It was definitely their "hit." The band was called . . . you guessed it, Stormy.

Stormy is force!
Stormy is force and thunder!!

All the while, nothing that could be seen through the heavy fog of this fake-wood-paneling home soirée would have indicated it was 1979 or that "My Sharona" could be heard playing from every corner on the rest of the planet. In this groovy pad it was the "Summer of Love," and not in a masquerade party kind of way. It all seemed very new to them, and to me. And I didn't see much of Mrs. So-'n'-So that night at that swinging teachers' party, but I did learn she was a damn awful singer. As Stormy's thunder squeaked through a Peavey tower all night, I borrowed the phone to call for rescue, by airlift if necessary. I waited for my mother at least an hour outside on the cul-de-sac. Had I known then that the literal translation for the French "cul-de-sac" was "the ass or bottom of the bag," it would have given form to what I suspected Mrs. So-'n'-So was seeing up close at that very moment "backstage," behind a thin bedroom door. I'd had my fill of the sixties that night. I was done with the Summer of Love. I wanted to go back to the future and watch *Welcome Back, Kotter* with the rest of the seventies.

Obviously, the internet has closed the geographic gap, and we all get the memo about current trends more or less at the same time now. But we still pass around mannerisms, symbols, and styles from one side of our culture and globe to the other, adopting them at varying rates, and applying our own interpretations. The music and style of the 1960s in San Francisco was all about rebellion. In 1970s' North Carolina, we were finally just conforming to what had already been established. We were saying, *It's okay. We get it now and we'll get on board.*

I try not to jump to conclusions about anything I feel I've seen or heard before. I try not to write off music my kids play me as "throwback" even if it closely resembles something that I thought was new when I was a kid. Sure, I want to put on the seventies' English band the Jam and say, *See! Your new little punk bands are just shiny versions of this!* But I'd be wrong. To diminish the new as nothing more than a rehash is a mistake. I'm reminded of Gertrude Stein's belief that "There is no such thing as repetition. Only insistence." Meaning: You can do or say something a second and third time, but it will not be the same experience again. Because the first occurrence, utterance, or expression of an idea has now altered the environment. So you can't repeat, not literally, but you can insist: *A rose is a rose is a rose is a rose . . .* The youth might co-opt a symbol, but it will likely have a different meaning the next time around, one that probably flies over the heads of the older generation. Hell, it was my generation who decided it would be fun if "bad" meant "good." As in, "that's one *bad* motherfucker."

We pass the same symbols down from generation to generation, and they migrate from place to place, as the meaning morphs along the way. We've all witnessed the journey of an artistic innovation that originates with a hip-hop group, before the idea is eaten by the indie rockers five years later, soon to be aped and sanitized by the corporate rockers, and ultimately wrung of its irony by Christian bands, a year ahead of its hipster revival. What used to be an embarrassing hole in the jeans of someone who couldn't afford new ones is now being marketed to rich people who are willing to pay big bucks for that hole. *A hole is a hole is a hole is a hole.*

I believe that when a piece of music (or any art) has been set free and released into the world, it doesn't matter if it was dressed in bell-bottoms or a jumpsuit. If its aim is true, if its heart is in the right place, if it's chock full of meaning, feeling, and intent, it might—just might—survive the journey over decades and cultural fault lines. Just not for the reasons anyone might have predicted. Writers, like parents, must accept that their creations will take on lives of their own.

BUT FOR THE GRACE OF MY
MUSIC TEACHERS

A FEW YEARS AGO, I VOLUNTEERED TO BE A SUBSTITUTE TEACHER FOR my kids' seventh-grade music class. Just for a day. That's all I had to do. I knew most of the kids in the class anyway. It should have been a breeze.

It wasn't.

If I didn't fully appreciate the public school music teachers of my youth before 11 A.M. that day, by noon I damn well did. As I stood before the class, a lifetime of experience performing in front of people went straight out the window. The forty-five-minute affair was absolutely exhausting. Kids, 1—Folds, 0. Animals, every one of them! I am no music teacher and I bow to each and every man and woman who is. I especially bow to the ones who can see that these children are not animals and recognize which ones could use a push, or a hand, like I did when I was younger.

Teaching school is by nature a one-size-fits-all sort of thing—that's just necessity. It's not "man-to-man defense," as they say in basketball. It's zone—there's only one of you defending against God knows how many rat bags. What strikes me looking back at my own childhood is how many of my teachers still managed to take on each student one at a time. How many of them managed to make it feel like one-on-one. These teachers that knew my name out of a school full of kids recognized that I loved music, encouraged and inspired me, reprimanded me when necessary, and kept me on a path that led me to a career in music.

I don't think most rock musicians appreciate the impact their music teachers had on their artistry. At least in my day, it just wasn't cool for a rock star to shout out to his music teacher. Rockers were supposed to be completely self-taught, rolling out of bed one day with messy hair and a bong, and suddenly—boom—they were the shit. I tore through music magazines at the 7-Eleven when I was a teenager to see if Gene Simmons of Kiss might give me some clue as to how he became Gene Simmons, or, more important, how he became a musician. Did he attend band camp? I did—was that okay? Should I not

Tenth-grade disciplinary slips (one of many). Apologies to my teachers.

admit that? Did he know what key "Calling Dr. Love" was in? I did! Was that okay?

I urge my recording-artist homies to have their own music-teacher appreciation week. Go to bat for the teachers, for their programs, their pay, and music education in general. Unless you really believe you learned nothing from them. In which case, go to bat for marijuana laws.

This is my thank-you to the music teachers who made a difference in my life. Not all of my teachers were good, of course, but we'll ignore the handful of shitty and mean ones. To the shitty and mean ones, I'd say, "You know who you are," but the problem is you probably don't.

1. All of my K–6 teachers at Moore Laboratory School. The teachers at my elementary school would regularly give us a break from our studies to teach us how to clap in rhythm, showing us musical notes on the chalkboard. Even though they were just regular teachers, not music teachers, they would turn the classroom into a music lesson for a few minutes. For some of us, it taught us the joy of making music in unison with other kids. For others, it was just a brain rest, like playtime. And we all learned basic rhythmic notation:

Tah = half note (or, for us, long)

Tee = quarter note (or, for us, short)

The teacher would write the actual note, as a rhythm, on the chalkboard, along with "Tah" or "Tee." We would clap along on the floor:

"Tah Tee-Tee / Tah Tah / Tee-Tee Tah / Tah Tah /"

That's 4/4 time—always adds up. Easy. Great music program, seriously. It required no more than a floor to sit on and a chalkboard and, most important, a teacher who knew just enough music to lead it.

2. Mrs. Rushing, elementary school band teacher. My first school music teacher was Mrs. Rushing. She noticed that this skinny-ass kid was definitely in need of something to sink his teeth into. She pulled me aside in third grade and suggested I take up an instrument, even though band didn't normally start until fifth grade. She encouraged me to study at home with a book she'd provided, and she said she'd check up on my progress periodically after school. If I practiced the whole year, I might be able to join the school concert band in fourth grade! She even drove me to the local music store with a broken snare drum, where I got to help the music-store man fix the instrument in the back room. The snare stayed at school, so I practiced at home with two sticks and a basketball. I got through a year's worth of Mrs. Rushing's tests in less than a month, came in one afternoon and performed a perfect buzz roll on the snare drum. She put me in the concert band in third grade. My other studies improved, and I felt way better about myself. Yay for Mrs. Rushing. She didn't have to take the time to get a little jackass on track.

3. John "Chick" Shelton, junior high jazz-band director. My next amazing music teacher was Mr. Shelton, but even the students called him "Chick." The music building of Wiley Magnet Middle School in Winston-Salem is now named after him. Chick was a round and rosy ball of energy, who probably had gone gray in his twenties. He had played trumpet in the U.S. Army Field Band years ago, before touring professionally in big bands. He was a straight-up jazzer with some street cred, having seen all kinds of crazy shit on the road, and he had an awesome sense of humor. He took approximately *zero* shit.

His Wiley Junior High Jazz Band was famous. He had this bunch trained within an inch of their lives. They rocked *The Tonight Show Starring Johnny Carson* theme song and the James Bond theme too. You have to understand, this was *off the chain* back in this era. A student band performance was always some Sousa and out-of-tune children's wind ensemble adaptations of Dvořák or Tchaikovsky. Not that interesting to a kid.

The finale of Chick's student jazz-band show, which I first saw in fifth grade, when they toured our elementary school, was the drum-set solo. It was the greatest thing I'd ever seen. The drummer froke out (past tense of "frokar," *v.*: "to freak"). Fireworks on the toms! We grade-schoolers also froke, like we were seeing the Beatles on *The Ed Sullivan Show*. I was determined to be the Drum-Set God too when I finally got to seventh grade.

But unfortunately I would have to audition against the heavyweight champion of all Wiley Jazz Band history. Wade Culbreath, the incumbent eighth-grade drumming legend, was the best kit player that Chick had ever seen come through the school. Damn him and all his talent and hard work! At thirteen years old, he was already as good as most pros. His dad led *the* local professional working big band, and Wade had probably learned to crawl with sticks in his tiny hands. Wade is now the principal timpanist for the Los Angeles Chamber Orchestra and taught for years at UCLA. So, in seventh grade, I stepped up to audition against the master, got my ass kicked, and went home with my tail between my legs.

But Chick encouraged me all year as I sat on the sidelines. He gave me listening lists, things to practice, and let me come to some rehearsals, even letting me fill in for Wade when he was absent. I learned a thing or two watching a prodigy such as Wade up close. And at rehearsals Chick didn't give Wade a free pass. He made him work for it. Kindly. He called Wade "Dumbhead!" He *threatened* to throw things at him, busted him for rushing, and so on—but always with a smile. Witnessing this, I actually felt a little relieved I had a year to prepare for my turn in jazz band. I wasn't ready in seventh grade.

The next year, I'd improved quite a bit, and that Wade

bastard moved on to the next school to terrorize his senior competition. I became the Wiley Jazz Band drummer, and the first rehearsal began with "Ben Folds, you *dumbhead*—you're slowing the whole outfit down with your damn sock cymbal!" Chick used antiquated words like "sock cymbal" instead of calling them "hi-hats" like everyone else in the twentieth century. If it was the sixties in most of North Carolina, in Chick's band room it was the fifties. Hi-hats/sock cymbals are that pair of cymbals next to the snare, which can be operated with a foot pedal. He also called the drum set a "trap kit." "Dumbhead! If you're gonna play the trap kit southpaw, get here early enough to turn it around!" I still use "trap kit" *and* "southpaw."

Chick retired after my eighth-grade year, and later, when I was in high school, he called on me to write horn arrangements for the Tony DiBianca Band, a professional local jazz group he was in, built around an electric accordion. Certainly they couldn't actually have used the garbage I wrote for them. It wasn't very good. But I had to copy each part by hand, transpositions and all, and get it in on time. Chick paid me for my time and went through the charts to show me what wasn't working. He was still teaching in retirement. He couldn't help it.

Years later, in 2011, Chick attended my induction into the North Carolina Music Hall of Fame. He and his wonderful wife had kept up with my every career move. The ceremony was delayed so that Chick, in his declining health, could make the trip one step at a time from the parking lot to his seat, smiling the whole way. It is not hyperbole to say that I wouldn't have been there if it hadn't been for him. He passed away in 2014.

4. Chuck Burns, senior high school music director. Chuck was one hip band teacher. We'd listen to my cassettes of new music after school and he would provide some really great perspective on the current music I loved. He taught me to listen to music for more than its fashion sense, by recognizing the connection between all the different eras and styles. If I'd introduce him to, say, the Clash, he'd point me to some Bob Marley, or even some gospel jazz to show me how much more similar these styles were than I'd thought. He facilitated my application to the University of Miami after I played him an album by the Dixie Dregs, a sort of Southern fusion jazz outfit who'd graduated from Miami's jazz program.

5. Minnie Lou Raper, senior high school orchestra director. Yes, that's her name—get used to it. Even *I* was able to. Mrs. Raper took our high school orchestra out of town constantly for competitions and concerts and insisted our high school take orchestra seriously. The marching band had always gotten the most attention, but Mrs. Raper encouraged me to focus on the orchestra instead. She also suggested that I audition for as many things outside of my high school as I could, so that if I wanted to apply for music school one day, I'd have a solid résumé. I followed her advice and piled on loads of first-chair regional orchestral percussionist positions, competition ribbons, and so forth. And, yes, it did come in handy.

Maestros, rockers, rappers, pickers, and grinners—where would all us dumbheads be without the right teacher at the right time? If you were lucky enough to have experiences like mine, go substitute-teach for one day and get your ass kicked. Then let schools know how much you appreciate their music programs and teachers. Tell your representatives while you're at it. Nobody ever did it alone.

CHEAP LESSONS

DURING MY SENIOR YEAR OF HIGH SCHOOL, I WORKED TWO SHITTY JOBS on the other side of town into the wee hours of the morning. I created constant drama with my girlfriend and wasted the rest of the time obsessively installing and reinstalling crappy car stereos or being kicked out of class for being a clown. My studies dwindled to nothing. Each afternoon when the final bell rang, I'd run to my car, hoping to hit all the green lights for my afternoon gig at Hertz Truck Rental. My title was "rental representative," and my desk was empty other than the phone with a typed script in case anyone called: "Hello. Hertz-Penske Truck Rental. How may I help you?" About once a week someone would rent or return a truck and I would fill out the paperwork, put gas in the tank, and back it into its parking space. I was a sixteen-year-old who looked twelve, sitting alone at a desk on display at the center of a ten-by-ten-foot Plexiglas cube, in the middle of a parking lot, in a truly dangerous neighborhood.

My 360-degree view at Hertz Trucks provided an important supplement to my high school education. I had front-row seats to crazy stuff, like pairs of shady characters frantically shuffling through the parking lot, each holding the end of a broomstick, from which a row of stolen portable TV sets dangled by their handles. This was back when TVs were big heavy boxes with handles. These vagrants were always gone too quickly to call 911. I just kept the door locked.

An arguing couple once parked themselves just outside, and I could hear every word of their domestic squabble through their closed car *and* my glass box. "I'll *kill* you, bitch!" Stuff like that. They could clearly see me and vice versa. I felt like a third wheel on a bad date. I saw ground-shitters, pants-wetters, and out-passers from the safety of my cube. There was one fellow who would have stumbled right into my desk but for the Plexiglas between us. His eyes rolling around spastically in his head, he pissed himself while pressed up to the glass and passed out practically at my feet, dozing there for a couple hours before hobbling away. I'm not sure why I needed to lock the door for that one.

At Hardee's (a sort of Southern junior-league McDonald's), I learned when *not* to call the police. While taking out the trash during my 6-P.M.-to-2-A.M. shift, I spotted a pair of legs poking lifelessly out of the mess in the dumpster. I, of course, called the cops. The whole affair ended with this man throwing up in the squad car. I thought the police were going to beat *me* with a stick for the inconvenience. The lesson seemed to be that if you see what you think is a corpse in the trash, never mind.

From then on, I would save 911 for real emergencies. For instance, when a family feud broke out in the dining area, sending the employees crouching behind the counter. Screaming hillbillies with baseball bats, a lot of shirts being ripped off, and shit breaking. The mother from one of the families was the meanest of the bunch and had the other mother on the floor, elbowing her face to a bloody pulp, ripping hair out, and squealing like an animal.

I should take a moment to explain that these Hardee's and Hertz scenes did not have to be part of my upbringing. This was self-inflicted. This was volunteer tourism. My own doing. Had I not been famous at school for being the class clown, maybe I could have gotten work in my own neighborhood, like everyone else. But when managers of local businesses asked their student employees what this Ben Folds character was like, I got a thumbs-up for being *HI-larious*! I was known for stunts like crawling out a window in the middle of a class or faking a speech impediment in another. Not the kinds of talents most employers are looking for.

But to be fair, I was a different person at work. I was a fine employee, possibly even an overachiever. The lifers at places like Hardee's recognize kids like me as well-to-do transient—here today, gone tomorrow to live the dream. And so, relative to these lifers, I was the fancy fortunate one. Perceived as eloquently spoken. A snowflake before snowflakes. Quite the contrast to how I was seen at youth-orchestra rehearsal, where I felt more like an underprivileged pine knot amongst the more refined.

At school I was part-time overachiever and part-time loser. I took all the advanced-placement college-credit classes. But by twelfth grade I was flunking most classes for not showing up. I was a hard worker, a class clown, an accelerated student, the token poor kid, the token rich kid. A jackass of all trades.

I was making some pretty awful choices, as kids often do. My father, understanding that his advice was falling on deaf ears, said I would have to just learn the important life lessons on my own. And he could only hope that they would be "cheap lessons"—that is, he hoped I would suffer severe-enough consequences for my actions that I might learn something but not so severe that I would end up losing a limb. I found the God of Cheap Lessons both an angry and a merciful God. He dealt all I could stand and left my limbs intact.

As young men are wont to do, I begged for trouble, though I never wanted to cause anyone harm. I wasn't roaming the streets looking for a fight (ha, can you imagine?), but unsupervised teenagers in adult's clothing can get in over their heads quickly. And unsupervised teen-age couples removing their adult clothing in the back seats of cars in dimly lit parking lots get in over their heads even faster.

And so my senior year was spent living a teenage nightmare with my first girlfriend. That nightmare—our abortion—became the sub-ject of the song "Brick," and much of what happened played out just as the song states. I sold some early Christmas gifts to pay for every-thing and I took my girlfriend to the clinic the day after Christmas. It's all laid out quite literally in the verses. What wasn't in the song were all the stressful un-singable details that plagued our lives while finishing high school. She and I both missed quite a bit of school that year, and nobody could figure out exactly why. But she had gotten pregnant early in the autumn and she was having an awful time of it all, pre- and post-abortion. I would try to help where I could. While I didn't manage my own homework, I did as much of hers as I could. We had kept the whole thing secret because we didn't think adults would understand or help. I would try and keep her from cutting her face with razor blades, which she did anyway a few horrible times. I was always worried that she might kill herself while I was at work. I was painfully aware that she was the one walking the hardest yards, but there was nothing I could do about it.

Over senior year I had recurring strep throat and mononucleosis and, along with the absences due to our situation, I ultimately didn't meet the attendance requirement for graduation. I had missed as many days of school as I'd attended. One morning, a few weeks after the abortion, I met my girlfriend in a church parking lot to give her homework I'd done so she wouldn't flunk too. It was pouring rain and she jumped into my car as I handed her a stack of notebooks. She lost it right there, screaming uncontrollably and shaking. I suddenly real-ized how very in over our heads we really were. We needed help. I was worried she was going to die, so I drove her to the hospital. A coun-selor took her in and alerted my mother, who happened to work next door. It was all a relief, even my parents finding out. A great weight was lifted. Once the secret was out, we were children again.

Our parents were more understanding than we could have imagined. They were mostly just concerned. I picked my girlfriend up from the hospital and she already seemed much better. She was talking, at least, and that was an improvement. I took her back to the church parking lot, where she got in her car to follow me to a Subway for lunch. As I stopped at a light, I looked in the rearview and saw she wasn't stopping. Her car continued full speed ahead, plowing into the rear end of mine. Both cars were totaled, though neither of us was injured. They were huge old cars. Cheap lessons.

My mother loaned me her Honda Civic to get to school for the next week, since the insurance company would not loan a car to a teenager. It was the first and only new car my parents ever bought. When I came out of class, the car was gone. It had been stolen. I made the dreaded call to Mama from school and she picked me up. She was unbelievably understanding.

That midnight, the cops located the stolen Honda, and Papa and I went together to claim it. It was wrecked. The windows were shattered, and human shit was rubbed all over the back seat. The whole car had been dusted for fingerprints and was unrecognizable. While filling out the police report, my father sought to inflate the value of the stolen contents, claiming there were valuable items in the car, which he and I both knew weren't there.

"Benjamin, you had probably five hundred dollars of cassettes in here, didn't you?" he said for show so the police might take note.

I looked down at my feet. "No. It was just one cassette."

"No, but of course it was a whole case, Benjamin! Probably worth hundreds! Tell the officer now, because he's making a record of it."

"No. It was one. That one with all the black powder on it— Madness, *The Rise and Fall*." I still have that cassette, stained with fingerprint dust.

Papa tried to get me to fib, to exaggerate, like everyone does for insurance claims. But I simply couldn't lie anymore, for any reason. I'd done it for too long and I never wanted to again.

She broke down
And I broke down
'Cause I was tired
Of lying

I saw my first girlfriend years later, while on tour in San Francisco. She's awesome and wise. I had spoken to her only once since high school, calling her in 1997 to make sure she was okay with the promotion of the song "Brick." She said she felt better knowing something positive could come from it all. I could breathe easier about its release. She implied her parents didn't feel the same about it. They felt I was profiting from everyone's tragedy. To them, I can only apologize. I write songs about what I feel. And I feel there could not be a more expensive cheap lesson than this episode.

PLAN A FROM OUTER SPACE

I WASN'T EXPECTING TO GRADUATE HIGH SCHOOL. I WAS FLUNKING MY classes and had missed too many days. So I was mulling over my Plan B options—summer school, community college, a job, maybe the Army—when out of nowhere I received an incredible, beautiful lifeline in the mailbox. It was a full-tuition scholarship to study music at the University of Miami. I had all but forgotten about Plan A, my application to music school, and the life I'd wanted to pursue. I read the letter over and over. I showed it my parents to confirm I wasn't misinterpreting it. Maybe I *could* study music and be a percussionist in a fine symphony orchestra. I just needed to convince my high school to let me graduate.

Way back at the beginning of the school year, before my girlfriend and I had gotten into all our trouble, before I worked two jobs while flunking school, I had auditioned for University of Miami, having read that the Dixie Dregs, Jaco Pastorius, Pat Metheny, Lyle Mays, and a host of other brilliant jazz musicians had either studied or taught there. Who'd ever thought of going to a university that taught jazz? And who had ever considered that making a living in music was possible? When you went to your guidance counselor in those days, they pulled out a few catalogs of schools and majors, and nothing about music ever came up, aside from teaching. Learning to perform music—original music—for a living? That just wasn't on offer. Therefore, it didn't exist.

But my jazz-band teacher, Mr. Burns, knew better, and he collected all the information I would need to audition to be a jazz performance major at U of M. The audition requirements were a few solo percussion pieces, like snare-drum études. Yes, there is such a thing as a snare-drum étude, and I crushed those. Some orchestral mallet percussion. Easy. But one that left me scratching my head was performing three jazz standards of different grooves at the drums, with a rhythm section. I didn't know any local pianist or bassist who could play jazz very well, if at all. And I really wasn't familiar with jazz standards myself. So, I went to an 8-track multitrack studio in the basement of Duncan Music, a local musical-instrument retailer, and I

Practicing piano in high school, 1984. In background, Scotty Folds's original painting of piano player.

made up three jazz "standards," performing them at the piano, bass, and the drums. I sent the cassette tape to the University of Miami along with my bundles of awards and certificates and forgot about it.

And now I found myself in the kitchen, holding an acceptance letter. And not only had they let me in, they'd given me a full-tuition scholarship. One of two full scholarships in the whole music school! I had all but given up the notion of pursuing music before that letter arrived. And now I had a beacon to follow. I knew I had to act on this gift.

I got to work convincing my teachers to give me another chance. I volunteered essays on the importance of my scholarship and about what I wanted to do with my life. I had come to appreciate their classes too late, I explained, but was willing to make up the work. I had a doctor's note for the strep throat. But I was still coming up a little short of convincing all my teachers to let me pass. So, I thought, I'd go to a therapist and convince them I had some emotional issues to further make my case. That sort of soft fraud was always persuasive with teacher types. I'd just act anxious for the shrink and he would excuse the rest of my absences. I chose the same therapist who'd seen my girlfriend.

During the session, which began as a stunt to allow me to graduate, my whole year came flooding back. As I heard myself recount the awful experience, I realized I had actually been through a lot. And by the end of the session, I was a puddle on the floor. He gave me the note, and much more. I was allowed to graduate, barely.

My parents dropped me off at the airport at the end of the summer and I boarded the first plane of my life. My mother later told me that my father cried as the plane took off. I didn't believe that, of course. Real men don't do that (or so I thought at the time). I made my way to my first baggage claim, picked up my 1950s' suitcases, which came from my grandmother's attic, and took my first ride in a taxi. I was too shy to question the cabdriver as he dropped me a mile away from the university, somewhere on U.S. Highway 1, but I managed to make my way to the campus. This was it. Plan A. It felt like I'd been delivered in a spaceship. I passed strange palm trees and heard people speaking in Spanish.

I took the second cab ride of my life a week later, to the Greyhound station, to retrieve a large cardboard box containing my drums, which, although I'd packed them myself, were now mysteriously accompanied by some of my mother's Rice Krispies Treats wrapped in tinfoil, stuffed between the Styrofoam packing.

The parcel, in order of its value:

Shipping cost > Rice Krispies Treats > cardboard > old shitty drum set.

For now, for the first time in my life, I could actually imagine a path to becoming a musician. A real working musician who performs and records music, not just teaches it. An artist who puts food on the table—something that I'd never witnessed outside of the radio and TV. I shuffled what happened in high school under the rug and promised myself to never speak of it again. I was now in the company of some of the best young jazz students in the country. These were my people, I thought, unlike the kids back home, who ranged from broke rednecks to aspiring law students from old-money families. Maybe I'd found home at last. I felt relief, a sense of pride, and the overwhelming sensation of butterflies that a kid gets when he's far from home for the first time. I set about establishing my new life, shaking hands with my new roommate and gearing up to learn as much as possible.

DROPPED AT EXAMS IN A COP CAR

FINAL PERFORMANCE EXAMS IN MUSIC SCHOOL ARE REFERRED TO AS "the juries." The test itself is called "the jury," and it's adjudicated by the staff, but you don't call them the jury—you call them the staff. It's like the way we call the main course "the entrée" in America. Make sense? Anyway, the University of Miami, renowned for its jazz program, took this jury thing up a notch by providing a jazz ensemble with a full horn section to accompany the student as he/she performed prepared pieces, exercises, and some sight-reading. The band did not stop or slow down for the student if he/she stumbled. It was keep up or perish. I understood that I would need to ace my jury each semester or risk losing my scholarship. *No problem,* I thought. After a semester of stellar grades, an accidental suntan, and a few pounds back on my bones, I was feeling pretty good about this one last hoop I'd need to jump through before heading home for Christmas break.

On the morning of juries, anxious freshman performance majors trickled in to wait their turn in the foyer of the old Foster Building, glancing one last time at their music, while the provided combo, made up of grad students, casually talked amongst themselves. A small team of disheveled professors seated themselves in a row behind a folding table, organizing their notes. Back then, the front of the Foster Building was mostly glass and the students and jury had a clear view of everyone who approached the building. My approach was particularly conspicuous. I was dropped off in a Miami Dade police car.

I looked like I'd shown up for *Walking Dead* auditions thirty years too early, plastered with an assortment of bandages, patches of blood showing through. My head felt swollen and my nose and bottom lip were full of stitches. My right hand, in a splint, hurt even worse. I had what they call a "boxer's break." I tried to rustle up some dignity with a casual goodbye to the police officer, as if we were old buds or something, as I sensed the tilting heads and widening eyes of peers and professors from the other side of the glass. I shrugged in the direction of the music building. No book bag, no music, no sticks or mallets. Just a blurry hangover, of equal parts beer and adrenaline from the previous ten humiliating hours.

Still in last night's clothes, which felt damp and permanently pasted to my skin, I hadn't had a minute's sleep. I stood up straight as I could, thrust what little chest I had forward, and walked the fuck through the big glass door. I made a beeline through my peers to my percussion professor. Everyone could hear every whispering word echo off the concrete walls as I begged for my test to be put off until the next week.

As it turns out, the University of Miami percussion department didn't play that game. In the professional world, you see, you'd just be fired for showing up in such a state and asking for the night off. So that was that. I would have to perform soon. How I would've loved to at least change my clothes or brush my teeth.

"Hey, Mike," I whispered to a kid next to me. "Man, I'm sorry, but would you mind if I used your sticks and mallets for my test?"

"Nah, sorry, Ben, can't wait around to get them back. I gotta run and I need these sticks for my next class."

"Okay, okay, that's cool . . ." I muttered, searching for a receptive face.

"Hey! John, can you loan me your sticks for my jury?"

"Dude, you stink."

This was it. The slaughter was nigh.

"Ben, turn to page five," instructed the band director. "This one is called 'Fusion Juice.' Stay with me."

He counted it off and the band burned through each measure. I did *not* stay with him. I was left in the dust, crawling around under the snare drum for the stick I dropped, as the band squeezed out some "Fusion Juice" with no drums. To this day, my Miami percussion professor, Steve Rucker, doesn't think it was he who went all *Whiplash* (the 2014 award-winning movie about a struggling jazz percussion student and his abusive professor) at that jury. He suspects it was the senior percussion professor instead who made me play with a broken hand. But I think that I should damn well have had to perform, broken hand and all. Because that *is* life. And in my decades as a touring recording artist, I have personally canceled fewer shows than I could count on that broken hand. Cheap lesson learned. Either way, Steve and I both recall my jury for the disaster it was.

So, here's the story of the previous night's drunken idiocy that led up to all of this:

On that night, the eve of my juries, some guy named Jim had taken a special trip down from the eleventh floor of our dorm to my room on the ninth. Nobody on the ninth floor really knew this fellow. Jim's ninth-floor trip, as we would learn, was quite premeditated. He was in search of someone his size to beat up (as you do) and had his eye on my roommate, Doug, who seemed to fit the bill. They were of equal builds, both a few inches shorter and thicker than I.

I imagine that in the hours before his trip to the ninth floor, Jim had been flexing shirtless in the mirror, with a cheap-beer buzz, making intense eye contact with himself, and whisper-shouting to his reflection. Getting himself stoked, psyched, *and* pumped, under a single bare bulb in his cinder-block bathroom. He seemed warmed up and mid-script when he made the scene.

I knew how important the next morning's juries were, but I'd never found it useful to dwell or cram the night before an audition or performance. It just made me more nervous. I'd prepared my ass off anyway, and I imagined it might be a good psych-out technique to appear cavalier to the other musicians. I was competitive that way. So at midnight on jury's eve, while the music students were practicing and commiserating about their jitters, the PBR flowed freely for the non-music students. And for me too. I took the opportunity to have a few beers myself while organizing my side of the room. I had just cleaned my desk and was coming through the door to empty the trash and, boom, there was Jim.

Jim was tan and jock-like and appeared a little anxious. His eyes were on fire and he was brandishing a fire extinguisher. It was all good, though. I was learning not to judge a man too quickly. Away from home for the first time, you discover that the way a fellow is when he's drunk is not necessarily a good indication of the kind of person he *really* is. People who are normally soft-spoken can suddenly become boisterously loud after only one drink, like this kid Jonathan, a studious science major who lost his shit every weekend, yelling, *"Nine sixteeeeee!"* up and down the hall. Our dorm was called 960 Complex, and I guess he was really proud of that. Hell, I'd just had a few drinks and was now walking around with a trash can, so I didn't think it was odd if a guy had a few drinks and went for a fire extinguisher. If that was his thing.

I was about to be hospitable and invite this odd man in. Doug sat cross-legged on his bed behind me, white-knuckling a pair of sticks with his face in the next morning's jury music, as Jim and I stood face-to-face in my doorway. I remember sort of bobbing my head, Southern style—*yup, here we are*—to fill the awkward silence, which was now going on too long. There was no *how do you do* or even *my name is Jim and I get really nervous when tipsy—oh, and I heard there was a fire.* Instead, he puffed up his chest, looked around as if calling an Iron John meeting to order. He took a hard, deep breath through his nose, the kind that nearly collapses the nostrils, and announced his intentions to hose my roommate with a fire extinguisher. He would then "kick his pussy ass," he continued. Maybe he said he'd kick his ass *first* and *then* hose him down. Something like that. Whatever. It just seemed absurd.

I'm not exactly sure what came out of my smart mouth, but it got a good laugh up and down the hall. And then the air got even heavier. It had officially become Real™ on the ninth floor. And there was no turning back. Jim was the lion, and I was the small man in a loincloth waiting to die in the middle of a Roman coliseum. It was a *National Geographic* documentary featuring a boa constrictor and a small rodent, with Morgan Freeman narrating. And there's no turning back once Morgan Freeman has spoken. Oh yez, it was *on*! And the shit would soon be going down.

Only I didn't yet realize it was "on." I may have been the only one who didn't quite hear what Morgan Freeman said. I didn't even get that rush of adrenaline and holy-fucking-shit-ness until moments later, when I was being pummeled. Back home my sense of humor had always kept me from getting my ass kicked. It always defused a situation like this. Joking in these situations can earn respect or break down the predator by making him laugh. *Ah, let the kid go—he's funny!* Not this time.

It turns out that Jim was an amateur boxer who was attending college on a wrestling scholarship. My little quip that made the hallway laugh was sort of like a ringside bell for this guy.

Ding!

I just stood there getting beat up in the doorway, holding that damn trash can for God knows how long, until my limbic system suggested to my right hand that maybe it should, you know, let go. But, then, my teenage ego suggested I advance and swing like a maniac—in the general direction of Jim. Which, I'm told, I did.

Jim seemed to be beating my ass and conducting an interview all at once. He was asking me questions between jabs, like, did I want "another piece of this?"—*pop pop!*—and what did I "have to say now, chump?"—*pop pop pop!* This was the best day of Jim's life. As he frothed in ecstasy behind a blur of fists, I reflexively hollered something I'd learned back home, like, "Yeaaaah, you little titty bitch, let's go!" I also stepped closer, making me easier for him to hit.

I remember bleeding all over the elevator and getting a last blurry glimpse of Jim being held back by a few other kids. He was freakishly pumped up and loud, still high off his conquest, pounding his chest and yelling, "Yeah, I kicked your fucking ass! *I kicked your fucking ass!*" as the elevator doors closed.

All said and done, this was a brief affair. In the time it took you to read these last few paragraphs, the whole event would have occurred four times over. I was soon off to the South Dade Hospital ER. Dressing my wounds, the doctor asked if the attacker had worn brass knuckles. Doug told him no but that Jim had had some really fat rings on his fingers. I called my parents collect from the pay phone in the lobby at 5 A.M. for my insurance information.

In the end, the nail in the coffin of what was once my dignity— the thing that hurt at least as bad as all those blows to the head—was what I learned in this exchange:

ME: "Damn, they say my hand is totally broken! I must have put a hurtin' on Jim too, right? He's in the ER too, right? I can't wait to see what I did to *his* face!"

DOUG: "Uh, he's fine. You missed him and punched the wall."

Me: ". . ."
Doug: "Twice."

Some said later that the loud snap of my second punch to the cinder-block wall, which had wildly missed Jim's head, had made one of the onlookers sick to his stomach.

DRUMS IN A LAKE

LEAVING MY JURY, HEAD HUNG LOW, I KNEW THAT MY SCHOLARSHIP wouldn't survive my awful performance. My time at the University of Miami would soon be coming to an end. My friend Mark tried to hatch a last-minute plan to unlock some of his personal savings to help me stay in school, but I couldn't accept that. No, I was cooked. So I did what anyone would do—I rolled my drums to Lake Osceola, which was right next to the music school, and tossed them in, one drum at a time.

This wasn't completely spontaneous, though. I'd been dreaming of chucking these drums for months. The truth was, the whole set wasn't even worth a bus ticket back home. The bass drum was so anemic that when a tom was mounted on it, it would collapse in on itself. I had to jam two pencils where the metal bass-drum legs had once existed, to keep the kit stable. But even then I'd have to steal resting moments in the music to pull the bass drum back in place, so it didn't inch forward each time I kicked it.

I'd first unveiled these drums in front of a class called "Fundamentals of Swing 101." Despite its insipid name, I found this class terrifying and intimidating, and it seemed to have been designed that way. The instructor, a gruff old-school jazz pianist, encouraged a sort of mean-spirited competition between students as a way to motivate us to improve. In an environment like this, my shitty drums were open season.

Each day, a few of us would be grouped into a small ensemble—usually piano, bass, guitar, and drums—and assigned a jazz standard to perform together. The rest of the class would critique. In fact, critiquing was most of the grade, so you'd have to say the right things when called upon, and the right things were seldom kind. The more scathing the takedown, the more catty the tone, the more delighted the teacher would become.

"Sound and balance, Mr. Folds?" he would call.

If Mr. Folds didn't rip the band a new asshole for being out of balance, then God help Mr. Folds. Conversely, when Mr. Folds finally got his turn to play, the same musicians would be foaming at the mouth to turn their steely knives on his broke-ass drum set.

Eventually I got my first turn to play in an ensemble for Fundamentals of Swing 101, and a famous vibraphone player from a successful fusion band who was buddies with the teacher came in and sat in the back to watch. I nearly shat my pants. Anyone who's spent any time in elevators has heard *this* guy. I must have gotten my teeth drilled to his music at least a few times, so I was starstruck. I'd never seen a famous person before. Well, there was that one local radio DJ at Hanes Mall when I was ten.

To be fair, as green as I was, as cheap as my drums were, I was no slouch of a musician. I was just more of a jack-of-all-trades than a technical monster. My creativity earned me my scholarship, but at music school it's all about being a specialist, since you can't really teach creativity. I was now supposed to be a technically proficient jazz-drumming specialist, I guess. My training had been orchestral percussion, but that wasn't really the thing at Miami, and burning through a jazz standard was not my strongest suit.

As the class was about to begin, the other musicians in my ensemble were putting away their cases and taking their places at their instruments. There were definitely no cases with my drums. Nothing to put away for me. As I sat at my garden of droopy plywood and tried to calm my nerves, the harsh critiques that I'd dished out to other students the week before echoed in my mind, and I shivered. Quiet order came over the class and I noticed a weird little sound nearby, an annoying high sizzling buzz, *sssssss,* just down to my right. What was it? Shit. It was me! It was *my* right foot on the pedal of *my* hi-hat cymbals (I'm a left-handed drummer, for all you drummers), trembling so fast it made a buzz roll. I shut it down and looked around to make sure my quivering cymbal roll had gone unnoticed. As my mind scrolled through the music I was about to play, the damn sound started up anew, surprising me as much as the first time. I had to stop it repeatedly. Taking my foot completely off the pedal didn't seem to occur to me.

As we began whatever cocktail-jazz garbage we'd been assigned, I felt myself losing access to all that had before distinguished my musicianship. The sense of danger, the playfulness. The humor and lyricism. All that stuff, though still in its crude form, should have been fostered and encouraged. I wasn't a virtuoso but at least I was original. Here in jazz school I was suddenly just some chump with a mean single-foot hi-hat roll and a sagging drum set. I could feel my inner musician retreating to the furthest reaches of my frightened soul.

When the tune was over, and I'd managed to drag it to half of its original tempo, the peanut gallery began to chime in. I'd expected the comments to be harsh, but they weren't even musical in nature. They were personal, about the scared look on my face, how the bass drum had advanced forward and I had to lunge to reach it. I felt I was being punished for not having the money for a slick drum set. And for my Southern accent. My North Carolina lilt drew further sniggers and eye-rolling—or, at least, that was my youthful perception. The proper criticism, I thought, should have been simple and obvious: *Ben's tempo dragged the whole song down.* Enough said. But because I didn't fit in, didn't wear the right clothes, didn't have the right way of speaking and, of course, the right brand-name drums, it was a personal pile-on. As the semester wore on, my performances in the class kept getting worse.

But I learned a lot about swing and music in general in that class, despite the quasi-abusive atmosphere. I learned how to pinpoint performance problems within an ensemble, which formed the basis of how I identified musical problems and their possible solutions during my time as a judge on *The Sing-Off,* a prime-time a cappella competition series that aired for a few seasons on NBC. Only, as a TV judge, I tried to bring some kindness to this method. All said and done, my experience in my brief time at University of Miami certainly toughened me up. It was an indispensable part of my education as a musician.

As I was chucking drums in the lake, I'd had enough of feeling diminished for not being a rich kid. I'd be happy to never be thrown to the Fundamentals of Swing wolves again. I was also tired of so many of the exchanges I had in Miami, where strangers would repeat what I'd just said back to my face in a mock hillbilly voice. And I looked like a skinny seventh-grade bumpkin in my secondhand flannel shirts (a decade early for grunge) and baggy jeans. Somehow the average University of Miami student of my age looked more like upper twenties, made for TV, with designer sunglasses and muscles. Tom Cruise in the movie *Risky Business.* It's like Miami wanted me to know that even though she was far south geographically, she was not culturally Southern or backward, and she made her point at my expense, daily.

As I rolled my drums down to the lake in the middle of the campus, I could feel some of these made-for-TV college bros turning my way, pausing to take note as I hurled the first drum into the water. Soon they began to cheer me on. I wasn't used to approval from this set. To be fair, I somehow hadn't really even registered them as human. For me, it was like the plastic mannequins that had decorated the campus suddenly came to life. And for them, it was probably like the little invisible nerd suddenly became a badass. I got a few backslaps and even a "Gimme five!" (This was 1984, prior to the "*high* five," which is performed above the head. A proper 1970s *gimme* five was, of course, executed at waist level.) Mark had his Polaroid camera and made a few snaps of the drums as they floated toward the far side of the lake, where the locals fished. I bowed to a few of my new frat-boy admirers. And for a moment I thought, *I might actually miss this place after all.*

Bass drum floating in Lake Osceola

MT. LABOR

MT. TABOR SUPERMARKET'S 1960S STOREFRONT SIGN AND THE SPRAWL-
ing brutalist structure beneath it seemed a little lost in time—even in
Winston-Salem in the year 1985.

> MT. TABOR: LOW PRICES WERE BORN HERE
> AND RAISED ELSEWHERE!

The manager, a dead ringer for Lyndon B. Johnson, glanced over
my application.

"What happened to your face, son?"

"I got my ass whipped, sir," I drawled, like an extra out of *Forrest
Gump*.

I was hired.

Maybe it was the "sir" part. It's always good to be respectful to
your elders, especially in the South. It was decided I'd start in January, when my hand was up to the task. It wasn't quite Christmas, so I

had a couple weeks of winter to acclimatize from the sun and fun of Miami before starting. On my way out, one of the younger scrupulously mulleted stockroom employees corrected the store's motto.

"Psst! Hey, kid: Mt. *Labor:* Low *wages* were born here and *raised* elsewhere," he whispered loudly with cupped hands in my direction, as a few of his bag-boy friends laughed.

For the next few months, I clocked sixty hours a week in that damn grocery store. Time slowed and the world outside the supermarket faded into oblivion. I came home exhausted each night. At first, I kept close contact with even the most casual friends back in Miami, whom I thought I might actually rejoin next fall. It seemed my friend Scott, an incredible singer who'd lived down the hall in my dorm, was suing the school after slipping in the dark in the dorm hall and breaking a vertebra. Big news indeed. And my roommate, Doug, had had a visit from the police. This was my fault. At the end of my semester I'd noticed a sign—STOLEN AUDIO EQUIPMENT! CALL IF YOU HAVE INFORMATION!—with a list of the missing equipment, posted in the music engineering department. I thought it would be funny if right next to it I posted AUDIO EQUIPMENT FOR SALE! MUST SELL QUICK—CALL DOUG GROBER, with the same stolen equipment listed at suspiciously low prices. Also, a fellow drummer by the name of Socrates, having recently attended a student Christian forum called "Rock Stars or Voices from Hell?," had decided to smash all his rock records. Apparently, the AC/DC and Rush albums he listened to had backward messages that might force the listener to smoke pot. I've never understood how that works. Why should unintelligible lyrics played backward be so persuasive? Besides, I'd listened to all of that music for years, never even knowing (or caring) what the lyrics actually were forward, and I had yet to smoke marijuana.

So this was my new life: a thousand miles north of my school, moving in slow motion, cutting open boxes of Mrs. Paul's Fish Sticks. I shared news and stories of Miami with the mulleted stockroom guy, as we placed boxes of fish sticks on a pallet. He agreed with me about the backward messages. "Sounds like horseshit to me," he said. Later, after work, he sent me home with a bag of weed—"Carolina Kick-Ass," he called it—with a lighter and some papers. He couldn't believe that I'd never tried pot. He also included a cassette of Yngwie Malmsteen, a famous Swedish heavy-metal guitarist who played a thousand notes a second.

Each night I'd come home, put a Stouffer's in the microwave, and retreat to my room. My poor parents. They thought they'd sent me off for good only four months ago. That had been their first taste of peace and quiet in seventeen years. But now, once again, there was one more shower to wait on before work, one more car in the driveway to move, and once again loud music blasting from my old bedroom.

"Maybe turn that down a little?" Papa politely suggested one afternoon through my bedroom door, after a couple of knocks. He asked about my plans for college.

"Well, if I'm going to go back to Miami, I'm going to need a scholarship," I said. "So I'm looking through some ROTC brochures and I'm thinking about the Army—"

"You're fucking high," he said. And disappeared.

Coincidentally, just prior to that moment, I had lit my first amateur-hour doob all by my lonesome, timing it with an overzealous inhale. The whole loosely rolled joint, a couple of inches of badly twisted paper, had gone up in smoke before any of it could reach my lips, all in less than a second. I'm told if you roll them tightly this doesn't happen. #ProTips.

Papa, of course, wasn't talking about drugs at all. He was just questioning whether I was cut out for scrubbing the barracks toilets with a toothbrush and following orders. I wasn't Army material, no matter what the recruitment officer had promised me about being in the field band. From the song "Army" (*The Unauthorized Biography of Reinhold Messner*, Ben Folds Five), written a good decade later:

Well I thought about the Army
Dad said "son, you're fucking high"
And I thought, yeah there's a first for everything
So I took my old man's advice

By February, the correspondence with my former Miami classmates slowed to a trickle. It all seemed more like last year's summer
camp now. My tan was all but faded. My stitches were out, and I'd
put away the jazz-fusion albums and the Ted Reed *Syncopation* book
that all U of M percussionists practiced religiously. I traded in my
thin-rimmed tiny John Lennon glasses for some thick black ones. I
was cleaning up spills on aisle 17 and bagging groceries like a boss. I
was doing what I was qualified to do—work at minimum wage. And
that's not hard luck. That's just life. Still, it's one thing to work shit
jobs in high school, when there's a theoretical life ahead. It's another
to realize the shitty job *is* your life.

Then there was the matter of the math:

$3.35 x 40 hours per week x the Rest of My Fucking Life =
Not Enough Dough for University of Miami.

So this is how it happens! I thought. *This is how you become the
manager guy who looks like Lyndon Johnson. You start out as a bag boy
and you just keep doing it until your nuts drop and your parents die and
leave their house to you. Frozen in time thirty years on, wearing the
same white button-down shirt, tie, and glasses, style and technology
changing around you.*

I shuddered.

Okay, maybe I managed to inhale a tiny bit of pot with all that
paper.

After work, I found solace listening to records alone in my room, obsessively, for hours on end, like I had when I was two. I broke out my

old punk and new-wave records, as well as new bands like the Replacements, who seemed to struggle to stay in time with three chords but understood life (so I thought), stories, pain, and irony. The Smiths too. In fact, "Frankly, Mr. Shankly" came out a year too late, or that song would have certainly been my best friend as I fantasized how I would quit the grocery store. But this was a rather friendless era, and this music was my only company. I didn't care if it turned me to Satan.

I'd found no such company, advice, or danger in the kind of records that students of academic jazz were trained to make—the music I'd tried so hard to love while at Miami. I had been understandably starry-eyed about my peers, who knew the cool scales, could play the jazz stylings of the masters, and had real gigs after classes. Even if I felt they were a little mean to me. But I now imagined those same cool kids aging into cocktail entertainers. I was beginning to suspect I'd dodged a bullet when I was sent down from jazz school. Had I been fucking high? Why had I chosen to study music I didn't even like?

I was beginning to rebel against academia, but I can now appreciate that my short semester at Miami provided me with an invaluable harmonic vocabulary, all still very much a part of my musicianship. Half my heart has always been in primal rock and roll, but the other half will always beat in odd time signatures, warmed by gratuitously intricate melodies and fancy harmony—all of which was introduced to me in music school. My defection back to Team Rock and Roll was, in part, a defense mechanism that helped ease the disappointment of having been chewed up and spat out of school.

But, still, something bigger was brewing.

Maybe I could/should finish these piles of song fragments I'd been sitting on, so I might make a living making my own kind of music one day? The only problem was, I hadn't come up with "my own kind of music" yet. Exhausted at the end of each day, I could barely get my shoes off, much less write a song. I remember telling Papa that I'd started nearly a hundred songs in my life but hadn't been able to finish a single one, at least one with words.

"Well, Benjamin," he said, "maybe it's just that you're not a songwriter."

He was right. At that very moment, I was not a songwriter. I was a fragment-writer at best. I was a broke college dropout who lived with his parents and called himself a songwriter. I decided at that moment that I would do whatever it took to finish songs—good ones. I forged ahead in my room after work with a notebook, no matter how tired I was. I finished verses in my head as I stamped prices on cans and pushed pallet jacks, grinding my teeth to the groove of my ideas.

But the more lost I got in my songs, the more I fell asleep at the proverbial wheel at work. I was still a kid you wanted to keep away from the power tools. My chronic daydreaming and fucking up started to become more apparent to my co-workers. Near the end of my three-month tenure at Mt. Labor, I was cutting open cases of canned meatstuff (that's exactly what it was called) and was so spaced that I didn't notice the teeming nest of white maggots that had covered my hands, making their way up my arms.

"GROSSSSS!" A stockroom co-worker snapped me back to earth.

It was like someone pushed up the "intense stink" fader on the mixing console of my olfactory system and hundreds of crawling white bugs suddenly came into focus. Whatever masterpiece I'd been dreaming up escaped out the top of my head.

I know how I'll get out of this shitty work, I thought one day while pricing apples. *I'll get a gig in one of those cheesy bands that play covers, like they have down at the Rhino Room. Certainly that must pay something. Then I can convince them to do some of my songs and perhaps that will lead somewhere?*

I could see it all as I double-priced the same apples by accident. I could hear the tinny PA system in the dive bar of my mind, as it played to a lonely scattered trio of people.

Ladies and gents, we are . . . Pegasus Rox! And that was Pat Benatar's "Hit Me with Your Best Shot"! Speaking of shots, folks: Remember, the more you drink, the better we sound!! Now, don't go anywhere, because we're going to play an Original! That's right, by our very own local boy Ben Folds!!! . . . Some feedback and a lone slow hand clap.

Okay. Maybe not.

Soon after the revolting maggot incident, I decided to quit Mt. Tabor Supermarket. *Fuck it.* It's not like I had a family to feed. I just walked in one day and gave my apron back like a total jackass, no explanation, and got in my car to drive to Charlotte to see a man about a synthesizer. Maybe the Clash told me to do it, I don't know.

Boj ruoy tiuq! Nnneb!
Boj ruoy tiuq! Nnneb!
Boj ruoy tiuq! Nnneb!

That's *Ben! Quit your job!* backward, for those who do not follow Satan.

THE EXISTENTIAL CHICKEN DANCE

QUITTING MT. TABOR SUPERMARKET FELT SO GOOD I FIGURED I'D TAKE it one step further and blow my meager savings on a new keyboard instrument. The Ensoniq Mirage. It was the first ever consumer digital sampler. It was like a combination recording machine and keyboard. You could sample any instrument you wanted or play pre-recorded samples from floppy disks (look these up if you're bored). I thought this was astounding! Of course, by today's standards the Ensoniq Mirage is a medieval machine. An iPhone can do all that and more, is smaller than the floppy disks themselves, and doesn't sound like it's going to break while it takes fifteen minutes to load in a simple low-res sound. At the time I thought this musical weapon might change everything.

I will be the next Thomas Dolby!

However, after messing with it for a couple weeks, I lost interest. So what if I could say a word, like "nineteen," and play it back on any pitch, "n-n-n-nineteen!" (Also look up the song "19," by Paul Hardcastle, 1985.) The novelty wore off quickly. I began to sense this piece of equipment was a procrastination machine at best. Songs were melody and words, not all the frilly production around them, I reminded myself. Until you've written a great song, who gives a damn how it's presented? Time spent sampling a washing machine or a car horn, looping it and playing a bass line with it, was time not spent on songwriting. *Focus, Folds! Finish your songs!* I was an idiot to have spent my money this way.

But just as the expensive keyboard began collecting dust in my closet, an interesting opportunity leapt out of the classifieds. A German restaurant called Veronika's was "desperately seeking" a live polka band to play at their grand opening. A real paying music job in the paper! I'd never seen such a thing! Local music ads were always full of garage-band auditions that didn't pay. I hopped straight in the car to answer this ad in person before it was too late. I brought my keyboard.

Veronika's, overlooking glamorous I-40, was positioned more like a Waffle House than fine dining, and it didn't seem close to ready for opening week. I walked through the open kitchen door in back, where I ran straight into Veronika herself.

"Can I help you with something?" she asked in a thick German accent, sporting paint-streaked overalls and carrying a can of Spackle. She and a small crew were doing touch-ups, setting up equipment and tables.

"Ma'am, my name is Ben and I saw your ad. I want to be your polka band," I said.

I explained that by using the new sampling technology I could imitate an accordion and play along with programmed polka beats on my newfangled keyboard—a one-man band, for a quarter of the cost. Plus, I added, I could learn pop songs and play them as polkas. A fun novelty. I brought the Ensoniq Mirage inside and gave her a quick demonstration. She seemed to like it and immediately took my measurements for a pair of lederhosen and wooden clogs, to be rush-delivered from the Motherland.

The pay was way better than at Mt. Tabor. One hundred and fifty clams a night, three nights a week! In one month, I would even earn enough to pay for the silly expensive keyboard. Then I could save for University of North Carolina at Greensboro, where, I had decided, I would give college the old college try once again in the fall.

It was midsummer 1985 and I had my first regular music job.

By the second hour of night one, the waitstaff were catching on that I only knew four polkas, which I brazenly recycled every twenty minutes. Their polite, automated waiter smiles soon gave way to scowls and rolled eyes, as they passed by with trays of weiner schnitzel and frosty mugs. But scowl as they might, the repertoire for my tenure at Veronika's would remain, stubbornly:

1. "Beer Barrel Polka"
2. "The Chicken Dance"
3. "Ta-Ra-Ra Boom-De-Ay"
4. "Edelweiss" (a waltz to mix things up, of course)

Rewind and repeat, bitches—I ain't learning one more polka!
I learned that it didn't matter how many times I played that damn "Chicken Dance" song. As soon as its first goofy strains of canned accordion oozed from my Peavey amp, the old folks would limp, wallow, or lumber to the dance floor, jam their thumbs in their armpits, and start flapping their elbows. And that's before they'd downed a few steins.

"The Chicken Dance" is Polka-Nip. Apply generously. #PolkaProTips.

Later, when the bell tolled drunk o' clock, I'd unleash my Rock Songs Over Polka Beat trick. (And the Veronika's staff thought it couldn't get worse!) If I'd started this job hoping I might date a waitress, I dashed those hopes with my music alone. And that's not to mention how flattering the Bavarian lederhosen must have looked hanging off my 130-pound frame.

. . .

Life as a college dropout cruised along as my electro-polka gig became routine. It was isolating. I didn't mingle with staff, and the restaurant clientele averaged in their seventies. My friends were scattered around the country now. Mama and Papa would return home from their jobs around the time I headed into mine at night. It was my first taste of the nocturnal lifestyle and I found I preferred it, even if it was a little lonesome.

With my parents out during the day, I could work freely and loudly on my songs. Though I wasn't happy with much I'd written, I did have a few I could live with. Two of them have survived: "Video" and "Emaline," although they sounded a little different then. "Video," which made its way onto the eponymous *Ben Folds Five* debut a decade later, started out as a strummy rocker in 4/4 rather than the 6/8 dirge it became, and "Emaline," which still sounds similar, used to have a lot of lyrics about shaving my head. (By the time of the song's commercial release on *Naked Baby Photos*—Ben Folds Five, 1998—those lyrics had given way to a story about dating an unusual girl who is misunderstood by nearly everyone and results in the singer's own alienation from friends.) I was also playing around with a waltz that became the song "Boxing." It was all instrumental then, except for the single line of the chorus, "Boxing's been good to me, Howard."

After a few months, Veronika's and the incredible Hi-Tech One-Man Fake-Ass Polka Band began drawing a regular crowd. Loyal and eccentric, the demo skewed gray and happy. It was nearly all couples, because, after all, who goes to a polka bar to pick up chicks?

My favorite regulars were an elderly couple, whose names I've long forgotten. Their eccentricity was worthy of a Tom Waits song. They cut a fine Viennese waltz, despite or perhaps because of the husband's wooden leg, which required a conspicuous kick to the side to straighten it every three beats. He'd fought in World War II. She'd been a schoolteacher for fifty years. They'd lived all over the world. I thought they were the best, and we often struck up a conversation on my breaks.

They even hired me one night to play a party at their home. They requested that I arrive ready to go in my Bavarian getup. And so I hopped into my 1976 AMC Hornet to make a long drive up into the middle of nowhere west of Winston-Salem, looking like an extra from *The Sound of Music.*

They make this ninety-minute trek weekly just to do the damn Chicken Dance and sling Spaten-Bräu? I wondered.

Their little home was perched on a peak in the foothills at the end of a winding dirt road. They greeted me at the door—he in coat and tie, she in an old-fashioned dress. There were party favors and the wife offered me a bubbly drink before I began. Being offered alcohol was still quite a compliment. I'm pretty sure I didn't even look old enough to drive.

As it was time to start my first set, I realized that no guests had been invited. This was obviously a private show. Just them, and me. *Okay. Slightly odd,* I thought, *but, hey, it's a paying gig!* I cycled through my four-tune repertoire for a couple hours as they kicked around the living room, with intermittent breaks where we sat and talked. It suddenly didn't seem so weird. They were just enjoying life. They told me amazing stories of being stationed around the world, and I sipped wine like an adult. This was way better than the grocery store.

As odd as playing private living room affairs for old couples with wooden legs might sound, there was one other couple who takes the cake (German chocolate, of course). I'd seen this odd duo plenty of times at Veronika's, though we'd never spoken. They had a habit of sitting side by side, facing away from the music. They never got up to dance. One night as I finished off my Power Polka Tetrad, which ended with a feeble theme and variations on "Beer Barrel Polka," and clopped my way back to the kitchen for my schnitzel dinner and a Coke, the pair beckoned me to sit.

The husband, who looked like Flanders from *The Simpsons,* motioned to an empty chair across the table. He had a loose tan corduroy jacket and wide collar. His wife was sitting next to him in a hippie dress, her hair stuffed underneath some kind of Amish-looking headwear. They were in their mid-forties, I would say. It all felt very serious and formal. They wasted no time on small talk. The man launched into a bunch of questions:

Did I think it was possible to read minds?

Did I know that rooms had memories?

Did I know what parapsychology was?

I was, they announced, looking at two parapsychologists. They then answered all the questions themselves. They also mentioned they taught at Wake Forest, but it seemed far-fetched to me that Wake had a department for this kind of gobbledygook. Maybe their day job was teaching something traditional like English and this was their hobby? At any rate, they seemed dead serious.

I'm going to put this weird shit into a song, I thought. (I never did.)

They felt obligated, they said, to warn me that I was doing everyone in the room a great disservice as I performed. They told me they sensed I was bored. They told me it was obvious that I thought I was better than everyone else in the room. And no matter how polite my outward demeanor, my inner smug boredom was harshing the mellows of everyone near. This mellow-harshing would radiate from me, into their lives, and to others, and so on. They even insisted that the knock-on effect of this sort of insincerity was at the heart of the world's problems. War, world famine, prejudice. I wasn't sure I wanted to take credit for all that!

They were there, they said, to teach me to appreciate the power I was wielding, because I had an unusually strong aura and charisma— *well, shucks!* Charisma carries with it responsibility. They suggested that when I performed I should always be present, kind, and engaged. They implored me to always remember that the intention with which you play each note has an effect on the people listening. An audience's time, presence, and attention are great gifts to a performer. I too had a gift to share, but it wasn't worth anything if I wasn't mindful. I should never sleepwalk my way through playing music, skipping across each note as if each one was a step closer to getting the fuck out of there. It was far braver to actually care, they concluded—to savor each phrase, to give something of myself, no matter what kind of music it was.

They had essentially declared me to be an existential chicken, not rising to the challenge of performing earnestly with intent. I knew better, they said, and they were certain I was capable of more.

To be honest, I thought they were pretty fucking creepy, and I wasn't happy I missed out on my schnitzel break. But I had to admit that some of what they said struck a profound chord. I probably *was* bored and smug inwardly, though I didn't think it was obvious to anyone else. I figured I was giving it the ol' showbiz treatment.

Wasn't I energetic enough?

Nah, that wasn't the point, they said. I just wasn't being genuine. I had to admit they were right. I *was* phoning it in.

When I had first taken the gig, I'd written off all Veronika's goofball clientele, those regulars who were so easily entertained by a shitty little fake accordion over an even shittier drum machine. But as I got to know them, I learned they had incredible stories to tell. The parapsychologists' words and advice, no matter how fruitcake they seemed at the time, planted a seed, or at least they reinforced something I was beginning to learn anyway.

A good thirty years later, from Veronika's German Restaurant to shithole punk-rock clubs, from Royal Albert Hall to Radio City Music Hall, I understand what these two were trying to tell me. They weren't even musicians, but it's a great lesson in music.

I promise you that performances, presentations, and public speeches will improve when you can acknowledge that your audience has made a choice to be there and to give you their attention. They've changed their plans, traveled, and paid hard-earned money, and you should never take that for granted. They have come, as a certain Billy

Joel (god*damn* he's good) once said, "to forget about life for a while."
Fade in a cheap digital accordion version of "Piano Man."

Being present and mindful is easier said than done. Sometimes it seems nobody is listening, and it's tempting to disconnect accordingly. Sometimes there's one heckler that overshadows the rest of the crowd. It's easy to be distracted by less-than-perfect situations, especially when you've turned your passion into an occupation. It's hard not to set your soul to "autorepeat" or "autopilot." I've been guilty of focusing on something wrong with my monitors, or some fellow I wish wasn't beatboxing on the front row in a solo piano show, when I should have been inside the music, appreciating that there were other human beings in the audience giving me their time.

It's always the easy way out, being an existential chicken. Not really being there. It's harder, it's riskier, to be present. But we should try like hell to be. And not just in music, but in every action and exchange in our short lives. I can tell you that when I inwardly acknowledge the effect that music and my presence can have on others, even the old songs seem new again.

And you don't have to kiss the audience's ass. You don't have to bust a move, tell jokes, or juggle. You don't even have to speak or smile. It's an internal thing—an intention that radiates out of you. It's humility and gratitude. It's about living inside the notes, and between them, and understanding that each of those notes may mean a completely different thing to each person in an audience. Once it leaves your fingertips or your lips, it's no longer yours. Maybe it never was.

At Veronika's with guest trombonist (not pictured)

OF MACE AND MEN

PAPA HAD BEEN CLEAR AS I HEADED TO VERONIKA'S WITH HIS CAR that night.

"Don't bring my car back home tonight on fumes again Benjamin fill the damn thing up *before* work not after and do it at the 7-Eleven close to home because I wouldn't stop in any of those places downtown especially late at night that's just *asking* to be mugged also keep the car doors locked for the stoplights too. Okay?"

Sure, sure . . . Eighteen-year-old me didn't need Papa's advice. I just needed his Chevy Suburban to cart some extra musical equipment. This truck was the workhorse vehicle Papa drove for his gig inspecting houses for the city of Winston-Salem, in the very neighborhood he advised me to avoid. He knew from whence he spoke. Shadowy figures lurked even in broad daylight in this strip of downtown off the highway near Veronika's, which is why he had an assortment of weapons tucked in the driver's door pocket.

I generally didn't bother changing back into my street clothes after work. Too much trouble. I finished the gig this particular evening, loaded out my equipment in full Bavarian getup, and pulled out of the parking lot of Veronika's to head home as always.

Fuel light! Oops . . . Forgot! Fumes! Must find filling station!

I pulled into a forbidden gas station on the dodgy side of town—a skinny teenager in lederhosen hopping down from a macho cowboy truck, well after midnight. But the gas station was well lit, and I made it snappy, taking note of a shadowy figure lurking around the dumpster. He was what I imagined a hobo from Steinbeck's *Of Mice and Men* might look like, in his ill-fitting soiled clothing with filthy clumped hair he'd probably cut in a bus-stop bathroom mirror using a metal lid from an old can of tuna. He was just limp-walking in a corner of the lot with his hands deep in his pockets, as one does at midnight. I figured he was at a safe distance and I made sure to look like a man on a mission.

After pumping the gas, I stuffed a few bills through the little hole in the foggy Plexiglas booth. The attendant's lifeless hand lazily dragged the money toward the register, barely looking up from his magazine. No stranger to the Plexiglas cube myself, I knew he probably saw all kinds of shit go down nightly, as he peered over his *Hustler* and sipped his tepid hazelnut-flavored coffee. I didn't even wait for my change or the "have a nice evening" that was mumbled through the distorted talk-back speaker.

The shadowy figure seemed to have moved on and I walked quickly back to the Suburban. Now, personally, I've never felt inclined to mug anyone, and I'm sure you haven't either. But, you know, if I saw someone dressed like I was at 1 A.M.? One hundred thirty pounds of Bavarian steel, all alone and carrying cash? I'm just saying. It would certainly be a good place to start a mugging career. From there, you could move up to more-difficult jobs, like snatching purses from old ladies.

I climbed into the Suburban, hit the auto door lock, and was nearly out of the parking lot when a chill came over me. A god-awful smell, like a goat soaked in dumpster juice, filled the car. I looked to my right with a start and snapped my head back to the road ahead, as if not looking at him would make him disappear. It was . . . the Shadowy Figure! He was sitting in the passenger's seat right next to me! *Fuck fuck fuck!* This was precisely what Papa had warned me about.

"They make you drive them to Mt. Airy"—Papa's words echoed through my head—"where they *take your car and cut your nuts off*."

I nearly shat my fine German leather.

I slammed on the brakes, halfway into the road, looking straight ahead, as he told me in a shaky tense monotone that I was to drive him to *Mt. Airy* (!), where he'd drop me off (without killing me, he added) and take the car off my hands. He said then I could "call my fucking mommy" to pick me up.

It's astounding that I didn't just get out and run to the booth for help. Certainly, even the jaded little man at the register would have let a kid in and called the cops? But that's not the way a teenage boy thinks. I glanced down past the nineteenth-century buttonless fly of my silly leather pants, which, by design, lay perpetually half open, and I surveyed Papa's driver's door war chest.

I had three choices of weapons, it seemed, and I weighed each option.

Okay. I knew I wasn't going to shoot anyone. So the derringer was out.

The Mace! That's the ticket! I thought.

Then I realized that if I sprayed inside the car, I'd get an eyeful too and wouldn't be able to drive.

Hmm . . . which one of these . . . But I had paused too long, and that made the Shadowy Figure nervous.

"Fuckin' hit it, kid, let's go!" he erupted, his words hitting me just before his nasty breath arrived.

I had to act quickly, and I opted for the knife, which I pulled out calmly in a show of confidence, as adrenaline shot through my wiry frame. Then I heard myself speak.

"Sir, I'm going to have to ask you to get out of my car."

I remained completely deadpan. I established full eye contact as I gripped the knife handle, the way a toddler might a fork. We were both still, and quiet. The motor was running. The turn signal was tocking away. It seemed like a long time, though I'm sure it wasn't. Just long enough to forget how I was dressed.

The stinky man looked me up and down, laughed, and tried to open the car door, but of course I had locked the doors when I got in. A pause. I fumbled around the panel of the driver's door with my left hand, my eyes fixed on the Shadowy Figure and my right hand still clutching the knife. The amount of time I was taking was making him even more nervous. Maybe as the Shadowy Figure had left home that night, his dad had warned him of nerd weirdo Bavarian serial killers.

They lock you in their Chevy Suburbans and cut your nuts off!

Who knows what he thought, but as soon as my left hand managed to clumsily locate the UNLOCK button, he slid out of the car in a hurry. He said I was lucky he didn't take that knife right out of my skinny hand and stick it up my ass, as he slammed the door with all the energy he would have beaten me to a pulp with. He returned to the shadows, Shadowy Figure that he was, perhaps having second thoughts about this midnight mugging career. I put my wooden shoe to the metal pedal and sped down Peters Creek Parkway with a giant knife pressed to the steering wheel, my skinny, hairy legs quaking beneath it.

AN ACCIDENTAL MENTOR

AS THE SUMMER OF 1985 DREW TO AN END, SO DID MY ELECTRONIC-polka-music gig, and I enrolled for fall semester in music school at the nearby and eminently affordable University of North Carolina at Greensboro. I don't know what got into me the day I took the placement tests for UNC–G's music school. I could have breezed through a good year or two of my basic music subjects and entered at an appropriate level, probably at about fourth semester. But I decided to answer just enough of the test to manipulate my placement as a second-semester music major, at the 102 levels. I just left the rest of the test blank and turned it in, even though I knew the answers. Unsurprisingly, finding myself in courses that were too easy, I became bored and started skipping class. I got a D-minus in ear training because, although I could sight-sing every note, I got stubborn and refused to learn an antiquated method called "solfège." You may know it, even if you've never studied music: "do-re-mi-fa-sol-la-ti-do." Like Julie Andrews sang in *The Sound of Music*.

Doe, a deer. A female deer.

That's actually all I know of that song.

Solfège was, I thought, for students who couldn't remember the pitches and intervals and needed the associative phonetics. It's actually quite useful for classical musicians communicating scale degrees in certain situations, but to me it was like training wheels that I didn't need. I was sight-singing the pitches anyway, and isn't that the point?

My most curious abdication during my UNC–G placement tests was the piano test. During that audition, I sat on my hands and pretended I'd never touched the instrument. I can't tell you exactly what was going through my mind. Maybe I was just ashamed to demonstrate how awful my sight-reading really was. Maybe I hoped that by starting over, I'd be forced to improve my reading, catching up on any bits of technique that I missed as a child. I guess we never fully understand the little self-destructive quirks that present themselves along the way. In any event, I was placed in first-semester class piano, in a roomful of non-music students who couldn't tell you which note was middle C.

The group piano class was conducted in a large semicircle of Wurlitzer electric pianos, all connected to one group mix of headphones. Every student's piano came through everyone else's headphones simultaneously, so you couldn't tell who was playing what. The bored instructor was tethered to his own wires and piano at the mouth of the semicircle, to demonstrate how to do things like pressing a key down and letting it up when you wanted it to stop. It was a one-finger-at-a-time affair, the way my father types an email. It was a fine opportunity for a keyboard-proficient class clown.

I tormented the poor grad-student teacher, whose job it was to teach us how the fingers are numbered and where to place our hands. When he wasn't looking my way, I'd throw in some kind of crazy jazz lick, or I'd re-harmonize the one-note melody we were learning, and I kept a pretty good poker face. When he realized he wasn't going to catch the joker, he begged for it to please stop. It was an interesting challenge to try and lay my hands on the keys as if it were a foreign language.

After a couple of weeks, the usual grad-student teacher took a day off, and in his place stood a disheveled old man. *This is really going to be fun,* I thought. I screwed around with the old fellow for the full fifty minutes, but he seemed utterly oblivious. *What an idiot,* I thought, throwing in a few extra ridiculous mocking riffs, with audible chuckles from the rest of the class.

As class let out, he stopped me at the door.

"What's your name, might I ask?" he said, very gently. In fact, the kindness he'd maintained throughout the whole class had begun to make me feel like a dick. I figured I deserved the smackdown he was about to deliver. Instead, he only asked if I would be so kind as to make a little time at 3 P.M. that day to drop by his office. Ah, I saw how this guy was. He was going to give me the afternoon to get nervous and then break me down in his office, alone, away from my peers.

At 3 P.M. sharp, he answered the door of his top-floor corner office, which housed a gorgeous mid-twentieth-century Steinway D concert piano, a library of beautiful scores arranged in floor-to-ceiling built-in shelves, and wonderful old photographs. Well lived in and loved, the office spoke volumes about this man's personality and life. Plus, it had great art deco windows with a view of Tate Street that almost made me like the school. It seemed he was big stuff at UNC–G. Who'd have known?

He introduced himself as Robert Darnell. He'd been in this office at UNC–G, he said, for forty years. His manner was bright and easy, if a little weary. He was the oldest member of the music staff, probably in his upper seventies. He led me straight to the piano.

"You don't sight-read very well, do you?" he asked.

I shook my head.

"I see. So these silly people placed you in first-semester piano? Of course! Damn shame." He placed a song by Stephen Foster on the piano music stand. "Do you think you could play any of this for me?"

I struggled, stopped, and shrugged, a little embarrassed.

"That's okay, that's okay!" he assured me. "Just get through the one-note melody for me. It's 'Swanee River'—you've heard it. Cheat. Play by ear if you need to. Just play the tune."

Easy enough. I could do that.

"Good! Good! Now play it like you want to. Any way you feel. Take your time. Add new chords, re-harmonization, counterpoint— have at it!"

I did that too. And then some. I mean, it wasn't like Oscar Peterson or anything mind-blowing. I just played in my style, the way I heard it.

The next words out of his mouth were: "How would you like a full scholarship to study piano under me for the rest of the year?"

I came in for what I assumed would be a spanking and instead was leaving with a full music scholarship? For being an asshole? I was blown away!

He explained that this was his last year at UNC–G. He'd looked me up that afternoon after class piano, and he noticed that I was a percussion major.

"With all due respect to the percussion department," he said, "you might get more out of time spent at the piano."

I went straight to my percussion teacher to tell him I was defecting to the piano department and received the tongue-lashing I thought I was going to get from Robert Darnell at 3 P.M. I was a quitter, the percussion teacher said. Obviously, I knew that. Everyone knew that. Or, rather, being called a quitter stung because I was already too tough on myself for feeling I didn't have the stamina to properly follow through on things—jobs, school, and, of course, songs.

The outrageous temper I'd displayed when I was little, punching holes in walls when I felt I wasn't good enough, had found another way out in college. And that way was inward. These lyrics from the bridge of "Boxing":

Sometimes I punch myself hard as I can
Yelling "Nobody cares," hoping someone will tell me how wrong I am

I felt desperately behind schedule on my life's journey at that point, missing semesters, switching schools and majors. I felt I was floating aimlessly. I often thought I'd need to be getting married soon, fast approaching twenty years old. Where did *that* come from? Sure, the South likes to marry 'em off young, but it's not like I was born in Victorian times. I think I wanted these stamps of approval, these certificates, so I could justify the perceived frivolity and hedonism of pursuing music. I was a kid who couldn't bear standing still, silence, being alone, and, most of all, uncertainty. Floating from school to school, major to major, with no plan toward my career, not a girlfriend in sight, was proof I was an absolute loser. A quitter, yes, I knew that. I didn't need a butt-hurt percussion director reinforcing it.

It was time for a proper teacher, a mentor, someone who could combine lessons of life experience with music. The year of studying with Robert Darnell was formative, empowering, and inspiring. But we didn't spend time focused on the piano like I expected. He told stories of his youth as a promising new young American composer. He'd met Aaron Copland, gotten awards and commissions, even taken a boat across the Atlantic to study with the famous Madame Boulanger in Paris. But he said the pressure had gotten to him and he'd suffered a serious nervous breakdown at twenty-three, from which he'd never quite recovered. He often told me I reminded him of a young version of himself and he worried for me, that I might have a nervous breakdown one day too. I suppose my being hard on myself was more obvious than I knew.

Robert Darnell's disposition was not suited for the life of a composer or a performer, so he had settled for teaching, which he never regretted. But he wanted to give me the tools to go out and do what I was destined to do and not settle for less. Sometimes he had me bring in my own songs and he would help me analyze them, considering alternate compositional, harmonic, and general orchestration options. He didn't discriminate against my rock leanings. He told me a wonderful story about a man who came to his grade school in Texas to demonstrate one of the first electric guitars. "The whole school was assembled in the gymnasium. We were dead silent as this man plugged a freakishly thin-looking guitar into a box, about ten feet away from him. You know, the way you would plug something into a wall!" Darnell said. "And then! He strummed a chord . . . and the sound came from *the box*! Yards away! Not from the guitar! It was a miracle. We were all amazed!"

Robert Darnell saw music as dynamic, ever changing, and exciting, and he was always curious and interested. He once asked me if I'd heard of a man named Eric Clapton. He was very interested in Mr. Clapton's playing but also in his singing, which Darnell described as "speaking on pitches."

"It's all he needs to do," Darnell said. "Tell his story by speaking the notes. No ornamental vibrato, no sustain. Very effective."

He asked to hear recordings of music I liked, so he could understand where I was coming from. This informal way of passing on experience, lessons on music and life, exchanging ideas—this accidental mentorship—was as new to him as it was to me. It was his final breaking from tradition before his retirement and a wonderful hand extended to me from another era.

We looked at scores and talked about how simple some of the most complex-sounding solutions often were. He knew very little about jazz, in the way that I had come to understand jazz, but he could sight-read a full orchestra score by cobbling a piano part together from all the orchestra parts. And he surprised me by playing back a Bill Evans phrase on the piano after hearing the record only once. I'd always thought classical guys didn't have ears.

Robert Darnell retired at the end of the year and I began to lose interest in the music department altogether. After experiencing proper mentorship, my music classes began to feel a little shallow and impersonal.

When I tell people that so much of my success in the music business is luck, I'm not talking about the luck of being discovered playing some club, or appearing on the right TV show at the right time, or running into some music mogul at a party. I'm talking about stuff like this, like meeting Robert Darnell, God rest his awesome soul.

I used to "photoshop" the same photo of Darnell every day before my lesson, across the street at Kinko's, using the same Robert Darnell photo, and bring them into my lessons.

LEDERHOSEN TO PINK BOW TIES

Death Onstage with Dignity

IN GREENSBORO IN THE MID-EIGHTIES THERE SEEMED TO BE HIGH DE-
mand for electric bassists who could slap and play ridiculous white-
man funk. I decided I would be the man to fill this void. If you can
play drums and guitar a little, you can pick up funk bass well enough
to work in a cover band. So I got myself a shameful Steinberger-copy
bass guitar from a pawnshop, for one hundred and fifty dollars. It was
a dreadful-looking futuristic black truncated stick with some strings.
And within a few weeks I was slapping that bitch like it owed me
money. I do realize that doing the electric slide with a cheesy bass
hanging high across the breasts and rocking the "white man's over-
bite" ain't exactly the portrait of dignity, but I felt it was an improvement over polkas. If I was going to be found at the bottom of a river
somewhere, the victim of a carjacking, at least I wouldn't be in leather
shorts, suspenders, and clogs.

. . .

Early on at UNC-G I found work in a lounge/top-40 band at an Italian restaurant called Giovanni's. The couple whose band it was fought openly onstage, while the sparse local audience howled and cheered them on. Everyone assumed it was an act. But the band knew better and we looked at our shoes in shame as they argued. Sometimes the couple would even stop mid-song and have it out. The husband would yell at the rest of us too—also a big hit with the audience.

"I had a smoke-blowin' show band in Las Vegas, you turkeys! I could have stayed there and wouldn't have to play with jokers like you!"

Giovanni, one of the owners—the other owner coincidentally turned out to be my cousin's stepmother—took me back to his office one night for a talk. With a gin martini in hand, he showed me drawers full of handguns and a special, sentimental place on the floor where he'd had sex with a famous female singer back in the seventies.

Giovanni told me, in his overly cultivated, gravelly *Godfather* accent, "One-ah day! One-ah day *you* gonna be ah-fuckin' famous, Ben Folezzz!"

Finally, someone sees this! I thought. *Thank you!*

Then he finished his thought.

"Yez! You-ah gonna be a famous . . . a famous *clown!*"

Well, not quite the kind of famous I was thinking of, but it was still recognition, I guess. He showed me pictures of himself as a young man posing with a comic by the name of Red Skelton. I would one day be like Red Skelton, he proclaimed. *"Clowwwwwn!"*

He said I was funny, much funnier than the silly couple I worked for, the ones with the domestic quarrel shtick. The Couple-Fighting-Onstage comedy routine had played itself out, he thought. Particularly the gag where the husband threatened to hit his wife onstage and the guitarist walked out. It seemed too real, he said. He preferred the moments when I sang "Rawhide" or moved to the piano for "Great Balls of Fire."

"That," he told me, "is why people come a-back!"

I respectfully declined his offer to take over the band, because I didn't want to shit on the couple who'd hired me, even if they were miserable to work for. I played the gig awhile longer before moving on, taking pickup gigs here and there, on piano, bass, or drums, but the extracurricular schedule soon took its toll on my studies. I struggled to make it to 8 A.M. theory classes after late-night gigs, often many miles from town. It was all too much so I decided to take some time from University and just earn money.

I took a gig playing bass and directing a house band at Pinehurst Golf Resort near Fayetteville, North Carolina, and lured a couple talented musician friends away from their studies at UNC–G to be the rhythm section: a drummer named Dave Rich and a guitarist named Millard Powers (who now plays with Counting Crows). This ensemble was pretty large, fronted by six singers. After a few weeks rehearsing volumes of medleys at our new home at Pinehurst, we were ready for opening weekend at their new spiffy nightclub. Opening weekend turned out to be our and the nightclub's last.

We were but one of many identical bands at their sister resorts. There was a format and repertoire to follow. One of the format's shticks involved a female singer flirting with the older golfers and bringing them to the dance floor. On that first night, our best female singer, following the script, approached a well-dressed older gentleman seated at a large table with his wife and friends, and pressured him to dance. A spot followed them to the dance floor as the audience egged them on. Then we all watched in horror as the poor man went into violent spasms, collapsing in front of the bandstand. A few doctors, who happened to be seated at his table, tried desperately to keep him alive before the paramedics showed up, to no avail. He was dead from a massive heart attack before the paramedics arrived.

At the end of the harrowing evening, in which the deceased was carried away under a blanket, we quietly rolled up cables and put

away our equipment. The place had cleared out, except for the band and some remaining staff. The local soundman, sporting a massive mustache and baseball cap, broke the silence with—and these were his exact words—"Well, I hate to say it, but you guys were *knockin' 'em dead* tonight," and exited the restaurant with his case of mics.

That was it for our Pinehurst gig, but the company found us work at one of their other resorts. We took a Greyhound bus to Schuss Mountain, Michigan, where we joined a large show band called the Schussy Cats—a Northern Michigan tradition. Suited up in pink cummerbund and bow tie, I was beginning to get the picture. Nearly all the cover-band gigs were corny. They'd seemed so appealing back when I bagged groceries and it was a pipe dream to put food on the table with music.

Our audiences at Schuss Mountain weren't afforded any more dignity than we were. They were called "Fudgies." "Fudgy" is a not-so-endearing term for tourists from Southern Michigan vacationing in Northern Michigan. The word was coined by Mackinac Island locals who made their living selling their homemade fudge to tourists and then mocking them for buying it.

That summer rockin' the Fudgies left me with what the Schussy Cat singers called "transition damage"—what you get from memorizing too many endless medleys with segues every fifteen seconds. I can't hear four bars of "Gary Indiana" without a mental transition into "Oklahoma," dovetailing into "Kansas City Blues," and so forth. If I hear a song with a state's name, I have to compulsively work my way through them all. It's a problem, still.

Transition damage and all, I'm very grateful for what I learned playing with these various cover-band gigs. You learn a lot about songs by experiencing what works about each in front of many audiences. Seeing when they get up to dance, where they sing along or point to their best friend while mouthing a phrase that means something special to their friendship. I put in my time as a musical mercenary—

Slapping my way through a wedding-band gig, 1989

playing radio hits, cocktail jazz, dance music, and requests on piano, bass, and drums. I believe, as undignified as it often felt, it was invaluable life (and death) experience. I highly recommend a couple of years of it, no matter how cool you think you are. The things you will learn.

I made a pact with myself upon returning to UNC–G to not take another paycheck playing music that wasn't my own. I had witnessed far too many middle-aged musicians who still carried their "originals" in their back pocket, harboring false hope that their own songs could ever see the light of day. Sticking around too long in cover-band world was a slippery slope, so I decided to take a considerable pay cut to wait tables at lunchtime instead, leaving my evenings open for starting my own band with original songs.

This was a leaner lifestyle. Gone were the days of eating out and buying new LPs, but working a day job seemed more dignified. Music could retain its sanctity for me this way, as I would never take money to play a note I didn't want to. Cover-band work had been a good run, but I gave a bag full of cheesy show shirts, ties, and various sparkled suits to Goodwill, and I never looked back.

MY SEMESTER OVERSEAS

RETURNING TO UNC–G, NOW WAITING TABLES, I WAS STARTING TO focus on a broader plan. I would get a band started while finishing up my degree in English Lit, seal a record deal, tour and record—the end. Something like that.

But my studies at UNC–G were interrupted by an opportunity that came via my childhood friend Anna Goodman, who was now attending Duke and playing French horn in the wind ensemble. You may recall my mention of a little girl named Anna who had inspired me to play piano back in second grade? That's the same Anna. Duke University needed a percussionist for their semester in Vienna, so instead of spending my birthday blowing out candles in Greensboro with my family, as I'd expected, I found myself with a roomful of strangers playing a student concert in Budapest, Hungary.

During my surprise semester overseas, I lived with a host family, studied German, and toured Eastern Europe (before the fall of the Berlin Wall) with the wind ensemble. I spent that wonderful semester walking the streets of old Vienna each day, passing the homes of Mozart, Beethoven, Schoenberg, and so many others, with my headphones playing XTC and Peter Gabriel. I regularly attended the opera, braving clouds of BO with cheap standing-place tickets, and on weekends hopped on the school tour bus to perform in cities around Eastern Europe. Bitten by the touring bug, I now wanted to travel more. I liked being surprised by what the next day might bring.

Fuck it, I thought. *In a few days, when this semester is over, I'll just go live in London and make my mark there!* I had an electric bass, a backpack with a couple changes of clothes, and about five hundred dollars in cash. I didn't know a soul in England. What the hell? Who needs a plan?

Here's a line from my song "Phone in a Pool." It kind of felt like a throwaway line at the time, but it now strikes a profound chord for me:

What's been good for the music hasn't always been so good for the life.

It's one thing to take risks playing music, where unpredictability is often rewarded, and another to take them in everyday life, where consequences are real. People often ask me if it's scary to make up a song onstage, dictating parts, on the fly, to a full orchestra. Well, no. It doesn't occur to me to worry about that. I have a jazz musician's view of mistakes. If you play a wrong note, you can always make the same mistake again on purpose and make it sound right. Insistence on the mistake can be quite musical. Indeed, "once is a mistake, twice is jazz," a quote often attributed to Miles Davis.

In life, however, this improvisational outlook, repeating mistakes to make them seem intentional, doesn't work quite as well. Being hit by a car, for instance, or getting married and divorced, are mistakes that don't improve with repetition. The fearlessness and cavalier outlook that allows me to just *go for it* in my music has caused me no small amount of grief in my life. I've had, perhaps, a few too many cheap lessons.

And so, at the end of my Viennese semester, I hopped from train to ferry for London, England—home to the music that had gotten me through high school and all my shitty jobs. British rock made sense to me, and so I figured it must come from a place that made sense. Anna thought it'd be fun to see London, so she joined me for a couple of days.

It was midnight when our ferry pulled up at Dover. I'd always wanted to see the white cliffs, even if it had to be in the dark under artificial light. Exiting the Victoria Station at around 3 A.M., we chose the first cheap hotel we could find. Over the next two days we spontaneously became a romantic couple, as young adults are wont to do when in close proximity for a few days. She flew back home before Christmas and I continued my London adventure, and though it was never discussed, I'm sure we both knew we'd be married within the year. It seemed right, even obvious, arranged somehow. We'd been best friends nearly our whole lives, and everyone who knew us both since grade school seemed to think we'd end up married. I could never tell any girl I'd dated (all two of them) everything I felt, but I'd always been able to do that with Anna. Being married in your early twenties was the Southern thing to do, something that assured everyone, including parents, that you could "be somebody."

But first I had to get to the business of making it big in London. I didn't even have a ticket back home. And why would I need one? After all, I was going to ace some auditions, join a great English band, write some hits, and live happily ever after. Then maybe Anna could return and get a job and we'd live happily ever after together? Who knows. I obviously hadn't thought this through.

That night's cheap hotel became my home for my entire time in London, and my entire time ended up being a few weeks. Resources were dwindling by the hour, but I made the acquaintance of a certain John Bartlett. He was the manager of the cheap hotel, and I remember his name because of *John Bartlett's Familiar Quo-*

tations. Mr. Bartlett could see I was struggling to make ends meet, and he admired the fearless audacity of my mission to conquer the U.K. with just a bass and some pocket change. He was kind enough to let me work for my room. Mostly, I just had to wrap the little breakfast trays in plastic wrap before the sun came up and plop them on the floor outside all the rooms. It turned out there were far more rooms than I knew. What looked like a row of multiple hotels was actually one massive shitty hotel with a number of fa-çades with different names. Maybe that was some tax-dodging scheme? Each morning I delivered old bread, sour milk, and a thimble of orange juice in a hallway the length of a city block.

One night after a day of tube trains and auditions, as I lay in my sunken ditch of a stained mattress, wondering when the poor old plaster ceiling might finally surrender and fatally wound an unsuspecting sleeping musician, John Bartlett knocked at my door. Choking back tears, his nose even redder than usual, he explained that something had happened. He couldn't say what, but he would have to leave in the morning, never to return. The drama! The new manager, he said, was not a nice man at all and I should leave soon. He offered to *give* me a few thousand pounds of cash so I could survive. This was tempting, because my bass amp had just literally gone up in smoke. It turns out that a hair-dryer converter is not sufficient to step up the voltage for a power amp. I had also yet to find a paying gig.

Out of cash, no place to stay, and no ticket home. I kept making mistakes, but I couldn't quite seem to make jazz out of this situation. I declined John Bartlett's offer and wished I had at least a little money to buy him his own copy of his book of quotes as a going-away gift. I still can't believe he hadn't heard of that book.

That night, after John Bartlett shut the door to my moldy room and disappeared down the nastiest, longest hall in London, I realized that soon this awful room would be a luxury I could no longer afford. Calling my parents for a bailout wasn't an option. Starvation seemed preferable to humiliation for a young man who'd yet to experience either. It was a matter of pride, since they'd predicted this London move wouldn't work out.

In the morning, after making a round of embarrassing collect calls to various friends across the U.S.A., I finally found a willing loaner to get me home. My friend Rob's mother was kind enough to help me out. In fact, his family had also previously given me a loan for a semester at UNC–G. Rob and I were childhood friends, from quite opposite sides of the track. We played a lot of music together and I spent a lot of time at their house, which was beautiful and large and had all kinds of nice musical equipment I'd otherwise have never had access to. I don't feel I thanked them properly to this day, so I'll say it again here. Those loans and the opportunities they afforded were invaluable, so thank you, Mr. and Mrs. Strickland.

Fitting easily in a middle economy seat between two wide asses somewhere over the Atlantic, I made the decision to drop out of college for good. I'd lost momentum. I didn't believe in it anymore. After being a working musician—hiring, firing, and paying bills—college was beginning to look childish. It now seemed like a meaningless hodgepodge of boxes to check to earn a piece of paper. It was time to concentrate on starting my band.

My father was not happy with this. It was the first time I'd ever heard genuine disappointment in his voice. He was damn near close to graduating college himself, just by doing one night class at a time for however many hundred or so years. If a severe dyslexic working two day jobs while raising a family was managing to graduate, why couldn't his son manage one more semester? But no. I was determined to start a band and get my music career off the ground. Now.

I then went to my mother for support in this decision. She didn't seem to be buying it either, until I told her that "continuing on my current path and finishing school just doesn't *feel* right." "Feel" seemed to be the magic word. She relaxed with a sigh that said, *Why didn't you say that in the first place?* I went back and tried the "college doesn't *feel* right" line on Papa, who thought that sounded like bullshit. He didn't approve but remained supportive of whatever I chose to do. He shrugged. Support with a shrug is probably the best response you can give a young man who's overly confident in his ability to make jazz out of his mistakes.

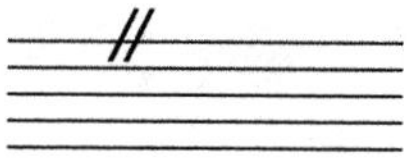

CREATIVE VISUALIZATION
OR USEFUL DELUSION?

THERE'S THIS MODE I GO INTO FROM TIME TO TIME. YOU MAY DO IT TOO. It begins with visualizing a seemingly impossible accomplishment as if it has already come to be. A trance ensues, mountains are moved, and soon it is so. When I can 'see' it, when I can just about touch it, a confident calm comes over me because I know it's as good as done. All I need to do now is put one foot in front of the other.

You may have heard this referred to as "creative visualization." Of all the self-help drivel I've read in my time, this is one bit of drivel I am down with. I get it. Results fueled by temporary delusion. Because the state of wanting to be something that you aren't or wanting something to be true which is not can make you a little crazy. After all, fantasy and reality that cannot be reconciled is, by definition, a little crazy. And being crazy saps energy. It's an uncomfortable itch. I believe that with creative visualization, it's that temporary state of craziness that pushes us to make the fantasy real, whether it's building a house, writing a movie, or running a marathon. We live inside the delusion that our fantasy is a done deal, and when we've finally made it so, we can stop being crazy. The itch has been scratched.

Part of the creative-visualization delusion for me is that I'm just a foot soldier following orders. It's the universe that wants it to be so, and so it shall be. I only have to follow through on my part.

Won't you look at me, I'm crazy
But I get the job done
I'm crazy but I get the job done

Of course, I accomplish goals without creative visualization. But it's harder to get inhuman amounts of work done when you're not crazy. It requires plain hard work, self-motivation, effort, and discipline. It requires setting short-term goals and all that, which is the standard way we execute a task. Incrementalism.

But this creative-visualization thing brings about vast changes, turns things upside down, and achieves the unachievable. And it's kind of weird, but I'd be nowhere without some useful delusion.

When I'm under the spell and direction of a creative visualization, I grow all kinds of courage I didn't have before. I experience sudden deafness to the word "no" and I pity the ignorance of those who utter it. I can power through embarrassment and shame. *Why should I care what they think?* Blindness to roadblocks sets in. Those roadblocks were Fig Newtons of my imagination in the first place! It's a little like this:

The audition has been won. I only need to practice and show up.

The book has been written. I just have to plant my ass at the type-writer and watch my fingers move.

It's like seeing it all in reverse.

I wish I could summon this state at will. I wish I could squint my eyes, imagine something, and make it so. But only a true believer can fall under the spell of creative visualization. You can make believe, but you can't make *yourself* believe. Creative visualization happens to me. I don't summon it. The greatest sincerity of desire will not alone make a thing come true. I just gave that last sentence a Victorian sentence structure to make it sound profound—but I think it's right.

For instance, I've always wanted to write a musical and have taken many steps to do so. But I haven't visualized it truly. I can't yet completely see and believe the audience coming in and being seated, and the lights going down, the actors singing my words. I only see some weak jazz hands. And I also see the realistic possibility of it closing in two weeks. Until I'm delusional, I'm not embarking on this ambition. I hope this visualization comes to me at some point, because I do have a great desire to make a musical.

I've actually found that I can often creatively visualize things that I dread—things that I don't even want to happen. Like firing someone or breaking up. Of course, it's really *me* who has made the decision, but it comes in the form of a vision, as I abdicate responsibility to "the universe," whatever the fuck that means. The inevitability of the firing shoulders some of the blame. It becomes one of those God-told-me-to-fire-your-ass things.

It wasn't my idea, Ted. I just awoke this morning and your firing was dancing before me like a Tupac hologram. What can be done? Pick up your shit and go.

See how that works next time.

I'd always been more comfortable with other people singing my songs, so when I visualized myself as a lead singer, I was terrified. I didn't believe intellectually I should be singing, but when I saw it with such clarity and inevitability, I knew that was the way. Similarly, when I went on my first solo piano tour years later, it was because I visualized it that way. I dreaded it. I shook in my boots. I had to convince my manager, booking agent, and audience of something I wasn't even sure I could do.

Retreating home after my aborted London move, I could suddenly and clearly visualize Majosha, which was to become my first serious band, as if it were already so.

It didn't matter what Millard or Dave, who'd played with me on those resort gigs, had going on at that moment or whether they also realized it was to be. The three of us would be Majosha, and we would soon be gracing stages and making recordings. I had already imagined the kind of house we would live in. I saw a van with shag carpet, road maps, and equipment rattling around the back. I visualized the gigs, an EP, an album, and even a manager. And by late summer, all those things would have materialized, powered by my useful delusion and a lot of hard work.

I was twenty-one years old. I had a high school diploma and mounting debt. I was a waiter of tables. And I was a bassist with a beast of a band that was hungry for new songs, over which I would gladly toil. In the middle of a Majosha recording session one night, as Millard, Dave, and I were rushing to finish our debut cassette EP, to be called *Majosha: Five Songs About Jesus* (none of the four songs on the EP were about Jesus), Anna and I casually announced that, oh by the way, we had gone to South Carolina earlier that day and were now married. They congratulated us, shrugged, and we got on to the next take. Anna was a good sport about the recording sessions taking precedence over a honeymoon and about living in the house with a nasty rock band. After all, she was the band's manager.

Anna and I were both ambitious and utterly focused on getting this band up and running. We lived and breathed the band and the business around it. Millard and Dave were more part-time about the whole endeavor, but, man, were we a fine trio! Musically, we were, as Dave liked to say, "tight as a gnat's ass." (He may have had personal experience with which to back up this metaphor, who knows— there are some things you don't ask a man.) Dave, who was a self-taught monster on the drum set, was the swinger, the bad boy of the band. He once had three girlfriends on-the-go simultaneously, all named Kim. I shit you not. He was three-timing multiple Kims. It became really stressful answering the phone at the band house.

ME: "Dave, pssst! It's *Kim* on the phone! She sounds upset.
What should I tell her?"
DAVE: "Which Kim?"
ME: "Am I supposed to actually ask her that?"
DAVE: ". . ."

Millard, the guitarist and singer, was quite the shredder of everything from jazz to heavy metal. He'd sit on the floor of the living
room—also his bedroom, through which everyone had to cross—
straddling a bong and playing a million notes a second through Rockman distortion. The Rockman was a little box that looked like a Sony
Walkman and allowed you to play professional-ish guitar sounds
through headphones or a stereo. It was developed by Tom Scholz, who
was famous for his rock band Boston. "More Than a Feeling"!

The three of us had played a lot of funk together as a cover band,
so that was naturally a big part of our sound, even though we all preferred English new-wave music and thoughtful almost-punk bands
like Squeeze or Elvis Costello and the Attractions. At our gigs, always
slightly insecure and wanting to keep the enthusiasm of the crowd up,
we'd reflexively do what had worked as a cover band. We'd break into
"The roof, the roof, the roof is on *fire*" when we worried our heartfelt
songs had been boring everyone. Then, when we had safely blown the
roof off the motherfucker, we'd shift back to a ballad like "Emaline."
It was probably a little confusing for the audience. But it's always
tough to debut earnest, unknown songs as a new band. It feels like
you're making everyone eat their spinach. You have to hold your own,
stay strong, and deliver your songs until they stick. But we weren't
that kind of band.

Majosha could be described, as could most bands, as a failure. That
is, we never "made it." The band was probably doomed from the start—
from the moment I chose that hideous name. We had heard "Majosha"
was a Native American word for "penis" (as if there was only one Native
American language). I highly doubt it's a word for anything at all, and

I'm not sure where we got that from, but maybe it gives further insight into how and what a young man creatively visualizes.

Majosha went through a few *member* changes (no pun intended), including the addition of Evan Olson, who was a total rock-star front man. We also went through a few drummers before settling on a fellow named Eddie Walker. I guess I kept creatively visualizing the

Cover of the cassette version of Shut Up and Listen to Majosha—*from L to R: Evan Olson, me, Eddie Walker, Millard Powers*

wrong drummer? After eighteen months of regional weekend gigs, we were beginning to get some attention. Majosha's self-released album, called *Shut Up and Listen to Majosha,* began receiving some airplay on college stations, and we even had some record-label interest.

But after all that hard work, and all the disappointments and successes, Majosha was growing in one direction, and my interests were growing in another. To put it bluntly, Majosha was at its best when we were rocking a drunken party, and I had higher aspirations.

And so I creatively visualized not being in that band anymore. I got sick of the whole thing and we were done.

WHERE OH WHERE IS MY VOICE?

I've Looked *Everywhere* and I Can't Find It!

AS GOOD AS MAJOSHA WAS, I WAS NO LONGER ABLE TO WRITE SONGS for an almost-funk, almost-indie, almost-Southern party-rock band and keep a straight face. I didn't want to feed my new songs to that beast anymore. The songs themselves were becoming the beast that needed to be fed. They had grown up faster than me, and I had to catch up. I still had to find my artistic voice.

By artistic voice, I'm referring to one's artistic thumbprint—the idiosyncratic stuff that makes an artist unique. It's not a precise science, and finding it is always a painful process. I think it has to be about subtraction. It's not a matter of cooking up a persona or style so much as it is stripping away what's covering up the essence, what was already there.

Sometimes it's just growing out of the imitation phase. Most artists have a period where they sound like their favorite musician, and once they've learned from that they can shed that effort. Sometimes the subtraction is about casting off a misconception about how music is actually performed, or how art is made. No matter what your particular subtraction is, the artistic voice you will discover will ideally be something you haven't seen or heard before. Because, miraculously, in a world with billions of people, you're still the only you. That's some cringeworthy self-affirmation shit right there, but it's just the truth. That impossible search for the voice is, in the end, about being yourself. It's self-honesty. And in those moments that the artistic voice shows its face, it's hard to imagine what was so difficult about finding it.

But it *is* difficult getting there. Added to the challenge of looking for something for which you have no prior example, once you find it, you're the only one who will never truly see what's special about it. What an artist has to offer is obvious to just about anyone else *but* the artist him- or herself. It's not terribly profound or abstract to say that the way we hear our speaking voice, reverberating in our own skull, is not the way we sound to others. We never get a chance to meet ourselves the way others have. It's the same with the artistic voice. It's something you feel in the dark.

When I'm working with successful artists—usually in the studio, that particularly self-conscious fishbowl—I can often see them working the angle they *think* is their calling card. And they are usually way off. Of course, they're pros and accustomed to finding their way back, so they snap out of it. But it's striking to witness. It's like when you ask a little kid why others like her and she says something like, "Because I'm funny! I make farting jokes in class." Well, if you ask her classmates, they may well tell you that they tolerate that class-clown crap but that actually, "I like Ethel because she's nice." They see her in a way her ego will never allow. Ethel never needed to act like the village idiot to make people like her. Being herself was all she needed to do. It can take some time to find the thing that lives in your blind spot.

As you get closer to finding your voice, you'll feel resistance. You'll want to retreat. It's scary to just be you. You may notice that criticism from others starts to sting more, because now it's personal. You're being seen and addressed directly, not through the sunglasses you finally removed. But once you've relaxed, you can apply the effort to the important part—that which projects and amplifies the expression of the real you. That's technique. And by the way, when it's said that someone is "trying too hard," we should take that to mean "trying too hard *at the wrong thing*." Once the wrong thing, usually affectation or tension, is stripped away, by all means, please try too hard. Try as hard as you can to express what you feel, and don't let anyone bully you otherwise.

I arrived at some kind of unique artistic voice in my songwriting, my piano-playing, and my singing at different times in my life. And I'd say the whole package came together rather late. And that I lost my grip on it and found it over and over again. It's still something I struggle with.

My songwriting clicked first. That's where I put the time in early on, enduring constant failure, mostly in the privacy of my bedroom. Imitating my heroes and then rebelling against them as I matured. Writing and throwing away hundreds of songs.

I came to a point in my musical development where I wanted to listen to albums that didn't exist. I wanted more than anything to hear a specific record and realized I had to be the one to make it. For instance, I wanted to hear a rock star who didn't need to cast themselves heroically. I wanted to hear a record where, for once, the singer wasn't always right. Where the rock star didn't have to always be the sexy one, the strong one, or the victimized party. Because even when on the losing end, they didn't seem to me to be showing honest vulnerability. They'd sing shit like, *Girl, I cried for you*. As if that revealed anything at all. Who the hell says that in real life? It's dress-up and playacting. Disingenuous vulnerability. Amanda Palmer has a fantastic verse that touches on this in her song "Grown Man Cry":

I'm scanning through the stations as the boys declare their feelings
But it doesn't feel like feelings
It feels like they're pretending

It's like they just want blowjobs
And they know these songs will get them

And, sure, it's fine to cry and it's fine to write about it, but she's right. It so often doesn't feel like feelings. I was highly suspicious of most rock lyrics. It felt like rock bands were selling a brand too hard. *What if you risked ruining your brand?* I wondered. Wouldn't it be riskier and more dangerous to admit that I was too shallow or too afraid to show feelings? Honesty like that, that didn't cast a singer in the most flattering light, seemed more like real-life vulnerability. It seemed sadder. Cultivating my vulnerability, nerdiness, and weakness, all in the *key of awkward,* is what eventually felt right for me. That was the imaginary record that I wanted to buy, that I would have to make myself. A great leap away from the herd, and toward my voice.

I learned to embrace lyrics that didn't match the music, gravitating, for instance, toward major keys (usually considered happy keys) with sad lyrics. You know, lyrics and music don't *have* to agree. The music can refute or ridicule what is being said, and I loved playing with that effect. That sort of contradiction reflected the way I felt life worked, and it also felt naughty and off-limits. I called it "breaking the law." And feeling bolder with each misdemeanor, I began to enjoy words outside the usual rock nomenclature. Even words more commonly found in a physics book, for instance, would probably be more compelling to me than dithering lyrics with lots of *baby, baby, baby, I'm so hurt.* Staid technical language might even be used to portray a singer who wants to divert attention from his true feelings. Not to mention that it's a shock to hear obtuse, jagged language in a song. We so rarely hear that, and it can draw you in. That's the impulse behind the waltz, "Boxing," that I wrote about Muhammad Ali and Howard Cosell. I knew it wasn't cool to couple a sports story with a pretty melody, or to write from the perspective of old men in rock and roll. I just wanted to hear *that* record and so I would have to make it myself. Since then the times have changed, and it's not as unusual to project awkwardness anymore—it's actually become fashionable. But when I was finding my voice, it was by feel, like learning my face with my fingertips in the dark.

My voice as a pianist had been evolving all along at another pace. Style is often steered by circumstance and necessity. When I was younger, trying to jam with loud guitars and drums on an unamplified upright piano in various neighborhood garage bands, I couldn't hear myself at all. The guitars could just turn a volume knob and blow me away. But one day when we played "China Grove" by the Doobie Brothers, while copying the original piano part I discovered the power of sticking the top of the piano range loudly and repetitively. I could finally be heard. And it wasn't the velocity alone that made the piano speak above the loud garage band. It was also a matter of what range to play, and when. I was like the runt of a litter who learns to bull in to get food. I can fucking stick it in any loud band and make myself heard.

My training as a percussionist also contributed to my style. Drums are traditionally set up with the highest drums to the left and lowest to the right. That's the opposite of a piano. But I'm a left-handed drummer and so I lay the drums out like a piano. Lower drums to the left and higher drums to the right. This has allowed me to play drums on the piano. My embellishments on the piano are rarely melodic flurries, which couldn't be heard in a garage band anyway. They're more like drum fills that I learned to play left-handed. Style by circumstance.

But what really gave me a voice on the piano was my songs, which were a product of my imagination. My songs taught me to play piano. What I learned and practiced at the piano was driven by my desire to play what I heard in my head, and my piano-playing became its own thing once my tunes fell into place.

I now had words, songs, and a pianist, but that wasn't enough. I needed to find a singer who could bring it all out. At first, I looked everywhere. Everywhere but under my own nose.

Where oh where is my voice . . .
my voice . . . my . . .
Ah! My voice! My physical voice? That damn buzzy thing?

It made sense for me to sing these songs I was writing, but I had one problem. I was a terrible singer. So I sought real singers to bring my songs to life.

To be fair, it's not that I had a terrible vocal apparatus. It's just that this God-given vocal instrument was not what *I* wanted to hear. It was too . . . me. Too scary to reveal. I made things worse by trying to disguise it, which resulted in my singing badly. I harbored a grave misconception that singing involved some herculean effort and strain in order to force it into something interesting. I thought this is what all the real Singers™ did. It turns out, singing *does* require effort, just not the kind I imagined.

I didn't understand singing at all, because I hadn't grown up doing it. It was like trying to learn to ride a bike in your twenties. I was ashamed to be seen trying. And so, as an adult, I contorted and distorted all the elements of phonation, from overbreathing to pushing my larynx up into my jaw. It was quite a feat turning an otherwise unique instrument into a distorted, airy squeak-box. *There must be some magic trick to singing,* I thought. *It couldn't possibly be as simple as hitting the notes and telling the story . . . Could it?*

I would nervously step up to the mic, choke out a few overwrought whisper screams, lose my voice, and walk away frustrated.

Where oh where is my voice? I squeaked to the heavens!

The first clue came from the cassettes I made for the singers in Majosha. Demonstrating a new song into a tape recorder, without feeling pressure to be a Singer™, I felt safe singing the melodies plaintively, in a way that simply elucidated the words and the intent. I was actually singing, but I didn't realize it because it seemed too easy, too obvious. It didn't hurt. *Doesn't it hurt to feel?* Those tapes were just meant to get the point across. They didn't *count*. But they sounded right.

Here's how the song goes. See?

"Pitched mouth noises," Frank Zappa once called them. Words with notes. I recalled how impressed my piano teacher, Robert Darnell, had been with Eric Clapton, who simply spoke the notes. But even as I began to discover I didn't need all that strain, I still couldn't always relax on command. As soon as it *counted,* I would get anxious and involuntarily revert to my old habits. It was an impossible nervous tick. It was my soul hiding being a rock. It took a while.

I like to say I suffered from a vocalizing disorder—something akin to an eating disorder, only applied to the voice. I suffered from a case of extremely low voice self-esteem, driven into me from youth. You know how you can hear that one awful comment about your body, at exactly the wrong time, and it can plant a seed in the center of your soul? That was what had happened to me with my voice. I guess feelings of inadequacy, like old habits, die hard.

You see, my father, with absolutely no mal-intent whatsoever, had always proudly insisted I had a weak and unlistenable voice. It was actually a compliment from his perspective. Raised poor in the macho South, he learned that real men don't go around singing. So Papa boasted that he also had a useless set of vocal cords, and the same went for my brother and me. We were all real men. Papa liked rock music just fine but considered rock singers "sissies" and "fruitcakes," mostly. Sometimes he gave them a pass because he figured they were laughing all the way to the bank. "Shit, I'd put on mascara and shake my ass in leather tights like a little girl for that kind of money!" he might say. So sure, I had to dig out of a little insecurity hole vocally, but I don't blame my parents for this. We are all a work in progress.

It was when I heard myself singing on the demo cassettes that I realized I had no choice. I had to be the singer. Now I could suddenly creatively visualize my songs making their way in the world. But I would have to grow a pair, lose a pair, whatever—it's all so confusing—and just sing. I learned to state the facts and nothing but the facts vocally. That's the way I shed the strained affectation. Pitched mouth noises, speaking the lyrics, letting the songwriting do the heavy lifting. I would be myself. A non-singer sort of singer.

There's an immediacy to hearing a non-singer singer deliver a song. It draws our attention, because we suspect the non-singer singer must *really* have something to say. Why else would they bother? Certainly not to show off their vocal gymnastics. We trust somehow that they're telling the truth. They've cut out all the sugar coating and they're telling us the way it is.

The non-singer singer was a sort of unmentioned genre. There were loads of them, only I didn't quite fit in there either. Non-singer singers always had a character voice. But my voice wasn't gravelly or odd like Bob Dylan, Leonard Cohen, or Tom Waits. I had a boy-next-door sound I hadn't heard much on records. One who definitely doesn't wear sunglasses and smoke cigarettes. I figured I had to just go for it, belly flop and all. I began to push this boy-next-door quality front and center. No apologies, no disclaimer, no effects to hide behind or defensiveness that would indicate fear. I was tired of being afraid. I embraced my fear so I could get my songs out there. I still do.

I began to record my new songs on a four-track cassette machine in my bedroom. I had one track for drums, one for bass, one for piano, and one for my newly discovered non-singing voice. I sang into the mic, almost in a whisper, so nobody outside the room would hear me. I locked myself away, wrote and recorded the songs "Jackson Cannery," "Silver Street," and "Underground" in one week, sometime in 1988.

This was, I thought, the real deal. It felt like a significant step forward.

After hundreds of forgotten songs, and humiliating adenoidal attempts at singing, I had found the first hint of my voice. And it was so much easier than I had imagined.

NASHVILLE—THE BEST
(PREFERRED) WAY TO FAIL

MY FIRST GIG SINGING MY SONGS AT THE PIANO FELL IN MY LAP. A local pop and soul singer by the name of Marc Silvey hired me to play bass for him on what is known as a "showcase" gig, which is basically a publicly attended audition for record labels. A chemist by trade, Silvey had made a home demo tape that grabbed the attention of record companies and music-publishing execs, who would be flying in from L.A., Nashville, and New York just to hear him play a few songs. If they liked what they saw, then he would become a signed recording artist. This being Marc's first gig, he didn't have many songs, so he casually asked if I might play a few of mine on piano as the opener. I didn't put enough thought into it to be nervous. I said, "Sure thing."

On Marc's big showcase night, Raleigh's venerable Rialto Theatre was full and buzzing. The local press had whipped up a lot of interest with stories of the talented young chemist who'd attracted so many big-city music reps. The lights came down, and I wandered out alone to the piano, unannounced. It was easy. There was no pressure or expectation. I just relayed the stories of the songs musically, speaking the pitches. I played "Jackson Cannery," "Tom and Mary," and a song that was never released, called "Half Asleep." After that I immediately ran backstage to tune my bass guitar before shaving my head with a number-two electric razor. I thought it was funny to play my little piano set with a full head of hair, then shave my head to be the bassist for Marc's set.

Following the showcase, a fellow who worked at BMI (Broadcast Music Inc., which is one of the three big publishing-licensing companies in the United States, the others being ASCAP and SESAC) pulled me aside and told me the labels were all flipping out about my opening set. Most had expressed interest in seeing me again on my own gig. He asked if I could manage to book something quickly while there was excitement. This was innocent beginner's luck, I suppose. I was over the moon at first. And then very nervous. Suddenly it *counted*. There were expectations! My next performance could determine my future.

I booked the first venue that would have me and I hired the two hottest local musicians around, hoping I could make it a real show and impress the boys and girls from the big cities.

Cue sad trombone.

A few months later, seated behind an electric piano in a conference room at the Carolina Inn in Chapel Hill, North Carolina, with a band I'd never even rehearsed, I faced an audience that consisted of a few music execs who had flown in, my family, and some friends, all seated on folding chairs underneath flat fluorescent light. It was utterly unnatural. I nearly puked the whole time from nerves. I relapsed vocally, trying again to hide behind effort and strain, adding embellishments and fake gravel that I couldn't pull off. Luckily, it was over quickly because I ran out of songs. The bored label execs in their hip sneakers had already migrated to the back of the room, where the food was. My BMI man worked the room afterward, but to no avail.

Well, with one exception. A small publisher/lawyer from Nashville named Scott Siman, who stayed behind after the room cleared—and, boy, did it clear—was interested in my music.

Scott invited me to Nashville, but Anna suspected he was a con artist.

"Is this man a lawyer or a publisher?" she asked.

I nodded yes.

"He's both? Hmm . . . That sounds worse. Anyway, Nashville is good at country music, not rock music."

All legitimate concerns, but I was undeterred. I ended up signing a deal—whatever it was Scott put in front of me, I didn't really read much of it. Technically I didn't sign without a lawyer, of course, because Scott served as my lawyer and my publisher all at once. I know, I know. It's a terrible idea. You should always get your own lawyer. And it's true that there were parts of that original publishing contract that became a massive pain in the ass down the road. Still, I must emphasize that Scott did not screw me. He was sincerely interested in developing talent, not taking advantage of it. I was lucky.

I was now a twenty-two-year-old married man with no other obvious opportunities, tired of waiting tables, ready to pay his debt down and take on the world. I was not to be detained or slowed down with caution or logic. I packed the old Volvo station wagon. *Cue *Beverly Hillbillies* theme song.*

Entering Nashville at the Demonbreun exit ramp, a newcomer like myself got an eyeful of a strip club that boasted 50 BEAUTIFUL WOMEN AND ONE UGLY ONE. A Music City landmark for decades. In the late eighties, Nashville was still sporting a culturally latent, seedy, early-seventies' mustache. Irony-free. The first night there I stayed in the Shoney's Inn, across from the Barbara Mandrell Country Museum, with creepy wax figures of the Mandrell Sisters displayed in the foyer. Everything in that neighborhood was surreal. There was a place around the corner called Houndogs. It was a hot dog stand manned by a fellow in a hot dog suit and an Elvis impersonator. In fact, a couple years later my car broke down right at Houndogs and blocked their business for an hour. You haven't lived until you've been screamed at by an Elvis impersonator until AAA shows up. On the next block was a bar with a mechanical bull that clacked through the night. This was a stone's throw from Al Jolson Enterprises Inc., which copied cassettes in bulk for songwriters making demos. It was owned by the son of the minstrel singer Al Jolson, famous for his blackface rendition of "Mammy." It's now Southern Grounds recording studio—I did some overdubs for Kesha there recently.

The musicianship I found floating around Scott Siman's demo studio, only a few blocks from the tourist freakshow, was outstanding. And they did music full-time! I kept getting this funny wink-wink treatment from the circle of talent that Scott was supporting, who hung out at the studio. They'd all heard my four-track demo, and they each waited until nobody else was in the room to tell me that they got my music but nobody else did. And they congratulated me on being Scott's new favorite. It was a little odd, but it was a whole new world of opportunity.

I slept on the floor of the Scott Siman demo studio/hangout shack. It was on the corner of 19th and Chet Atkins Place. The comers and goers at this little studio included a then-unknown Keith Urban, who was pounding the pavement to be taken seriously as an Australian in country music. It wasn't going well at that moment. I'm pretty sure Keith also slept on that studio floor, but he doesn't remember that. I, in turn, don't remember suggesting he and I write songs together, only to end up making him my "tape op bitch." I left him running the studio equipment so I could perform everything myself, as Keith recalls. There was the late Will Owsley, later known as simply Owsley, who made a few great records of his own and played on many more. Tommy Sims, who went on to write big songs like "Change the World" by Eric Clapton, would come in and play bass and Moog synth bass. I could keep on with the list. It was exciting.

What wasn't exciting were the shitty demos made in that studio, which woke me up at 9 A.M. each morning. How's a nocturnal rock musician supposed to sleep with some sappy song called "The Winds of Change" playing on repeat in the next room? In my sleeping bag on the floor, I covered my head with my pillow as I got a glimpse of what a musical sweatshop Nashville was. It was like they were making shitty greeting cards with some follow-the-numbers music behind it.

The Nashville musicians seemed all too happy to treat creativity like a nine-to-five job. By the time a song like "The Winds of Change" might make its way through the bowels of the Nashville system and onto the radio, the original writers probably wouldn't even remember they'd written it. Songs were a commodity—*crank 'em out*. Although the structure of my publishing deal resembled the standard old-school Nashville sweatshop deal, Scott assured me that our plan was different. I was writing for my own career, not for others. He didn't expect me to tailor songs for other artists to get "cuts" on others' albums. No greeting cards for me.

My regular monthly royalty advance was about a thousand bucks. After two payments, I could afford an upstairs one-bedroom apartment on 18th Avenue South near Wedgewood, and Anna was able to leave North Carolina and join me. We broke into a fit of joyous laughter in the grocery store when we realized we could afford two boxes of cereal instead of one. Anna took a Kinko's copy gig and I spent the days writing. I recorded demos in the studio when I was lucky enough to get a slot. Otherwise, I worked at home with my bass guitar and notebook.

I wrote songs like "Philosophy" and "The Last Polka"—which would be on the *Ben Folds Five* album six years later—sitting in a chair in the living room into the wee hours. But Scott wasn't blown away by my new material. The songs were okay, he said, but the demos were too rough. I would have to learn the fine art of the Nashville slick-assed demo. And he made it clear that I wasn't to play any live shows in the meantime. It was a small Music City, and the word would get out if I were to play a show that got mixed reviews. An impressive demo would be my calling card to interest labels. Then I'd blow them away with a surprise attack from the shadows in a single

showcase! Erg, there's that "showcase" word again. It made me slightly ill. Why not just call them gigs?

Nashville demos were like an extreme version of a normal studio recording. Everything a little louder, a little brighter, with more effects. Just push the MORE button to rope 'em in. It's a little like the way TV screens are sold in Best Buy or Circuit City—they look impressive in the store, over-sharpened and over-saturated, until you get them home and find they've made your favorite classic movies look more like cheap wedding videos. That's how I felt about those Nashville demos. They sounded impressive cranked up loudly in the music exec's office, but in the real world they sounded cheesy. Then you'd hear the same singer at a bar being himself and it would blow you away. The talent there was outstanding. I just didn't quite agree with all the methods.

My demos, on the other hand, sounded the way I thought a demo should sound. Shitty. Why spend your soul on the demo? If you're going to put all that time into it, why not call it an album and be done? I figured I should try to get on board with this glamour-demo business like I was told, but my demos got worse as they got slicker. And I knew it. Trying to impress was also resulting in some of those old strained vocal aberrations. I was sounding less like me again. I began to write less, and I spent more of my time riding my bike, running long distance, and buying stacks of one-dollar LPs down on Division Street. And as I engaged less and less with my publisher, my publisher became slower to write those advance royalty checks. My time as the new favorite was up.

Scott had become more interested in my friend Millard, who had just moved to Nashville. Millard and Will Owsley, whom I'd introduced to each other, had started up a project called the Semantics, playing clever power pop on Nashville demo steroids. Scott was rightfully impressed. It was damn good. I was in Scott's office with a roomful of local music execs one afternoon when he put in a cassette demo of a song I'd written called "Kalamazoo" and sat back to watch their reaction. Tired of all the slick demo business, I'd gone back to my evil four-track cassette ways. "Kalamazoo" was rough, a sort of jazzy and melancholic piece. Not at all commercial. One exec rudely asked Scott to "please take that shit out of the tape player." With me in the room! Scott quickly ejected mine and put in the Semantics tape.

"Now, that's music!" they all concurred, banging their middle-aged heads to the slickest demo Nashville had ever heard. Not that the Semantics didn't make great music. But ouch, you know.

Most of what Anna had feared about this Nashville move was coming true. Tension between the two of us was building as I settled into the clichéd Depressive Slack-Ass Musician™ while Anna, with her degree from Duke University, was paddling ferociously just above minimum wage at the copy shop to help make ends meet.

One day, as we browsed through the one-dollar record section at a store called the Great Escape, I spotted a Kate Bush LP collection I had to have. Anna reminded me that buying it would make us ten dollars' short on this month's rent. But like a naughty schoolboy I took our last ten bucks, plopped it down for the records, hopped on my bike, and left Anna in the dust. Twenty minutes later, with "Wuthering Heights" blasting out of the stereo, I heard Anna marching loudly up the steps to our apartment. When I opened the door she punched me in the jaw. Hard. Black-and-blue bruise and all. I deserved it. If I could go back in time, I'd punch myself. Nursing my jaw, I straightened up and got back to work. I needed to get as many songs as I could done before I was dropped from my publishing deal. I lent my musicianship to various other artists, and I played on some Semantics recordings. They were my friends, and although I didn't like my new place in their shadow, their music was good and I was happy to drum for them.

Meanwhile, a local rock duo called Fleming and John was making waves. Their gigs were incredibly inspiring. They often had a string quartet in tow, and once they brought along an African dance troupe, just for kicks. John Painter, who later arranged strings for the Ben Folds Five albums, was the most talented arranger I'd ever met, and

Fleming McWilliams had one of the biggest rock-star presences I'd seen up close. She's still one of my favorite singers in the world. I will always file those shows under "legendary." Re-energized, I realized how badly I missed the old-fashioned grassroots approach that Fleming and John were taking. They were actually doing it, while I was held prisoner in a demo studio. I needed to play gigs.

After a year of abstaining from public performances in Nashville, as my publisher had insisted, I put together a piano, bass, and drums rock trio called Jody's Power Bill. It didn't seem natural not to be playing my songs in public, so I enlisted my friend Tom Spagnardi on bass and Morgan Davis on drums and we started rehearsing a set. You might recognize the name Morgan Davis from an extremely filthy song I wrote years later, called "The Secret Life of Morgan Davis." I want to formally apologize to Morgan about this song, which had absolutely nothing to do with him. His namesake in the song was an entirely fictional character who sneaks out each night on his wife and acts out all his disgusting fantasies until sunrise, when he "wipes the coke and lipstick off his fat hairy chest" and "crawls in bed with his sleeping wife." Apologies to his wife too, and to his family and friends, while I'm at it. Actually, let's just make it an apology to anyone who's ever heard the song. It's truly gross. And it's one of my favorites.

Still in financial debt from the Majosha days, I decided to borrow *more* money, for a small baby grand Baldwin piano. I figured I'd just carry it to gigs. Anna, ever the manager, booked Jody's Power Bill into a place called 12th and Porter. We built a small following with our guitar-less rock, and I got good practice moving the piano.

At this point, Scott Siman probably didn't really know what to do with me. I kept writing wordy, uncommercial songs and was probably ruining his plans by playing shows. He sold my publishing contract to the legendary country-music producer and executive Paul Worley at Sony/Tree Publishing. Paul had stopped by 12th and Porter one night and caught me pounding "Purple Haze," in no shirt, no shoes, and with ridiculous fake tattoos drawn all over me. I don't think Paul stayed to hear any of my original songs that night, but he was sold on the audacity of my Jimi Hendrix piano performance and gave me the keys to Sony/Tree's full twenty-four-track studio facility, with free rein from midnight to 9 A.M. He didn't claim to understand my music—he sensed it was good, and he was probably doing a solid for Scott Siman.

The first song I delivered to my new publisher was the now completed waltz "Boxing." I had made a piano-and-eight-piece-choir version of the song, singing all the vocal parts in the stairwell for extra reverb. I proudly marched into Paul Worley's office to play the recording. He listened with interest, and some confusion. This wasn't the "Purple Haze"–style piano mania he'd expected. And . . . how on earth did I manage to make this state-of-the-art studio sound as bad as my messy four-track demos? I hadn't noticed, but for each of those eight harmonies, along with their doubles, I'd managed to record the air-conditioning unit in the stairwell sixteen times. It was a very noisy recording.

I spent the next year as a Sony/Tree songwriter, learning the studio from the ground up, nearly every midnight to eight in the morning. I learned how to align, demagnetize, and edit on the twenty-four-track analog tape machine, which I would put into record mode in the control room, then run as fast as I could out to the piano, bass, or drums. Often, John Painter would come add extra stuff. He also showed me the beauty of the Big Muff pedal for distorting the bass guitar. That seemed to help make up for the lack of electric guitars in my songs. I splurged on a string section from time to time, which either John or I would arrange. In that studio I wrote "Underground," "Uncle Walter," and "Missing the War," and a whole bunch I've forgotten.

Even though it was 1991, the music world was still solidly stuck in the aesthetic of the eighties, and seemed like it would stay that way forever. If you ever come across some of Nirvana's first early-nineties TV appearances, you'll notice their grungy style is totally out of sync with the slick colorful TV studio sets they're awkwardly performing on. In the eighties, rock bands might have to perform in front of fake brick walls with bad graffiti or with big-hair dancing chicks from

workout videos ornamenting the shots. In pre–Kurt Cobain Nashville, a nerdy, cussing, and pounding pianist with no vibrato didn't
seem ready for that kind of prime-time scene. The pop-music world
was still too slick.

Delivering my songs to Paul Worley was nearly as deflating as
delivering them to my old publisher, Scott. I admired Paul personally
and professionally, but he was so distracted by things like piano-pedal
squeaks and the air-conditioner noise on the stairwell vocals. He
rarely offered feedback on the actual songs. In retrospect I can see
that he had the instinct to know I was onto *something*, but as a country musician, he didn't feel qualified to comment on my brand of
music. It was a whole other style with a lot more chords and notes. He
did, however, feel qualified to comment on the production.

"What's that distortion on the bass? Where are the guitars? Wanna
put a *little* 'verb on those vocals?" he asked politely.

Meanwhile, Paul had signed my friends the Semantics to a publishing deal and he had a proposition. I could join the Semantics as
their drummer, add a few of my songs, and Sony/Tree wouldn't drop
me. My music was proving utterly uncommercial, but perhaps it
would add just the right touch to the Semantics. Plus, I'd get a fat
record advance, because the Semantics were going to be signed to
Geffen Records for a fuck-ton of money.

Anna was working two jobs and I was about to lose my income. If
I agreed to Paul's offer, I'd get a nice check, keep my publishing deal,
and land some of my songs on a major-label release. If I declined, it
was back to square one, waiting tables. Against every fiber of my
being, I joined the Semantics in L.A. for rounds of meetings with
their prospective producers.

I was out there for a couple of weeks and I didn't like it. I didn't
like it one bit. I didn't like the big name-dropping label guy we met at
the Palm Restaurant, sitting at a table under his own portrait. I didn't
like all the producers' sales pitches or their compulsory black turtle-
necks tucked into blue jeans. I didn't like the Semantics arguing over
whose song had been the one to get the record deal, or who would sit

"gun" in the limo. But this was the L.A. rock business, I guess, and I was beginning to wonder if they were all wearing diapers under those jeans. In truth, I was being a total sourpuss and I was looking for things I didn't like—because it wasn't *my* gig. I soon bowed out and the Semantics got a new drummer, Ringo Starr's son Zak Starkey.

I was now twenty-four years old, with increasingly concerned shrugging parents, added debt on a baby grand piano, a tenuous publishing deal, some great studio experience, and, of course, that high school diploma. And I was soon to be a divorced man. Anna had been working multiple jobs, all of which she was overqualified for, in support of my failing music career. Prospects of a record deal were going backward, not forward. I was becoming a Debbie Downer.

During my time in Nashville, I found myself increasingly sluggish all through the day. I wondered sometimes if I had some kind of disease. I just couldn't stay awake. I had no appetite. I'd often stay in bed well past noon, as there was no schedule to conform to. Now I was thinking about leaving Nashville altogether, but Anna wanted to stay. The strain of it all, and the obvious imminent diversion of paths, was becoming all too clear. We would be separating.

While in L.A. with the Semantics, I'd been told there was someone who actually liked my music, up in the Sony Publishing offices in New York. Her name was Kerry McCarthy. Feeling uncertain about my future, I gave her a call. She actually approved of my sloppy demos and she told me she wasn't the only fan of mine in New York. She'd been passing my tapes around the city for a while. Had nobody told me this, she asked? She suggested I come up, meet some people and play some shows, and was confident that Sony New York would assume my publishing contract if Nashville didn't want it.

Maybe New York *was* more my speed? I put a few things into the old Volvo station wagon and had awkward goodbyes with Anna. As I turned onto the highway at Broadway downtown, a familiar sound came over the speakers.

What is this? I know I've heard this somewhere!

Then I recognized that damn song. It was "The Winds of Change"!

The country greeting card that had ruined my sleep way back when I'd first arrived in Nashville and was bedding on the studio floor! It was squeaking through the old Volvo radio just the way I remembered it! It was one of those moments that make you think life *is* but a dream.

That shitty song and I had spent time sharing a sleeping bag, and now I guessed we were traveling buds. We'd both made it through the bowels of Nashville, and as I was being shat out of Music City by way of I-40 East, I cranked it up and shook my head, choking back a few tears every hundred miles or so.

FROZEN ON A SUITCASE

I sat here on my suitcase in our empty new apartment til the sun
  went down
Then I walked back down the stairs with all my bags and drove away
You must be freaking out

THIS IS THE SECOND VERSE OF "DON'T CHANGE YOUR PLANS" FROM *THE Unauthorized Biography of Reinhold Messner* (Ben Folds Five, 1999), and it's pretty much the scene on my last day in New York City, in November 1993.

But let's cinematically freeze this little man on his suitcase.

I'd like to honor my two years in New York by closing my eyes to see what images light up before me. The same way I write a song or watch for lightning bugs. I'll list them as they appear.

Okay. Here goes . . .

• Drops of sweat staining open classified pages, searching desperately for work while living in a one-room attic apartment in Montclair, New Jersey.

• The smell of the subway system, and how it sticks to the skin. And a neighbor who tells me in his severe Jersey accent, "My friend, that smell's what I call the wax!"

• Snatching the wig off my friend Ana's head onstage in the musical *Buddy—The Buddy Holly Story,* in an improvised moment that nearly got me fired. Laughing, unable to deliver lines. (You see, I'd answered an open call in *The Village Voice,* and when the company saw I could play most of the instruments and do a little acting, I was hired to do everything but the role I auditioned for, which was, of course, Buddy Holly.)

• Looking at an empty wonderful open-loft apartment for rent out in Williamsburg. The apartment, which rattles beneath the train, is cheap (*those* were the days!). I'm thinking I can start a band and move there with my new drummer friend who works in the tape room at Sony. (I didn't end up moving there.)

• Times Square, and that weird row of movie marquees on 45th Street with messages about the end of the world, and seeing a transvestite slammed against the Port Authority wall by a cop. Blood everywhere.

• Police clearing people who blocked the sidewalk on St. Marks Place, there to get a glimpse of Jeff Buckley at an alcohol-free café called Sin-é, where he performed each week. Capacity: forty. The sound of his voice too good to describe.

• The faces of my four actor friends from *Buddy* coming to support me on Wednesday at Sin-é. My crowd is about twenty people shy of capacity. Broken keys on my Wurlitzer electric piano.

• First blue glow of morning on St. Marks Place and a shirtless muscular man with long hair whirling a rope above his head like a helicopter blade—at the end of the rope was his pit bull, sailing around him in circles, hanging by his teeth.

Here's one more.

• A Christmas card from my friends Rob and Rob, a couple who also worked on *Buddy.* The card was a cartoon of them both dressed like Santa and dancing with their asses pressed together. It read "Bells on Robs' Tails Ring."

That's actually a pretty good summing up of my time in the New York area. But there's one week that I shouldn't leave out. The week that led to my sitting on a suitcase, right before I left town.

So let's keep the poor little man frozen on his suitcase for a few more moments and back up to a gig I'd played the week prior.

The Bitter End, on Bleecker Street, is legendary for being many performers' first New York gig. From Woody Allen to Lady Gaga. But it's anything but glamorous, or even cool. Mostly you'll see cover bands trying out their originals, hoping to be discovered, six to ten bands a night. Such was my experience. And having just rocked twenty people, mostly friends and families of the other acts that night, I went to collect my fifty bucks, only to be told that I owed the Bitter End a hundred. The soundman had discovered the strings I busted on the house Yamaha piano and was charging me fifty bucks apiece, which I didn't have. My single guest that evening was a music manager named Alan Wolmark, whom I'd met recently in the elevators of Sony Publishing. He saw me struggling to deal with the Bitter End management and he stepped up and took care of it. I don't know if Alan paid the club manager himself or if he just told him to leave me alone in some convincing New York language. Alan and I sat down, had a drink and a chat. He seemed very interested in my idea to start a piano band, no guitar. I explained it wouldn't be a jazz trio, like you might expect, but would have distorted and grungy bass and drums. It would be a piano band for the nineties. One that rocked.

Nearly a week later, Alan and his wife, Annette, came rocking up to Sin-é, where I had established a Wednesday-night residency. Alan and Annette had plenty of space to park their motorcycles, because, unlike Jeff Buckley's gigs, mine didn't spill out into the sidewalk.

They sat down right in front of my Wurlitzer electric piano, expanding the crowd to about six. When I finished my set, I was introduced to Annette and prepared to receive my compliments, but instead Alan said, "Not so good tonight."

"Really?" I laughed, assuming he was joking.

"No. Sorry. I'm very serious. It wasn't at all what I saw at the Bitter End. Not very good."

Actually, I had to agree. I'm a real-piano player, and not an electric-piano player. I felt like Keith Richards being forced to play banjo. The Bitter End baby grand Yamaha, even out of tune, was far more exciting. But New York was not the place to lug a baby grand around, and so I had to make do with an electric most of the time.

North Carolina, however, brimming with musicians and great rock venues, *was* a place you could lug a piano around. The commercial music world was completely upside down in 1993 with the indie/grunge revolution. No music scene was more liberated than Chapel Hill, North Carolina, which never quite got on board with the polish of the eighties in the first place. As soon as Nirvana, Pearl Jam, and that host of others busted the mainstream door down, all eyes were on places like Chapel Hill, where records were made—rough-and-tumble ones, not demo tapes.

I told Alan that as I listened to Liz Phair's new record the night before, it felt as though my "people" had arrived. Finally, some grit, some antiheroes, contradictory lyrics, rough edges, imperfect singing—something new. My rough plan had been to move to Brooklyn where artists were taking over cheap lofts and start a band, but a storm of creative visualization was gathering again, and I could so clearly envision a band back in North Carolina instead. Alan egged me on.

"Do it," he said. "What have you got going here? Just go while the time is right."

"Well, what about my plans for a band here? My upcoming theater auditions?" I asked, since this old man (he was in his early forties!) seemed to know things. My work in the musical-theater piece

Buddy had gotten me into Equity, the stage-actors union, and that was opening up a few opportunities. Alan saw those opportunities as distractions. I should be focused on my music.

"Nah. Do it. Go back to North Carolina."

Annette nodded. I suddenly noticed how much leather these two were wearing.

This spontaneous plan had a hole in it, though. Anna was flying up to New York the very next day. She'd gotten an impressive job at MTV. We'd been separated for nearly two years, but we were still a sort of team. She had even come up to visit while I was living in Montclair, New Jersey, and I had been happy to introduce her to my new friends as my wife, even though I doubt I'd ever mentioned I had a wife before. We were winging it. Being buds isn't enough to sustain a marriage. The shame of divorce was the last tiny thread holding us together. We were both solidly on separate paths. Either way, I had just scored a free house-sitting gig in a wonderful three-story brownstone in Jersey City—an easy commute for her new job. And, separate beds or not, it seemed like a good arrangement.

Now we can unfreeze the sad Ben on the suitcase and keep the reel running.

. . . But what's this? He still looks frozen. He's not moving.

Well, that's because I actually sat on that damn suitcase, frozen in indecision, most of the day. I didn't move for hours. Anna was to arrive in the late afternoon, and the plan had been to hop the PATH train into the city to see an MTV taping of *Nirvana Unplugged*. Yes, that one. That morning, however, my creative visualization had crashed my entire nervous system and I found myself paralyzed on my luggage. Should I stay or should I go?

Every selfish cell in my body said, *Go to North Carolina now! It's time! Leave a note! Anna will be fine! Start the car and GO!*

There were some decent unselfish cells in me too, but those cells were being shouted down by the majority. The decent minority tried to hold a filibuster and explain that leaving a Southern girl who's just come to town, still technically my wife (and my best friend), in a slightly suspect neighborhood, without at least sticking around a week to help her set up—well, that's plain wrong. Couldn't I stay and see this Nirvana TV taping, help get Anna settled, have a discussion, and then leave in a few days?

But then I thought, what if those few days led to endless wallowing in indecision, with all that back and forth, hot and cold, for months on end? What if someone gave us one of those awful *Save Your Marriage* books and we wasted a year on marriage therapy? I could end up stuck in New York another year while some other piano band took my rightful spot. Anna and I had been separated for so long it all seemed like a done deal. We were over. Why the charade? Just go.

I learned something about myself at that moment, frozen on that suitcase, clutching a set of keys, as the sun inched across the floor. I realized, when it came to my musical ambition, I was not going to be stopped. I had been fooling myself if I thought I was taking my career in stride, that I didn't have some very lofty goals, or that I was always a nice guy. All along I had really been one of those assholes who was out for himself. That creative-visualization stuff? That was pure unadulterated ambition, dressed up in some pseudo-spiritualism. Sure, I was a hard worker and I was polite and fair. Kind, courteous, empathetic, a good listener. All of that. But all that good-guy-from-N.C. shit always melted away at the first threat to a music career that I believed was rightfully mine. I was ready to admit that. Sitting there on that suitcase was about coming to terms with who I was and what my priorities were.

Moments of self-honesty are often laced with selfishness. I'm not proud of my selfishness, but we've all seen how acts of honest selfishness can often unblock the way and liberate others to live their lives. At least then everyone knows the truth and can carry on. I've reflected on this moment many times when considering the amazing man that Anna soon met, to whom she's still married, and the two wonderful kids they had, who are now themselves nearly adults.

It was midafternoon when I finally unfroze and stood up. I left a note for Anna and gripped the handle of my poor beat-up beige luggage. In white tube socks and Teva sandals (yes, laugh all you want), and a massive backpack on my shoulders, I started the old Volvo and headed toward the Jersey Turnpike. Heading south for an all-night drive to North Carolina, I could see through the leafless trees along I-95 that the holiday season was already gearing up. There was even a nativity scene at the truck stop where I grabbed some junk food for dinner at midnight. You always notice the holidays more when you feel the most alone.

I was twenty-seven years old, alone as alone could be, with more highway in my future than I could even yet imagine. I was off to find a drummer and bassist, a van with which to move my piano, and a small rental house in Chapel Hill, where in a few months a deputy sheriff would serve me my first divorce papers while my new neighbors watched. But I didn't yet know what lay ahead, beyond the headlights of my Volvo, as I sang along to its distorted radio with one hand on the wheel—the other brushing tenacious white donut powder off my lap.

Merry Christmas 1993.

BFF

COMING BACK TO NORTH CAROLINA, MY TO-DO LIST LOOKED SOME-
thing like this:

1. Call around to get names of bassists and drummers. Maybe
an accordion player?
2. Find house to rent. Chapel Hill? *Maybe* Asheville?
3. Find a van for moving piano/touring.
4. Pick up piano and other stuff from storage in Nashville.

This list looked quite similar to the one I'd made a few years ago,
before embarking on Majosha, only the circumstances had shifted. I
now had more experience, many more songs, and some friends in the
business. And I felt the music scene itself was changing quickly in my
favor. I'd felt very out of step with the music of the eighties. The polish, the theater, the style and content. But the winds of popular music
now seemed solidly behind my sails. Overnight, my boy-next-door

musical voice felt relevant. It was as if "my people" had risen from the rubble after Nirvana blew the roof off the music business, and they had infiltrated the mainstream.

It wasn't just grunge that Nirvana ushered in. They introduced a far-less-formal way of looking at things. Music was suddenly less slick, more cerebral, *like my music*! On my all-night drive down I-95, I was hearing music like "Divorce Song" by Liz Phair, "Low" by Cracker, and "Linger" by the Cranberries. On commercial radio! I felt confident that my years of music-business rejection were solidly in the rearview and that what I had to say would now be granted a listen.

I pulled into Winston-Salem just before the sun rose. My parents weren't expecting me, so I waited for daylight in the Cloverdale Shopping Center parking lot with the car heat blasting, an apple, some chips, and a Mountain Dew. There was one other car in the lot, and I recognized the man sleeping in it from kindergarten and grade school. We caught up briefly. He had just left his wife and was sleeping in the parking lot, trying to decide what to do.

It hadn't dawned on me yet what it would mean to be divorced and officially on my own. It was only a week ago that I had first considered moving back to North Carolina. Before that I didn't have any particular vision of the future. It had been some vague, unlit horizon. Now it was a blinding white page. We all experience a small handful of these moments in our lives, and as scary as they are, they should also be cherished. Electric stillness. Between chapters, between storms, completely up in the air. That split second between breathing in and breathing out. This is also the headspace I associate with the birth of new songs.

Once the sun came up and I had a morning nap at my parents' apartment, I learned they too would be soon getting a divorce. During a more stable time in my life, this news might have come as more of a shock. But the ground was shifting beneath my feet. I was also grateful I still had parents, even if they weren't together anymore.

Happiness, health, and following your path suddenly seemed more important than marital status, belongings, title, or home address. I only hoped that this was the best for them as we all lurched into the unknown.

Not wanting to wallow in too much feeling, I did what I always do when things get overwhelming: I got busy. There was a band to start and a music business to conquer. I started with the only call that would be necessary, and that was to my brother, Chuck. He knew all the local musicians, and they all knew Chuck. Chuck's band, Bus Stop, was doing quite well. They had even done a national television contest. When I described to Chuck the kind of bassist I was looking for—a rocker who wouldn't be afraid of some distortion and shredding, who could sing and looked good—Chuck told me to look no further than Robert Sledge. Robert's band, Toxic Popsicle, had made quite a splash regionally. They were part metal, almost jam, kind of onslaught-of-percussion rock, and some Perry Farrell on top? I guess. I hate to describe music like that. Look them up—Toxic Popsicle. Or take my word for it. They were good.

I met up with Robert in Greensboro, where he had just moved in temporarily with his parents. His life was also up in the air. We snuck into a practice room at UNC–G to meander through some fairly pointless jamming, which told me very little about his musicianship as we "rocked out" mindlessly with his portable amp and a student piano, on a G7 chord. He had a high tenor voice, which he wasn't shy to use, and he was ready to start a band. Plus, he had been considering a move to Chapel Hill anyway, so he offered to go in on a rental house. This was good enough for me! I could check that one off. Bassist. Next.

A few days later, I went on a mission to Chapel Hill to find a house for Sledge and me to rent. After exhausting the classifieds, which flapped around in the freezing wind as I tried to pin them down with a Sharpie, I took a break from the pay phone to slip inside a warm little café, and that's where I ran into Darren Jessee. He was twenty-three. I'd met him before once, in Nashville, but I'd never heard him play. We shot the shit for a while and I decided that he had art in his bones. He said he sang and wrote songs too. He seemed like a rock star to me, and, most important, he was in limbo and available too, just having moved to Chapel Hill. November 1993: Less than a week back in North Carolina and I had my bassist and drummer sorted. Gotta love that creative visualization. Now on to reality. *What do we actually sound like together?*

A couple weeks before Christmas Day, the three of us had a little jam together in the house where Darren was living. It was the first Ben Folds Five rehearsal. We didn't have mics or anything. You really couldn't hear what was going on. It just sounded like noise, but I didn't care. I could visualize it all, like Johnny Depp as Ed Wood, shooting scenes in one take and moving on as the crew scratched their heads. Certainly I wanted to vet a band a little more than this? Robert phoned me afterward to recommend a couple other drummers, and Darren also called, with the name of another bassist. Each understandably assumed that we were still in audition mode. But I wasn't interested in slowing down or looking before leaping. I reported back to Alan that we had a band and would be ready to play gigs soon.

Within the first couple weeks of January, Robert and I had found a suitable small brick shitbox on Isley Street, within walking distance of everything. We outfitted it with as much padding and soundproofing as we could manage—blankets, old mattresses from a dump. I even walked around the neighborhood, knocking on doors, explaining we'd be practicing. I gave the whole neighborhood my number and told them the phone sat right next to the piano. All they had to do was just give us a buzz and we'd stop. But, of course, after a few rehearsals, some asshole had already called the cops instead of the number I'd given them.

Seeing the squad car pulling up into the driveway, we toned it down and quickly segued into some cocktail jazz—a spotty, quiet version of "The Girl from Ipanema," which we let go on a few bars too long after the first knock at the door. The officer apologized for having to bother us. After all, the rest of the town was full of loud rock bands. The policeman said he found our cocktail music refreshing. He didn't see any reason we couldn't continue, as long as we kept it down. When his car was out of sight, we cranked it all back up. We'd just spontaneously and seamlessly gone from an early version of "Jackson Cannery" to smooth jazz via a sort of mind meld. We didn't need to telegraph anything to make sudden musical changes together. It seemed there might actually be something special about this band.

Robert's musical personality, which was an important key to the sound of our band, took a few rehearsals to reveal itself. Having spent years playing heavy distorted music, Robert had turned his interest to jazz. I guess this piano band seemed an opportunity for him to class up his musicianship some. I tried to egg him on to play the way I'd heard him play before, distorted with a guitar pick, but he remained stubborn for a few rehearsals, playing a traditional tone with his fingers. But soon he cut the easy-listening crap, put some Satan back into his playing, and settled into the Sledge™ I associate with our albums. And once unleashed, his sound turned out to be way bigger and crazier than anything I'd imagined. Nobody sounds like Robert. He's capable of great sensitivity too, but even in a ballad his playing holds a certain tension. It bursts at the seams, often bordering on musical antagonism, as if the bass guitar were strutting around the arrangement thrusting its chest, threatening to beat the other sounds up. That makes things happen! Robert's bass-playing wakes a song up like I've never heard.

Darren brought an organic lyricism that dignified my songs in a way I hadn't considered. There was Max Roach in there, Charlie Watts. He grooved, but he wasn't the band timekeeper. None of us were. We slowed and sped, maybe more than any commercial band I've ever heard. You could never get away with that these days, in an era where everyone seems to have been born with a Pro Tools grid ticking robotically just inside their sphincter.

I was the one who often wanted to push the concept of Piano-Band-That-Rocks™ to the point of breaking the songs. It's ironic because these were my songs I was willing to trod on, and I was probably the most old-fashioned in the band. My songs bordered on Broadway style when arranged and performed "normally." Maybe I was compensating for that by asking for distortion and bashing cymbals. Darren was always reminding me about lyrics and dynamics, by playing, not explaining. Robert worked to animate and energize the arrangements.

Fortunately, the two had very different vocal qualities and ranges, which is actually ideal for group vocals. Darren's voice was deeper and more resonant, Robert's more cutting and higher. Mine was right in the middle, and our blend was immediate. I soon found that we could get a few distinct alternate vocal timbres by trading positions and placing Darren's falsetto above Robert's chest voice. My lead vocal could segue into a backing vocal between lyrics, making it sound like we had more singers that we actually did.

Everything seemed to be falling into place. I'd call it 25 percent idiocy, 25 percent intuition, and 50 percent luck. I felt the window of opportunity might be short and so I was going for it at a cavalier, breakneck pace.

So let's wheel out that line from "Phone in a Pool" once more:

What's been good for the music hasn't always been so good for the life.

· · ·

These hasty decisions were obviously very good for the music, and that was invigorating and inspiring musically. But when the dust settled at night, I found myself personally overwhelmed, a bit confused and blue, thinking of that little fellow frozen on the suitcase. This was not at all what I would've envisioned just a month before. What was ahead? What had I left behind? One of my first nights in our rental/rehearsal home, I sat for a while at the piano in the kind of silence I've always been so uncomfortable with. Then I filled that silence by softly repeating a middle C and the F above, in a perfect fourth, simultaneously and hypnotically, perhaps to soothe myself. It might have been for an hour, I'm not sure. I don't normally write songs in one sitting, but this one was finished before I went to bed. It was called "Sad and Free," but when the sun came up I decided I'd instead call it "Evaporated."

> *Woke up way too late feeling hungover and old*
> *And the sun was shining bright and I walked barefoot down the road*
> *Started thinking about my old man*
> *It seems that all men wanna get into a car and go—anywhere*
> *Here I stand, sad and free*
> *I can't cry and I can't see*
> *What I've done*
> *God, what have I done?*

THE FIRST ALBUM—BOTH OF THEM

FROM JANUARY TO MARCH 1994, ROBERT, DARREN, AND I REHEARSED like the wind. The songs I'd been bumbling around with for years were coming to life, one at a time, with each session. On one breakthrough rehearsal we looped the chorus of one of my older songs, "Eddie Walker, This Is Your Life," playing it over and over. We'd discovered the power of pretty three-part harmony over a distorted rhythm section, which became a sort of trademark. The song had never sounded like that before. It was set free!

I likened our method of brutish musical arrangement to an American Tourister suitcase commercial I'd seen when I was a kid. It featured a gorilla jumping up and down on the luggage to show how tough the product was. I theorized, my songs would have to prove they could survive in this jungle of sound. The lyrics and the vocal would have to compete in the noise, rather than being coddled. If they were still intact, like the luggage, they were ready for consumption. This rough treatment of my old tunes created an interesting effect. Built on satisfying chords, well-thought-out arrangements, and centered at the piano, my songs could have easily been mistaken as undiscovered seventies' pop songs. But we buried that gooey center inside a fashionable grungy structure. I exaggerated my wilder style of piano-playing, and it all became one big ball of sound. I found this exciting and liberating and I looked forward to writing new songs for this beast. But for now we were creating a set for our first gig in March, so we concentrated on putting our stamp on my existing catalog.

We didn't yet have a band name, and Alan was calling every day to push that decision along because we would need to be called *something* for our first gig. We went through many cringeworthy ideas, as bands do. I think one of mine tops the list of god-awful band names: Dear Rosetta Stone. What? I also recall suggesting Uncle Plastic Bitch. A little better, but still. I still don't know if inserting my name into the band name was the right thing to do, but at the last minute I told Alan, "Let's go with Ben Folds Five," at least to get through the gig. I had built momentum as a solo artist in Nashville and New York, where we would be doing many of the first gigs, and the band was an extension of my four-year story from Nashville to New York and now Chapel Hill. So it made a degree of sense.

Predictably, Alan asked, "Why five? There are three of you." That became the leading interview question we would have to answer for the next five years.

"I don't know. I think it's funny," I answered, which became the answer I would always give.

"Well, I've got a great sense of humor," Alan said (and I will never let him forget this), "and there's *nothing funny about that name!*"

That settled it. Ben Folds Five it would be. I'm not sure Robert and Darren were quite convinced. Until now I had sold this whole venture to them as a band—all-for-one-and-one-for-all style. And here I was advocating for my name to be front and center. The tension that built between us over our time probably had some roots in this.

. . .

We would need to have some music to sell at gigs, so we soon made a two-sided single on 45-rpm vinyl. We recorded "Jackson Cannery" and "Eddie Walker, This Is Your Life" on sixteen-track analog and mixed it all the same night with Caleb Southern, who had a little nighttime share with a studio that made advertisement music. Caleb, a soundman at the Chapel Hill (technically Carborro) rock club Cat's Cradle, was becoming locally famous for his work with bands like Archers of Loaf, Metal Flake Mother, and Zen Frisbee. Great, simple production. We drove our two mixes to United Record Pressing in Nashville to have a few hundred seven-inch 45s pressed, creating the sleeve at Kinko's from an old picture of my mother playing bongos when she was fifteen.

"Jackson Cannery" single cover art, self-released, 1994

By the summer of 1994 we had some gigs in New York that Alan had set up. Some interested label people from Caroline Records attended one at the Lion's Den and asked for a copy of our demo. "We don't have a demo," I explained. "A demo is like a business card or a shameful eight-by-ten Hollywood headshot. We make records." I told them we had a vinyl 45 (even though not many people in the nineties had a record player—it was all CDs) and he could pay two dollars for the record just like everyone else. I wasn't kidding. I added that we would never record a song more than once because "it stole the soul of the song." Alan ended up giving Caroline some of our rehearsal tapes, so they could actually hear our songs.

We soon signed with Caroline and settled on producer Dave "Stiff" Johnson. Approximately a year after I'd gotten up off that suitcase in New Jersey, we were in Conshohocken, Pennsylvania, with a tiny budget, freezing our asses off and making our first record. Stiff Johnson, like any good producer, worked hard to rein in some of the insanity of our arrangements. We were rough around the edges and he worked to keep our tempos steady, to slow things down and keep us "in the pocket" when we got carried away. He got us to streamline our parts and placed us far away from each other so that piano mics didn't pick up drums. He got me to sing more earnestly, and sometimes very softly, to highlight the lyrics. And in the end, he balanced us more correctly so that the bass wasn't buzzing through the arrangements, the piano was simpler, and the drums less jazzy. He placed the music in the background and featured the voice. Sometimes he would suggest adding guitar. We certainly questioned this from time to time, but none of us had nearly his experience in the studio. We felt we should follow his lead.

Kerry McCarthy, who had picked up my publishing contract in New York, was now helping navigate our career, and she came down to visit on the last day of our mix. She was very excited to hear what we had done, and I was excited for her to hear it. It had been an intense couple weeks of recording and learning. I still file those sessions under "damn good times." Kerry listened to the first few songs and disappeared back into the tape room. When I caught up to her, she was crying. I'm pretty awkward at helping weeping friends with problems. I figured she'd just had a breakup. I took a deep breath and asked her what was wrong.

"The whole thing," she sobbed. "It doesn't sound like you at all. It sounds like three old men. It's awful."

. . .

A few days later, back in Chapel Hill, Robert, Darren, and I sat in the living room with a few beers, playing the studio mixes over and over, trying to convince ourselves the album was great. We theorized that Kerry must have been expecting our record to sound just like a gig. We assured ourselves that's not the way it works in the studio. Studio and stage are two different animals. Besides, some of our favorite records of all time sounded more formal than the live performances.

Darren suggested we pop in a cassette recording from a recent show for perspective. *Good idea,* I thought. I expected the tape to sound like a bad live recording, which would strengthen our resolve to stick by the more restrained studio versions. But not so. Not at all! The performance on that cassette was on fire! Yes, it was low-fi fire. But it was unique, energetic, and it popped out of the speakers. Damn. Kerry had been right. The album we'd made *didn't* capture who we were. What's worse, we'd spent the entire budget on it. Playing our studio mixes back once more our hearts sank.

We considered the possibility of using that live cassette tape as the record, but Kerry had a better solution. She would get us three thousand dollars and we could record some more with Caleb Southern, who had produced our seven-inch single. To say that's not a lot of money for a record would be a tremendous understatement. Under normal circumstances it might have paid for one day in the studio with a few extra expenses, but Caleb worked it out for us to get five days. The label insisted we stay focused and just concentrate on a couple of songs—a few of the up-tempo ones. Chaz Molins, our label rep, came down for a day to keep an eye on us, to make sure we stayed focused on the agreed-upon songs and got the right results. But as soon as he left, we went for it and recorded the entire album again, plus a few extras. All rhythm tracks and guide vocals were done in two days. Having spent a day putting on a show for the label, we had one day for the vocals and one to mix.

• • •

The experience was the complete opposite of the Conshohocken sessions. This time, we embraced all the things that any proper producer would want to fix. I recall sweating like I was playing a basketball game, catching my breath between passes. The more we broke the law, the better it sounded when it came back through the speakers. Caleb worked to bridge the difference between our live sound and the more well-behaved album we'd just made in Conshohocken. He understood the upside-down balance that made us tick—too much distorted bass, too much background vocal, and a slightly buried lead. He came up with ways of capturing the uncapturable, and he nailed it. I've rarely been as inspired as I was hearing what we recorded with Caleb. It really seemed like something new.

The day of our marathon twenty-four-hour mix, neither Caleb nor I left the building or slept. When I finally hit the bed, for the first time in two days, I was struck with fear that I wouldn't ever wake up. I was so tired, the pull of sleep was so hard, that I honestly believed I was going to die. I thought, *At least I finally made a good album! Good night, world!*

Once they heard what we'd done, Caroline Records forgave us for recording more than was agreed upon. Our entire session with Stiff Johnson went on the pile with all my other demos and literally into a vault. And my theory on demos, and how you shouldn't record songs more than once, went on that pile too. It turns out demos aren't evil—recording songs multiple times doesn't steal their soul. I just hadn't been doing it right. I was playing it too safe when recording. I needed to *break the law* and I needed accomplices. In Robert, Darren, *and* Caleb, I'd finally found the dangerous co-conspirators with whom to collaborate.

I'm not suggesting that Ben Folds Five's debut is a damn masterpiece. But I'm very proud of it. We were backed against the wall and went with our gut. It changed everything for us. From then on we would only do exactly what *felt* right. Too much compression, you say? Eh. Too many notes? Too much pounding? Out of tune? Speeding up? Actually yes, fuck it, why not? We decided we were allowed to do whatever the hell made us happy. There's no doubt in my mind—if Kerry hadn't cried, if we hadn't made the whole album again in such a frenzy, had we not cast all conventional wisdom aside in that last-ditch effort—the first Ben Folds Five album would have been our last.

WELCOME TO THE GODDAMN
MUSIC BUSINESS

Called in sick one day
Stepped out my front door
Squinted up at the sky and strapped on my backpack
Got into a van
and when I returned I had ex-wives and children, boxes
    of photographs
—From "Free Coffee," *Way to Normal*, 2008

DELIVERING THE MASTER OF OUR FIRST ALBUM WAS LIKE TOSSING A
grenade in slow motion. It was like we sailed it through an open window at Caroline Records in the dead of night and it landed with a
light *clink* somewhere in their tiny New York City office—followed by
a week of quiet . . .

Then.

Shit blew up. Things changed.

If there was a Broadway musical of my life, the delivery of the first Ben Folds Five album would be the end of act one. Not because the success of that album was overwhelming, but because, as of that day, I was officially a recording artist, and that alone made me feel a little more at home in my skin. I could take "aspiring" off my job description. I wouldn't have to hide the fact that I was a musician from prospective landlords and employers. That voice in the back of my mind that was concerned my parents would always worry about me could hush. I was no longer a tumbleweed with a demo tape begging to be heard.

I would have breathed a sigh of relief had there been a split second to process it all. But there was no intermission after act one. I was shot out of a cannon directly into act two before the audience could even return from the bathroom. Gone were the late nights of writing at a notebook in my bed, surrounded by empty album jackets, pizza boxes, and balled-up pieces of paper. I'd enjoyed going to sleep as the sun rose. I'd enjoyed reaching for my glasses at 2 P.M. and stumbling up to get a burrito and a Coke for breakfast. I'd thought it was funny to be an adult who was constantly reminded by strangers that he should tie his shoes.

Now it was different. I found myself waking up with the rest of the working world. It started with early mornings to take phone calls from the U.K., remaining tethered to the phone until the West Coast had concluded business hours. Back in this era of the music business, the three months prior to a new-album release were jam-packed with business and promotion for the band and label—if you were so lucky. For the first time in my life I knew what I would be doing the next day, month, and even year. We had plans. Plans to eat up every ounce of day and night we could handle. Every silent space would be filled and I would always be on the move. And I knew I could handle it all, so I said yes to everything. I was given the Script™ and was happy to follow it note for note. It went like this, robotically: "record-tour-record-tour." Amazing. No need to ruminate on life and my future. This *was* the future, and it was full of plenty to keep me busy.

I stay focused on details—it keeps me from feeling the big things
—From "Still," *Over The Hedge* soundtrack, 2006

The buzz about our soon-to-be-released debut album set off interest from major labels who wanted to buy our yet-to-be-conceived second album. Before our first album had even hit shelves, we found ourselves consumed by the process of major-label courting for the second one. But sleep could wait. In a business like this, I figured, you get one chance if you're lucky. I was twenty-eight years old and nearly aged out of the rock business. All of this, I figured, was happening just under the wire.

Some mornings I'd open the front door to discover stacks of massive boxes containing every record Warner, EMI, or Sony had ever made. Each label that was pursuing us had their entire catalog sent to my house. Just that alone was overwhelming. I was used to a normal life of acquiring one album at a time, listening on repeat for weeks until I could afford the next. Now I suddenly owned more than I could ever listen to. Hundreds of CDs spread across my living room floor. I'd play ten seconds of each, tossing them around the room like confetti while opening the plastic wrapping of the next. But record-bingeing wasn't as satisfying as I would have imagined. I felt like an out-of-control CD junkie, trying to soak up all of recorded music history in spare minutes.

As the setup period for the first album raged on, the front yard became my office. I'd pace around outside with my old-school chunky wireless landline phone, bullshitting my way through interviews. I spent all day talking about myself. I'm sure my next-door neighbor must have looked across the yard like, *what a douche,* as I wore a line in the grass, spouting God knows what kind of crap.

Front-yard office, Chapel Hill, 1994

Between press calls, I'd get updates from Alan on the major-label bidding war, names of the last five people to say I was great, the daily list of five-star reviews, who would be at what show, and what opportunities couldn't be missed.

It was an exciting day when Alan called to tell me we had our first national review—exciting for a few minutes, anyway. It was a glowing review, in *Entertainment Weekly,* and Alan read the whole thing to me over the phone. They rated the album an A-minus, a rating that, he added, wasn't given out "like candy." But it was candy, all right, for my little ego. Alan read all the good bits again for emphasis. It soon occurred to me to ask the obvious: "Was there another review this week with a higher grade?"

He flipped around the reviews section a bit. "Yes," he said. "A band called Garbage."

"Garbage, huh? So, what's *their* grade?" I asked.

"A-plus."

Innocence lost. You learn quickly that no sales number, no review, no award, will ever be good enough.

• • •

Alan kept me constantly up to date on all the amazing developments, like how many records had shipped. As long as the figures continued to rise, which they did, I was happy. Offers poured in from everywhere for things I'd never dreamed of doing. I'd grab my calendar as he added shows, turning each month ahead into a black page. It was all good news all the time. Every call-waiting beep was like a bell at the county fair, winning more and more prizes. *Yippeeeee!*

It was on an afternoon of such exhaustingly ego-inflating calls that I put one on hold and hit CALL WAITING to receive the next goody. But this wasn't the standard welcome-to-our-showroom-of-prizes call. It was Dave "Stiff" Johnson, the producer of the abandoned and vaulted version of our album. We hadn't spoken since the mix.

"Hello, Ben speaking," I answered.

"Well, well, well! Mr. 'Ben Speaking'! Mr. Ben fucking Folds! Welcome to the *goddamn music business!*" Dave shouted maniacally, almost as if he were singing. "You're gonna do just *great* in this cutthroat business, you fucking asshole!"

Oh no! It seemed *nobody* had told Stiff that we had rerecorded the whole album. He hadn't even received a courtesy call or letter—not from management, the label, *or* us. Dave Johnson had to find out for himself that not a second of his production was to be found on our release. He had just read about it in a magazine, picked up the phone, and was dealing me an earful. It's possible my neighbor could hear him through my phone too. But Dave was right. And I needed to hear it.

It seemed my new place in act two of my life elicited far more intense reactions than I had experienced before, both good and bad. My decisions now affected others. I guess it's called responsibility—not that special. It's just that being chewed out for being late to wait tables never quite had the emotional torque I had gotten from Dave Johnson. This wasn't just *Life as Usual + Fun Prizes*. It was a mixed bag.

I'd never been popular before. I'd never been a success at anything or had strangers cling to me in case I had something to offer.

What must it have been like for pretty girls back in school? I wondered. *Or just for someone who runs a popular local restaurant?* Because people who wouldn't have given me the time of day before were now pulling me aside to talk my ear off, with this wild look in their eyes. More than once I hid in a stairwell at an obligatory New York or Los Angeles music-biz party just to get some quiet—to grab a moment where I wasn't looking out of a fish-eye lens watching some stranger's mouth move as I nodded. There was the other side of that coin too, as certain old acquaintances now seemed to subtly exude a whiff of resentment or outward bitterness toward me. I wondered if I was imagining it, and that in itself began to get into my head.

I've never experienced an ass-kissing quite like the one Robert, Darren, and I got on our first record release, when we were a clean slate, all potential, no string of failures—or successes. The new "it" band, the band to watch. We weren't famous yet, but word in the biz was we might be soon. *Get in while you can!* I remember needing assistance from a couple of security guys for the first time, pushing fans back just to get to the stage for our third gig at the tiny East Village rock club Brownies.

Some of that intensity at the beginning stage is due to the fact that an artist is still accessible when they're the "next big thing." And those who want to hitch their wagon to you understand this very well. Once you get going and become professional, you don't look like prey anymore. You adjust, and things normalize. You learn who your friends are, and the sharks disperse to find the next new thing to latch on to.

This sudden fame, or promise of fame, wasn't all bad, of course! There was also plenty of earnest excitement and innocent attention. It was wonderful at times. It's just hard for someone who's not used to causing such a fuss to figure out how it all works. But it did get to my head some. Luckily, I was in my late twenties for this and not my late teens. I can't imagine how those who make it much bigger, much younger, can possibly cope. Hats off! Because there are so many levels to celebrity and ours wasn't even megastardom—Elvis or Beyoncé style. Ours was on a much smaller scale, even at the height of our career. But our ascent began back in another era, much different from now, when the money was flowing, when video budgets were a quarter of a million dollars, and a band like ours sold forty thousand records a week without blinking. Prior to the internet, a rock band reached audiences through a limited number of outlets like radio, TV, and magazines. And overnight we were pouring out of all of them. So, yeah, it was all quite a big deal, at least to us. I was damn near numb for most of it but kept my balance by remaining centered on the task at hand: the music and loading my own piano into rock clubs. The social part, the immersion in quasi-fame, sent my soul running for the recesses of my skull, where it crouched in hiding for years.

The thing about "making it" in the music business was best explained to me by my friend John McCrea of Cake, who put it this way (roughly): "Being a rock star is, of course, every fifteen-year-old boy's dream. You wish for it when you're young. And just when you're too mature to be a rock star with a straight face, *that's* when the wish is granted and you get the job." I don't believe John meant he had wisher's remorse. But the opportunity to ride the bull for a while in the goddamn music business isn't something you turn down, especially when you're otherwise qualified to bag groceries and wait tables. It's just that as an adult, you question the dreams of your fifteen-year-old self.

I often thought about what John said, and years later I wrote a song called "Draw a Crowd," where I likened achieving fame to ordering a package that arrives once you've forgotten you ordered it. Haven't you ever been surprised by an Amazon order that appears on your front porch—something you ordered drunk last week and never thought about again? *Whaaat? A book on identifying North American birds . . . ? Oh! Right! I'd totally forgotten. . . .*

I ordered something
It took a while
This morning something
Was on my doorstep
What's this I'm holding?

Time capsule order?
'Cause I'm a brand-new man and I don't think I want it!
—From "Draw a Crowd," *The Sound of the Life of the Mind,*
2012

I have drawers full of youthful photographs of Robert, Darren, and me from when we were the next big thing, doing our first TV shows, gigs big and small, business meetings, and fancy parties. It was quite a roller-coaster ride. In fact, these old photos remind me of the actual roller-coaster photos they try and sell you for ten bucks as you step off a ride at Six Flags—your very own snapshot of yourself and some strangers captured by automated camera at the most thrilling turn. Around you, twisted, terrified expressions of those hanging on for dear life, as well as the calmer expressions of the more stoic passengers. And, of course, the ecstatic faces of those having the time of their life, frozen in time with two hands in the air and eyes on fire. When I see our old touring photos, I'm not sure which roller-coaster passenger I am. The brave one with hands waving over my head, or the one clutching the safety bar in fear, looking like he might be ill. But this music-business ride was what I'd asked for, even if I'd placed my order as a teenager. And it had now arrived on my front porch along with all those boxes of free CDs. I was in the goddamn music business.

HAND ME THAT PIANO

WE'D GOTTEN THE MUSIC-BIZ THUMBS-UP. THE GATEKEEPERS OF THE industry allowed us passage to the next round and we would proceed until apprehended. The hype men and women of the music business were chanting and beating drums, as was the ritual. But even an anticipated debut album is a drop in the ocean of music releases. The mortality rate in the world of new music has always been grim. Those images from biology class of hundreds of thousands of sperm competing to survive come to mind. It was time to earn it or be sent home in shame.

We loaded the Baldwin baby grand piano into our converted Ryder box van and hit the road with old-school folding road maps. Analog, baby! Of course, cellphones weren't a thing yet either, so we had to get directions and discuss load-ins with the club owners on the landline before hitting the highway. But it was this hard work, these long drives, the shitty food, the sleeping on the floors of bad hotels, that was my lifesaving counterbalance to all the ego-stroking. It kept us honest, as the old-timers say.

Our old yellow van was outfitted with a generator, a sofa nailed to the floor, a small TV with a built-in VHS player (with an array of absurd seventies' kung fu movies and the silent film *Metropolis*), a mattress over the driver's cab, and some plywood cubbyholes for our bags. I usually drove, because I was too nervous to let anyone else do it. I kept awake by making myself moderately ill with as much Mountain Dew as it took not to fall asleep at the wheel and die. It was a lot of time in that van, and it was becoming more obvious that we only just met each other a year ago. Our days were now spent in each other's back pocket, our finances were tied, and we each pondered our changing lives as highway after highway unfolded, eight or twelve hours a day. Darren would put headphones on when he didn't want anyone talking to him. They were like a sign that read PLEASE DO NOT SPEAK TO ME, OR EVEN LOOK AT ME. Good idea. Soon we all had headphones on all the time, and I suspect they weren't always connected to music.

The audiences grew as we pedaled west. The buzz of our piano rock band spread through word of mouth, college radio, and press. I'd never seen most of the country before we crossed it on tour that first time. It was exciting to watch the familiar East Coast landscape give way to the flat West Kansas plains for what seemed like an eternity, until mesas began to spring up around Utah. We were glued to the windows. This was Wile E. Coyote shit we'd only seen on TV! I don't believe any of us had ever been west of Tennessee.

We could afford one hotel room a night for the three of us and our new tour manager, Trey Hamilton. His three important qualifications were that he lived in the house behind mine, was a great guy, and was exceptionally unemployed. He got on-the-job training on our first time out. He and I tackled most of the loading and the unloading of the baby grand piano, recruiting Robert and Darren for those moments where it took four bodies to get it up a ramp.

Here are words that no one has ever said before:
"Please saw my legs off" and "Hand me that piano!"
—George Carlin

There are some good reasons there haven't been many successful piano rock bands in mainstream rock and roll. If nothing else, grand pianos are not exactly portable and they're damn near impossible to amplify. But we were learning that if something didn't make sense, it might be worth exploring, because it meant nobody else was doing it.

We could afford one tuning a month when we started touring regularly. I'd carry a tuning hammer and do my best to get unisons close to in tune. I regularly broke bass strings, which would fly out of the piano and straight at Robert or Darren during the set. I learned how to "splice" these broken strings back into the piano with a special knot and some treble string. Once, when we were playing in subzero weather in Minnesota, the hammers were so frozen that the piano sounded like a harpsichord for the first half of the show. Steam bellowed out of the instrument like smoke. When the hammers thawed out, they were soaking wet and the piano became incredibly dull. During that same cold spell, on a day when it was forty degrees below zero, we got the piano down the ramp into the middle of a snowy street, panicked from the unfathomable cold, and just left it there in the road, watching downtown Minneapolis traffic avoid a baby grand piano. Not something you see every day.

The piano's place in rock and roll has always been interesting to me. Its associations with being middle-class living room furniture, church-choir accompaniment, a classical or jazz instrument, make the instrument nearly antithetical to rock and roll itself. The music and culture that the piano symbolized was the very thing that the rockers were rocking *against*. Anyone who's ever rocked the piano has had to be somewhat irreverent and even violent toward their instrument in order to be accepted in the world of rock and roll. You must sacrifice your piano to prove your rock-ness.

Each decade there seems to be room for one or two irreverent piano rockers. I'm not talking about career balladeers, like Barry Manilow or Neil Sedaka, whom I love. Or even artists like Tori Amos, who definitely kept the instrument alive when few others could. I'm talking about straight-up rock-and-roll pianists. Across rock history, you can still boil it down to Jerry Lee Lewis (who was willing to light fire to his instrument just to prove he rocked), Little Richard, Elton John, and Billy Joel. You *could* add Leon Russell, Dr. John, and Billy Preston, but you're headed to blues and jazz territory, where piano is more welcome.

Of all those just named, none had often rocked sans guitar. Most of those piano rock songs were actually dominated by guitars. The piano was usually sprinkled over the top while the rest of the band did the real rocking. If you deleted the guitars on Elton John's "Saturday Night's Alright for Fighting" or Billy Joel's "Only the Good Die Young," for instance, they wouldn't rock so much anymore. The piano in these songs is brilliant, but it's not what's driving the track. I knew of no precedent for a full-time guitar-less Piano Rock Trio in the mainstream when Ben Folds Five began.

However, there were a few moments in rock history that hinted a piano rock trio *might* work. One was Emerson, Lake & Palmer, a very successful late sixties/early seventies prog-rock trio from the U.K. They sometimes limited themselves to piano, bass, and drums on their records but mostly relied on the distorted B-3 Hammond organ, which probably has more in common with guitar than it does piano. Elton John's live record *11-17-70* is the best and perhaps only example of a whole album made by a piano rock trio that I knew of before my band, over twenty years later. *11-17-70*, captured before a small studio audience for radio, was released later as an afterthought, once Elton had already become a superstar. It's one of my favorite albums of all time. His bassist, Dee Murray, and drummer, Nigel Olsson, were off the proverbial chain. Elton's playing is James Booker, Allen Toussaint, Little Richard, Leon Russell, and Jimi Hendrix all rolled into one. Some of the most brilliant rock piano-playing ever recorded. It makes sense that Elton didn't make his commercial records as a trio—it's limiting and difficult. I was thankful he left that stone unturned. It left an opening. But *11-17-70* rocked in a sparse and laid-back seventies way, and a full-time guitarless piano rock trio would need to be more of everything if it was going to compete in the nineties.

Ben Folds Five could have stuck with mid-tempo songs and the ballads. Darren used to joke that if we did that and sold pink T-shirts that said SOFT ROCK in large puffy-cloud font, and then just made the music that matched that, we'd be a bigger hit. Indeed, that would have been a reasonable formula. And easier. Because the ballad is where the piano has always dominated and where it still wins today. Who can walk through a mall or airport without hearing a solo piano ballad like John Legend's "All of Me" at least once? It's no surprise that the piano power ballad "Beth" was hard-rock band Kiss's biggest hit. The power ballad became the radio slam dunk for metal bands during the seventies and eighties, with a piano appearing from nowhere to take center stage. But those bands started out by getting your attention with loud guitars. (It's of note that Ben Folds Five eventually broke mainstream with "Brick," which served as our power ballad. This was by design, as Alan, a veteran of record labels and quite the rock historian, had always envisioned releasing two rockers like "One Angry Dwarf and 200 Solemn Faces" and "Battle of Who Could Care Less" first and then delivering "Brick" as our "November Rain.")

"Revolution is exhausting," Kevin McCloud, the great presenter of the U.K. television show *Grand Designs,* told me recently through my TV, to which I replied, "Amen!" from my sofa. The unpaved path is damn hard going—it's as simple as that. And our first hurdle was just booking the gigs. Club owners didn't want a piano anywhere near their club.

"Yes, sir," I'd explain politely over my 1990s' landline. "No, it's a real piano, not an electric one. . . . Right . . . Yes . . . A baby grand, not an upright, and we move it ourselves. . . . Hello?"

Dial tone.

The clubs that had their own house pianos onstage were of course more receptive to booking a piano trio. But those gigs seemed to always go pear-shaped for us. Expecting jazz or blues, the audiences were sent running for the exits, holding their middle-aged ears. We stopped booking those early on.

Some of the rock venues were excited about the novelty of a baby grand piano on their stage, but mostly we were met with complaining, frowny faces, and eye-rolling. And just because we'd booked the gig didn't mean they were going to let us play when we showed up. There was a house soundman in Atlanta who, after trying in vain to get an "acceptable" sound from us, threw his hands up.

"This is not up to par. It's not professional!" he said. "And there's too much hum coming out of your piano mics! I can't let you perform tonight! I mean, would you make your record like that?"

I said that yes, actually, we'd just made our record exactly that way, hum and all, and he begrudgingly let us go ahead. I guess he figured if our brand was "the band that sounds like ass," he'd push the faders up and hope for the best. The gig went great.

Our first real tour was opening for the Smithereens. After the first couple of nights, their crew stacked all their road cases in front of the loading door and parked a van in the way so we couldn't load in. We couldn't get the piano by their blockade. I guess they just didn't want the hassle that night. If I could get my hands on an electric piano, they said, we'd be allowed to perform. They refused to budge, and we sat the night out. When we rolled up to the next day's gig, it was the same thing. Blocked again. The band's stage manager was waiting for us with arms crossed and a what-the-fuck-are-you-sissies-gonna-do-about-it grin on his face.

I made a beeline straight to him across the length of the sticky beer-stained rock-club floor. I was sick of being treated this way. Robert, assuming *the shit was about to go down* and fearing I'd be beaten to death, rushed protectively to my side, the dear man. I stopped a few feet from the stage, looked up straight into the dude's sunglasses, and spoke earnestly.

"What you did last night was rude. Rude and . . . selfish. And . . . and . . . and it really *hurt our feelings.*"

Dead silence.

How does a man commence an ass-beating after "it really hurt our feelings"? Not exactly fighting words. I thought I had the tattooed tough man in emotional checkmate. That is, until the tattooed tough man responded.

"Hurt *your* feelings?" he said, his face suddenly becoming human and vulnerable. "You guys think you're better than everyone, don't you? You don't think we know what you say about us? You think we're soooo stupid and soooo washed up? Your smug little sense of humor . . ." He paused and looked around, gaining momentum. "You never say hi! Nothing. You never once on this tour have even acknowledged the opportunity we have given you. The opportunity that the Smithereens have given you. Not once! Not in person, or from the stage." He took another deep breath and finished. "No fucking respect! That hurts *our* feelings!"

It turns out he had a name too—Chopper. We had a genuine talk after that, and the road hard-rock guy that was two clicks from kicking both our asses became our bud on that tour. Chopper even helped us load the piano each night thereafter. It turns out tough rock dudes are people too. Who'd have known? Another cheap lesson for us. This one in manners. When you're opening for an established band, maybe you shouldn't act like you own the place.

At the same time, something tells me Chopper wouldn't have had such a problem with us if we'd been a tattooed guitar band that, instead of a piano, had a quarter-ton model dinosaur with red lasers shooting from its eye. I don't think he would have blocked the load-in for that shit. No, it wasn't so much the inconvenience of the piano that the local crews had an issue with. It was, as I mentioned before, what the piano stood for. And I looked like a piano teacher at that time, or even an accountant, with my short hair and ordinary clothing. Me and my pain-in-the-ass middle-class living room furniture. We were another tribe—not from Planet Rock and not to be trusted.

But we were, in most ways, just like all the other struggling indie bands, earning it one gig at a time, with all the daily and nightly eight-hour drives. Four dudes sharing a hotel room. The terrible diet, the cheap beer, the constant dick jokes. It was all the usual baby rock-band stuff, just add a baby grand piano, which was the great liability, financially and physically. It added strain to every element of the day.

But by the end of each set, as I took a running body slam into the piano, smiled politely, and flipped off the audience, Robert's earsplitting distortion lingering a few beats too long, reminding everyone that we were a goddamn rock band, the great piano liability had become an asset. Mission accomplished, we'd have the scratched-up baby grand on its side, navigating the six-hundred-pound beast through the audience, which always got its own applause.

Hand me that piano.

Diving into the keys sometime circa 1997—Ben Folds Five

WHATEVER

FOR TWO YEARS WE CROSSED THE U.S.A. AS MANY TIMES AS WE COULD in support of our first album. The few breaks we'd originally scheduled were filled with chasing unexpected success in other countries. The first single, "Underground," cracked the top 40 in the U.K., and so we were off to Europe. Fan mail from Japan—a territory where the album hadn't even been released—tipped us off that our record was becoming a hit there on import sales alone. In a few months we found ourselves in Tokyo, signing autographs in front of a two-story-tall Christmas tree (I'm not sure it was even Christmas, but anything goes in Japan!) decorated with our CDs. And one early morning around 4 A.M., when I happened to be home off tour, my phone rang with an on-air call from Triple J national youth radio in Australia. "Underground" had landed at number 3 on their yearly top 100. I wasn't sure if it was a prank call, so I went back to sleep, but as it turned out, it was legit. We soon followed the good news to Australia as well.

Press was constant during the touring, done from pay phones in clubs, bathrooms, and on the side of the highway. I once got stuck in a sandstorm doing phone press in the middle of the desert. The van had dropped me off and was going to find food. I had to leave the phone dangling by its cord, make a break for it, and find a trash can to hide behind. That shit stings!

One morning, a limo with a journalist and photographer met us at our motel outside Phoenix and handed us each legitimate NASA space suits and helmets to don for a photo shoot. We took turns poking our heads out of the limousine sunroof in our space helmets, like three little boys. On location somewhere in the Sonoran Desert, the photographer explained that the photograph would look best if we walked in step. Running backward with four cameras clacking around his neck, he snapped away, shouting, "Left-right-left-right!" while we marched around the 110-degree noon desert in space suits. The resulting piece in *Spin* magazine likened the arrival of our indie-rock piano trio to exploration on the surface of Mars, and the accompanying photos were well worth the near heatstroke. I thought they captured the feeling of the era pretty well.

But all that talking about ourselves to rock journalists got old. So we got grumpier, and more sarcastic. We became a PR nightmare, with many journalists saying they'd never interview us again. It's just that so many of the interviews seemed impersonal and inane after a while. On our first trip to London for press, I had a glance at the massive British weekly music magazine with whom we were about to speak. It was geared for fashionable fancy English fans. It was a little intimidating for three Southern fellows on their first U.K. tour. I noticed that the magazine's most recent interview, with the English rock band Oasis, featured a quote set in massive bold colors, taking up a quarter page: IF YOU DON'T LIKE OASIS, WELL, THEN YOU'RE SHIT! So when I couldn't think what to say in the middle of our otherwise-normal interview with this magazine, I blurted, "If you don't like Ben Folds Five, well, then you're shit!" And what do you know? That quote got the same bold quarter-page treatment. The other weekly U.K.

magazine had us pose with wax figures at a London wax museum, which was unique until the next album, when the same publication had us do the same shoot with a different photographer. I guess they'd forgotten.

Another constant on the tours supporting our first album was the presence of label execs who flew in to various shows across the United States, interested in signing us up for our second album. We met the famous producer and head of Interscope Records, Jimmy Iovine. He'd flown in on a private jet in time for the end of the show. Our meeting was brief: "Hi, wish we could have seen the show. I'm Jimmy Iovine. Do the right thing!" He dealt a punishing handshake and, *poof,* he was gone! Seymour Stein with Sire Records, equally legendary, took us out to dinner somewhere along the way. You weren't a real band until you had dinner with Seymour. Belle and Sebastian even had a song about their Seymour dinner, appropriately named "Seymour Stein." I think we met most of the big record-label names on this tour.

We eventually decided on Sony 550, a relatively new major label. And I'm not sure whether 550 realized it or not, but we really didn't know what we were doing when we insisted on absolute creative control. Record execs were known to intervene in record production, which is understandable when investing millions in a band of nearly no experience. But many labels went way too far and got up in the artists' proverbial creative grill, which is what we feared, so we asked that they stay out. Of course, there's a middle ground, but we were becoming wary of compromises. The extremes were working for us. The late (very great and missed) Polly Anthony, who was the head of 550, and Ben Goldman, our A&R man, honored our extremism and didn't involve themselves musically.

We were given free rein over our budget, which we spent purchasing or renting recording equipment and soundproofing my seven-hundred-square-foot Isley Street shitbox. The record company was even okay with Caleb Southern as our producer, even though he had very few recording credits to his name. I'm sure no other big record

Caleb Southern in the kitchen (control room) in Isley Street shitbox. Recording Whatever and Ever Amen, *early summer, 1997.*

company would have allowed any of this. In fact, the competing labels had told us as much. They'd have insisted on a "proper" studio with a seasoned producer checking on our progress regularly.

The result of letting us run wild was an album that wasn't exactly stylistically cohesive. That may or may not have been a strength, but it certainly made *Whatever and Ever Amen* unique. Profanity-laden songs like "Song for the Dumped," with its chorus, "Give me my money back, you bitch . . . and don't forget to give me back my black T-shirt," sat side by side with "Brick," my story of high school abortion. The new more-serious approach took a moment to get used to for our fans.

I remember one night, as we were recording *Whatever,* some neighbors had gathered at the back door of the house/studio, eager to hear what we were up to. They were perplexed by what they felt was an overly whiny, plodding piano ballad. "She's a brick and I'm drowning slowly" droned through the speakers in the kitchen, which was Caleb's makeshift control room. To our neighbors, this was proof of selling out. Where was the fuzz bass? The pounding piano? They didn't think this was any fun at all, and they didn't mind telling me so on my back porch.

I didn't quite understand what they were talking about. This wasn't insipid. It was new and dangerous. "Brick" was a song about teenage abortion. It was true and raw. Anyway, it didn't sound like a radio hit to me at all. It was recorded in a few live passes on an out-of-tune upright piano, while Robert made his first attempt at double bass and bow, all on about six audio tracks live in a small bedroom of the house.

But the two extremes—loud joke songs and dead-serious ballads—sitting on the same album presented a sequencing challenge. It was unusual. Can you take a band seriously right after they've been shouting "kiss my ass" over and over? Normally an album has some in-between material for glue, but we had two opposite gears. So do you make Side A funny and raucous and Side B serious and introspective? We decided to mash them right up together, one extreme next to the other, no apologies. It was an honest snapshot of where we were.

Half the album represented our time on tour, slogging it out in drunken rock clubs. The other half, the ballads, was new. It came from introspection inspired by travel and changes in life. We found, returning home to record after nearly two years away, the Piano-Band-That-Rocks routine was wearing thin. It didn't seem natural to us anymore, all that excessive bashing. We felt like windup monkeys on speed. The crowds dug it, but certainly there was more to music, more to life, than that. And we'd just spent two years with beautiful, melancholy music, like Elliott Smith and Sebadoh, streaming into our *don't fuckin' talk to me* conversation-blocking headphones. Music that seemed to speak to what a young man feels when life is changing all around.

We had over a month to record *Whatever and Ever Amen,* but it ended up feeling rushed because so much of it was written in the studio. The pace at which we worked gave me less time to second-guess the new, more personal material. I reached for whatever was on my mind that day. "Selfless, Cold and Composed" was inspired by an honest and scathing handwritten letter I'd just gotten from Anna. I had her letter on one side of the piano lid as I scratched the lyrics out quickly next to it.

It's easy to be easy and free when it doesn't mean anything
You remain selfless, cold and composed

She was saying my affable, happy-go-lucky approach to our split wasn't because I was able to be magnanimous. It was because I didn't care. I wasn't affected by it. If I'd actually given a damn, she said, I'd have been moved to raise my voice, or say something mean. Just once. I'd never considered that, and it hit home for me. "Selfless, Cold and Composed" was a song to myself, as if from Anna's point of view.

Come on baby now throw me a right to the chin
Just one sign that would show me that you give a shit

I was a little timid about these quieter and more serious tunes, but Darren was particularly encouraging of them. Much of his song-writing was very introspective. The chorus of "Brick" was one of the unfinished songs Darren had told me about when we met for the first time at the coffee shop. Back when I sensed he had "art in his bones." Everyone was too busy to pay attention to my lyrics while we tracked, so I felt safe. But by the time we were mixing, I found myself sinking into my chair and blushing—was anyone noticing these lyrics? Too late. It was headed out the chute to millions of listeners. It was like a doctor giving you a shot by surprise in the middle of his explaining how he's going to give you the shot. It's done—it wasn't that bad, huh?

The last song written and recorded for *Whatever and Ever Amen* came from a challenge from my girlfriend, Kate. After we'd been dating a few weeks she told me she was positive that her name could never be used in a song, because it wasn't a musical name like "Michelle" or "Cecilia." I disagreed. "Kate" seemed musical to me, in a staccato sort of way. I decided to make the song "Kate" a giddy and nearly exhausting list of wonderful things to say about Kate. Although when you listen carefully some of them aren't that impressive: "Every day she wears the same thing"—*pretty amazing, huh?*—and "She hands out the Bhagavad Gita!" Of course, anything she did was impressive to the singer with the crush, and that was the point. The punch line at the end is "And she speaks! And she breathes!" as if just speaking and breathing were glorious accomplishments. Of course, she did cool tricks too, like producing rainbows when she smiled and playing "Wipe Out" on the drums (inspired by Karen Carpenter drum solos I was obsessed with). It turns out writing a song with a one-syllable name wasn't such a challenge, but writing one with nothing but kind things to say, with no irony or sarcasm, was. Being nice in a song felt like *breaking the law* somehow in the nineties.

At around midnight on our last night tracking, I was coming up short on gratuitous compliments that rhymed. I called up Anna, who could always think of nice things to say, and she added a few lines to the lyrics. I sang my parts at around 1 A.M., Robert and Darren sang theirs at around 3 A.M. while I was in the other room throwing clothes and equipment into boxes, and we flew to Nashville as the sun rose, to record some strings before mixing two days later. There was no time to think. If *Whatever and Ever Amen* is a good record, it's because it's an honest, naïve document if nothing else. It's rare for big-budget records, with so much at stake, to be allowed to be real.

I WANNA BE . . .

KATE AND I NEVER MANAGED TO SHARE AN ADDRESS, OR EVEN OPEN our wedding gifts, which were still piled in her parents' basement. Our marriage and divorce happened over the course of the *Whatever and Ever Amen* release and its promotion. We were both incredibly impulsive, and it all seemed like a great magical thing until the reality hit that we had no idea what we were doing or who the hell we'd each married.

Toward the end of our brief marriage, Kate met me in New York, so we could actually spend some time together on a rare week off. But I spent every hour arranging for and rehearsing a string quartet we were adding to the band for the H.O.R.D.E. tour, one of the more prestigious traveling rock festivals of the nineties. I was terrible company. At night I'd sleep for a half hour, then get up, flip the light on in our tiny hotel room, and work on the arrangements, while she pulled the pillow over her head in bewilderment. Then I'd sleep another half hour, get up, and arrange some more until the sun came up, before darting off to the rehearsal room all day. While we were out to dinner one evening, she pointed at an old couple at another table. They looked dour and jaded.

"That's us," she said. "The way we are now. Only *they've* been together for forty years." She was right. I recall her using the word "existential" a few times that night, and her observation made it into a song years later:

> *See? We're damned by the existential moment where*
> *We saw the couple in the coma*
> *And it was we were the cliché*
> *But we carried on anyway*
> —From "You Don't Know Me," *Way to Normal*, 2008

As "Brick" was becoming a hit, Kate and I met in Los Angeles, where we sat with a cheap lawyer to draw up our divorce papers and divide any belongings. It was mutually respectful and caring. We had lunch and went our separate ways.

For many years after, when friends would suggest to me that perhaps I should date normally, like everyone else, have the advisable get-to-know-each-other phase, and *then* maybe consider marriage, the advice fell on deaf ears. By my mid-forties I had had five significant relationships, which is probably average. Four of those ended in marriage—that's *not* average, and it's definitely *not so good for the life*. Each impulsive act, as exciting as it seemed at the moment, came crashing down, taking more of a toll than the one before. Rather than take stock of my feelings about it, and be honest with myself so that I could correct my mistakes, I just dug in with work.

The twenties, for anyone with the luxury of time to brood, can be laced with a constant low-grade sadness, always humming beneath it all. Biological clocks, coming-of-age, wondering, *Is this it? Have I missed my calling? Why are the hangovers worse? Have I passed the love of my life in a crowd somewhere on lunch break—like two ships in the day?* My method of dealing was an emotional fuse that would blow all too quickly, turning my whole system numb anytime my twentysomething low-grade sadness would crescendo and become too much. That's the feeling I remember the most from these years—being numb. Numb is what you become when something *should* hurt, but either the brain doesn't want to know or the nervous system thinks better of it. The word "numb" comes up a few times in my songs in that era. And the fuse-blowing concept is also closely related to another emotional defense mechanism I wrote about in the later Ben Folds Five song "Narcolepsy." In that song, any emotion, any feeling, good or bad, is just too much stimulation and puts the main character into immediate emotional sleep. I believe many young men are like this.

> *I should warn you—I go to sleep . . .*
> *I get upset or happy—I go to sleep*
> *Nothing hurts when I go to sleep*

I considered it a good metaphor for my understanding of depression as well:

> *I'm not tired. I just sleep.*
> —From "Narcolepsy," *The Unauthorized Biography of Reinhold Messner,* 1999

Some have suggested that maybe my questionable impulses were driven by my need to have something to write about—that perhaps songwriters like to invite some extra heartache from time to time. That's the "Phone in a Pool" line, only in reverse.

> *What's been good for the music hasn't always been so good for the life*
> =
> *What hasn't been so good for the life could be good for the music.*

We musical artists do, after all, get paid to be a moody bunch. Sometimes that can cause snowballing drama in real life, hopefully cheap lessons rather than tragedies like overdoses, suicides, drowning in a river.

Looking back, I think those rash decisions were attempts to wake myself up and feel alive. I worried I was a robot, a machine. I had a hard time being present. Most of my waking hours were spent locked into a repetitive task or thought, as life went on around me, like when I was a toddler who could watch records spin for eight hours. It felt like people were always knocking on my space helmet, asking if I was having the time of my life. *Life? What? Actually, no. I can't even see out of this thing!* Just the tin-can sound of my own breathing and an occasional *beep.* I wanted to snap out of that. Any thrill that kicked me into feeling had great appeal. Especially a *risky* thrill.

More again from "Narcolepsy"—it can read a little melodramatic without the music to balance it—it's actually sung by the background vocals—but it conveys the sentiment:

Dreaming in streams
Flowing between the shores of joy and sadness
I'm drowning
Save me, wake me up

I recall a Frank Lloyd Wright interview where he confessed that he never had the "father feeling" for his children. He said he had that feeling for his work instead. That doesn't make Frank Lloyd Wright terribly likable, but you have to admire the honesty. If I'm being just as honest, I would have to admit that as badly as I wanted to be married, I didn't have the husband feeling. I had incredible and brief crushes, but it was my music and my work that I was married to. However, when my children were born a few years later, I found that I had the father feeling for them. Very much so. Turns out I wasn't a robot after all.

But for the touring that lay ahead upon the release of *Whatever and Ever,* I was probably better off being an emotionally narcoleptic machine, staying numb and focused. Because that kind of touring leaves little space for a real life, much less coupling with another real life. Rarely more than four-hour sleeps, with no privacy, and no real life outside of work. Constant travel. I was quite happy with that, or as happy as a robot can be.

THROWING STOOLS
(AND OTHER MONKEY BUSINESS)

ONE OF THE MANY CHALLENGES OF A ROCK PIANIST IS BEING TETH-
ered to the instrument while everyone else is free to roam the stage.

As the venues got bigger, in order to help assert my front-man-
ness, I began to stand while playing the piano, which necessitated a
sort of a lunge position in order to reach the keys, use the pedal, and
sing into the mic simultaneously. I found I got more force into the
piano this way as well. This physicality became a big part of my musicianship. No longer having much use for the stool, I discovered the
fun of hurling it at the piano at the end of songs. It became a shtick.
As the stool struck the piano, Robert and Darren punctuated it with
a noisy bass and drums explosion. It looked violent, but the stool
rarely even scratched the piano. The soft padding of the seat was all
that actually made contact with the keys. It was for show. It expressed

just the right amount of irreverence to justify playing middle-class living room furniture in a rock band on a big stage.

Our first television appearance in Australia to promote *Whatever and Ever Amen* was on a big morning program called *Midday,* whose older demographic had absolutely nothing to do with the youth-radio audience that embraced us in the first place. Upon landing in Sydney after twelve hours of Qantas economy-class joy, we downed some caffeine and were wheeled to the Channel Nine set to rock some confused housewives.

The *Midday* show was pretty typical of the morning-show formats you see around the world. The host at the time was a woman named Kerri-Anne Kennerley. Her sidekick was a pianist named Geoff Harvey, who sported a big gray beard and a drive-through headset. He directed the music as he interacted with Kerri-Anne. After our line check and the compulsory quick powder touch-up, we went straight to live broadcast. Seated at our instruments, we heard an old fashioned "four-three-two . . ." The curtain rose and we found ourselves face-to-face with what Australians call the "Blue Rinse" set, which refers to a product that maybe takes a little too much yellow out of gray hair. The median age of the audience appeared to be seventy-five.

As I happily sang "shit" and "ass" on daytime TV, and Robert and Darren assaulted a horrified studio audience with booming distorted bass and deafening cymbals, I couldn't have told you the name of the show. Or the hosts' names. I got my introduction to Geoff Harvey moments after I broke the stool over what turned out to be his personal piano. I only learned the name of the show later, after we'd been tossed into the street outside the studio.

As the last note of our performance finished reverberating around the studio, about a quarter of the audience clapped tentatively. Soon, Geoff Harvey was making his way across the room, beet-faced and furious, launching a barrage of interesting Australian profanities.

"You fuckin' ungrateful Yank! I'm gonna rip your head off and shit down your bloody neck! The *Midday* show gives you exposure, mate!

And you think you'll just ruin my bloody piano as a fucking thank-you!!" he shouted.

The flying stool might have been theater, but Geoff Harvey's angry march across the studio to kick my ass on commercial break was not. My tour manager and crew all rushed to my side. Harvey's crew, who he later told me were ex-servicemen, did the same. And Robert, Darren, and I were quickly shoved into an elevator and up to the green room. Over the television in the green room, we could see Geoff Harvey ranting directly to the camera on live TV as his co-host, Kerri-Anne, sympathized. Channel Nine should never have an American act on their stage again, as far as Geoff Harvey was concerned. There were plenty of pianists who lived less than a mile away from the TV studio who were Australian, more deserving of exposure, and had ten times my talent, he said. But the Americans had money and so we came over, broke equipment, got a little publicity, and congratulated ourselves. His rant was accompanied by multiple replays of the piano-stool toss, as it broke into pieces over Geoff's shiny Yamaha.

Darren took in about thirty seconds of Geoff Harvey's freak-out before disappearing down the hall to the stairs. We followed to see what he was up to. By this time, Kerri-Anne and Geoff had moved on to interviewing a dog trainer, or maybe discussing recipes for a casserole. Darren all but tripped over himself trying to get his pants down in front of Geoff's camera so he might grace Australian TV with a few moments of his bare ass. Security grabbed Darren before he got there, and within seconds we were standing out on the sidewalk, our belongings sailing through the door close behind.

The timing of the broadcast and the whole incident turned out to be fortuitous. Universities were on break that week, so thousands of bored Australian students were watching the *Midday* show for the first time. Our album debuted the next week in the top five in Australia. On the flip side, I lost my endorsement deal with Steinway & Sons, who were supposed to provide us baby grand pianos on tour. The next day at the Prince of Wales, a legendary rock dive in St. Kilda, instead of a Steinway we found a note on the stage that began:

"To the management of Ben Folds Five, Due to the behaviour of your artist . . ." Now without Steinway's involvement, around which we had planned our tour, we had to convince piano dealers to deliver pianos to the various dives on our schedule. But they'd heard about the show, and each dealer suddenly required a bond for the value of each rental piano. It was an expensive tour.

The next year, when we were touring Australia again, Geoff Harvey had come around to Ben Folds Five and even had a few nice things to say about us on air. He now understood that throwing stools was just a bit of show business. He and I met at a hotel bar, had a pint of beer, and talked like civilized musicians. He left early to go to the hospital for the birth of his granddaughter. He's a good bloke.

The greatest, or should I say most shameful, stool-toss-gone-wrong happened in Porto, Portugal, at a big rock festival. It still makes my soul hurt to think about. We were playing the same stage as Nick Cave and Pulp, and I felt like we needed to make an impression. So I climbed some pretty tall and precarious speaker stacks at the end of our set to deliver the grandest of all stool tosses. This one didn't go well. It was, of course, another rare case where the piano wasn't a rental or our own. This time it was the personal property of the local promoter. Or, rather, it was his grandmother's late-nineteenth-century Hamburg Steinway B. I should have known by looking at it that this wasn't a rental piano. It was obviously an antique, the only Steinway the kind promoter could source in Porto. He'd been excited to host us and wanted to give us the best Portugal could offer.

Back home, we always made sure to have extra-light stools for throwing. But the Portugal festival had provided a massive stool, which was heavy as hell, and unwieldy. I struggled to the top of the speaker stack with it, took aim from many yards away, and watched in horror as the toss went woefully pear-shaped, the steel side of the legs colliding with the beautiful walnut piano. The Steinway's ivory keys splintered and sprayed on impact. I felt like a DICK and even worse when I found out it was a family heirloom. Doug, our tour manager, locked me in my trailer to protect me from the promoter, who wanted to do to me what I'd done to his grandmother's piano.

When I got back home, I purchased an old Steinway with ivory keys. You know, ivory—from elephant tusks. They're illegal now, have been for years, and they should be. I had the keys extracted and sent them to Portugal. I never communicated with this man, and I hope he was able to restore the damage.

The stool toss lost its luster for me after that. I did less and less of it and was more careful about it. But years later, in 2005, well into my solo era, I was performing "Landed" on the *Late Show with David Letterman* and relapsed into my old stool-throwing ways. "Landed," a mid-tempo song, suddenly felt excruciatingly long and underwhelming for TV. I can appreciate why most acts bring the lights, the moves, even some prerecorded tracks. Anything to keep attention, since the actual content of a song often seems to evaporate on television. My anxiety that I was boring millions of viewers kicked in, and I reflexively hurled the stool at the end of the song, a completely incongruous afterthought, given the introspective music I'd just played.

Mr. Letterman wasn't the type to make small talk with musical guests on commercial breaks, or really with anyone unless the cameras were on. I'd played *Letterman* a good five times by this time and had never once spoken to the fellow, so I was surprised when he appeared to be heading directly for me across the studio at the end of the song. He asked me if I was okay. I thanked him and told him I was fine.

"Then why did you throw things at the piano on my show?" he asked.

"Oh, that was just theater. I figured it made better TV," I answered.

"That doesn't make sense," he said. "Have I or anyone else here done something to upset you?"

I didn't want to argue the point with a hero of mine, but it *did* make sense. On major-network television, with its extremely valuable advertising time, you get a split second to make a memorable impression. Perhaps chucking a stool at the piano wasn't the best way to go for the song "Landed," but the instinct *does* make sense. It also makes sense that David Letterman, like Geoff Harvey on the *Midday* show might be confused by such a display. It's just easier to offend at the piano. Smashing guitars has been an institution for forty years, since Pete Townshend shocked audiences in the sixties. We all get that now. But the last time anyone saw someone rocking the piano, it was probably Elton John, and all he had to do on stage back then to freak people out was wear crazy sunglasses and stand on the lid a few times. In comparison, my stool-tossing didn't look like show business. It read more like violence against family furniture. It was cussing and throwing things in church—a petulant brat throwing a tantrum. That's the way it came off to anyone who hadn't seen our whole show.

If I may flatter myself for a moment with a broad comparison to one of my favorites: Early in his career, Randy Newman was a bit misunderstood. After a few poetic, ironic, beautiful albums with no real hits, Newman broke internationally in the late-1970s with a massive *perceived* novelty radio hit called "Short People," which unfortunately defined his career for a while. When I was a kid I saw him play it on *Saturday Night Live,* and he followed "Short People" with something that he probably felt made better TV than any of his serious and nuanced pieces. He sang "Pants." A song that repeats "I'm gonna take off my pants" for three and a half minutes. It *does* make sense that he chose to do that. Because what can a piano player who doesn't get up and dance, whose songs are too poetic and nuanced for prime time, who isn't a career love-song crooner, do to be noticed on mainstream TV? Threaten to take off his pants? Throw stools like a monkey?

OUR TURN TO RIDE THE BULL

AS BEN FOLDS FIVE GOT OUR TURN IN THE MUSIC-BUSINESS RODEO, riding our stylistically schizophrenic album from diminutive shitbox in Chapel Hill to the top of radio charts, we found ourselves with the opposite of the Randy Newman problem. We'd been rocking, snarking, distorting, and ironic-ing our way through the rock dives of America, but we were about to be defined by a painfully introspective and vulnerable song about teenage abortion.

In the summer of 1997, Sony 550 released "Brick" to the same radio format that had given moderate play to our first two rockers from *Whatever and Ever Amen,* "One Angry Dwarf and 200 Solemn Faces" and "Battle of Who Could Care Less." Their accompanying rock videos each cost literally one hundred times the budget of our first album. This new format that had embraced us was called "modern rock," and it specialized in indie rock gone mainstream. It was all-rock, all-grunge, all-day. Modern-rock stations were receptive to playing "Brick," which would be the format's first piano ballad, but the listeners weren't so convinced. It seemed that a wintry-sounding tale of abortion set on the "day after Christmas" wasn't an appropriate soundtrack for the sun-and-fun of June 1997, and so the song was pulled after a couple weeks of lukewarm reception. Our label blamed themselves for having promoted "Brick" in the wrong season.

Whatever and Ever Amen–*era publicity photo*

By the time "Brick" sank (like the title) on summertime rock radio, we had been hitting it nonstop for quite a while. So we were given a month off as the business folks figured out what to do about the state of our album, which was stalled with no real radio traction. We needed a breakthrough. Touring with a baby grand wasn't going to be sustainable, and the label wasn't going to keep investing forever in a band who didn't yield a significant hit.

Time off sounded miserable to me, but Robert and Darren had the right idea and took the break to get their heads together. I just didn't know what to do with myself for a whole month. I couldn't sit still, and I was still reeling from divorce. So, what the hell. I decided to record the pain away and made an experimental LP under the moniker "Fear of Pop" in Bloomington, Indiana. It was a sort of "techno" album, except with all organic instruments. There were no synthesizers or programming. I performed layers of repeating beats and riffs on mostly acoustic instruments, running around the studio like an insane child as Caleb chased me with mics. One song was a faux seventies' cop-show theme, and to keep it real I had assistant engineers doing donuts in their cars around the parking lot as we recorded it. We even beat up an old truck with baseball bats and recorded that too. There were distorted pianos, backward drums, and singing through a talk box like Peter Frampton. The talk box is a tube that blows loud distorted guitar into your face so you can mouth the words and make the guitar speak. It vibrates your teeth a lot.

The raw tracks of Fear of Pop were a clusterfuck of sound that was unlistenable. But that was just the first part of the plan. The intention was to complete the composition by muting select tracks—the way you would carve a sculpture out of a log. A subtractive approach. The mixes became the performance, which was what had fascinated me about the new techno music in the nineties. This side project consumed each hour of every day for my entire month off. I didn't believe in processing emotions and getting proper sleep. I'm still glad I made the album.

During that month, Alan and the label decided they would rerelease "Brick" in the colder months that the song itself evokes. Polly Anthony flew to the big radio stations herself, which was unusual for a label head. That was some real and rare commitment. Sony 550 just acted like we hadn't released the single in the first place and pressed RESTART. It worked. I'm convinced that without their persistence we would have been headed home with a dead record by the new year.

When we resumed touring in December, Alan came backstage

after a show at American University, in Washington, D.C., to tell us we were invited to play *Saturday Night Live*. That's the only moment I can remember thinking, *Damn, I've actually made it.* It seemed the fix was in and "Brick" would be a hit. *SNL* had been the pivotal TV performance for every rock act I'd loved when I was a kid. I held this in higher esteem than I would have any award, opportunity, or endorsement. This one *counted.*

Our *SNL* performance was on January 10, 1998. We were told that the music-biz machinery would kick in right after *SNL*, and what was already a shit-ton of airplay would quadruple. I cringed. "How many times can radio listeners stand to listen to that song?" I asked.

"A *lot* more," Alan explained. "A real hit gets pummeled with airplay. Just wait!"

After performing a ploddingly unlistenable version of "Brick" on *SNL*, I kicked myself all the way through the cast after-party. Not even being seated next to Samuel L. Jackson was sufficient consolation for having performed so badly on such an important show. I don't think I said a word to anyone. I just sulked. Our crowd pleaser "One Angry Dwarf" had been cut last minute, due to a rare instance of *SNL* running overtime, which sucks because we *killed* that song in the dress rehearsal. But oh well. It seemed their *Titanic* movie skit went too long and we would have to make our stand on live network television with a quiet ballad on upright piano. Going out to play "Brick" cold fucked me up badly. In trying to keep the tempo slow and make sure the song was sad, we went way too far, and the song dragged. My nerves kicked in harder mid-song as I realized how bad I was sucking on this legendary show. As we hit the bridge of "Brick" I just *knew* we were finished for good.

Following the *Saturday Night Live* after-party was the traditional *Saturday Night Live after*-after party, which I also attended, continuing my drinking and mental self-laceration. And by sunrise, I, along with a panel of drunken entertainment strangers, had decided to fly to Australia for my next month off—I would leave that day.

"Just do it!" One of the crowd egging me on was a girl with whom I'd recently gone on a few dates. And she offered to go with me. *Why not?* I booked the flights as soon as I stumbled back to my hotel room at 9 A.M. I called Alan from the airport, bitching incessantly about how our career was *cooked* because "Brick" was the wrong song. I told him that we were "going to be like that fucking *Walking in Memphis* guy!" (As if being Marc Cohn, a brilliant songwriter, was some kind of death warrant.) I then called my answering machine back home to hear the long train of friends and family who called to say that they'd just seen me on *SNL*—and asking if I was okay. See? Cooked.

Once I got to Australia I rented a car to drive all the way around the perimeter and face some of that quiet time I'd been avoiding. The girl I'd flown down with decided to go in a different direction from me. She mainly wanted to see Ayers Rock. I drove off to do a lot of sitting on cliffs alone with a notebook to try and get my head sorted. Because something in my life wasn't quite working. I was getting big prizes like I'd always wanted, but I was more and more miserable. *How clichéd,* I thought. And I've always hated whiners. Especially successful rock whiners. I figured clichéd solutions for clichéd problems.

I drove the coast of Australia with my Moleskine and camera, climbing around on cliffs, taking rides in hot-air balloons, even trying a bungee jump, and sleeping in cheap hotel rooms above pubs. I was a young man at sea—a good melodramatic metaphor for a lost young man. Marriage wasn't the right anchor, and I must have written that a hundred times in my little journal. I was aware I should avoid relationships for a while. But I did contemplate the possibility of having kids. Even without a partner, maybe. I could ditch the piano tuner and hire a nanny. That might give me a real human concern outside of my work and save me from being a robot. *Ah, maybe not,* I thought. *Hell, I don't even have time for a dog.*

Of course, old patterns die hard, and at the very end of the trip I met a yoga teacher in Adelaide by the name of Frally. After less than forty-eight hours together, I heard myself as I blurted out, *"We should have kids!"* She seemed to think that was pretty funny. Well, at least I hadn't proposed. Yet. Before I returned to the U.S.A. to ride the bull up the pop charts, I heard a report on the radio of an American tourist who had to be airlifted from Ayers Rock due to heatstroke and severe sunburn. I found out later it was the girl I'd flown over with.

The following eighteen months are a blur, and what I remember mostly makes me sad. But there are a few things that stick out that make me smile. Like Mama co-hosting a Mother's Day MTV show called "Mother's Cut" with Ol' Dirty Bastard's mom. The two moms got on amazingly, and Mama was a natural! She said she thought I "sounded like Elvis." Classic! I also have fond memories of touring with Beck and Elliott Smith. Once I asked Elliott if he could play his song "Angeles" at some point on the tour. I loved that song—I still get goosebumps just hearing the title. Elliott said he was sorry, but his band hadn't learned that one for this tour. A couple hours later, in our shared dressing room separated by only a thin curtain, Elliott played the whole thing for me solo, so I could hear on the other side.

I also have a fond memory of reading our first really bad review in the U.K. It was of a live show at Shepherd's Bush Empire. Most of the piece was dedicated to personal jabs at me. The way I talked, what I wore, how the audience and I deserved each other for being such twats, my sagging weak chin and wimpy shoulders. This reviewer didn't let up on me for two pages. After Robert got through the brutal review, getting more and more upset with each word, completely steamed and ready to fight, he exploded, "What an asshole! He never mentioned me once!" There was a pause in the airport and then the three of us laughed until tears came. Maybe we were just tired.

In all honesty, the chart-climbing, platinum-collecting, famous-people-meeting, and world-seeing blur of 1998–1999 doesn't go in my "good times" file. Now, with a bit more experience, it's easy for me to understand why this was. And the reason is not that damn sexy. In fact, it's downright elementary: I was just *tired* and I needed some sleep and good advice. I needed to slow down and even probably get some help. It's something you need sometimes in a world that moves so quickly. Self-actualization is a bitch, and so is jet lag—two years of perpetual internal clock abuse. There are some things that can't be solved with a notebook on a cliff.

I don't want to sound like a little whiny bitch. I can certainly appreciate how amazing all this was. How fortunate we were. It was a trip of a lifetime. But the success felt like a detour, oddly. A fluke. When I first sat down to write this book and reflected on this peak time of Ben Folds Five, it was difficult to identify what lessons, if any, could be gleaned and passed on. *Hmmmm, I learned how to do interviews with wacky morning DJs, how recoupable budgets work, and where to do my laundry in Paris.* I wasn't so sure I learned much more. I was mostly on autopilot, in survival mode.

By mid-1998, Frally had come from Australia to join me on tour with Beck. By the end of 1998, as *Whatever and Ever Amen* was winding down, an exhausted Ben Folds Five had a stack of awards waiting in various cardboard boxes back home. We attended the MTV awards, and our nomination was announced while I was in the bathroom trying to stuff toilet paper into my fancy new shoes, which were making my heel bleed. So it's probably best that we lost that one to Green Day, because security wasn't going to let me back in while the cameras were rolling anyway. On that trip to L.A., we found out Frally was pregnant. I guess this is what I'd asked for, brooding on those cliffs, the way I'd asked to be a rock star when I was fifteen. This package was definitely on its way, due to arrive in nine months, in July 1999. Would it be a boy or a girl, we wondered? Well, as it turns out, it would be *both*! *Twins*! A triple anchor, an instant family to keep the piano-playing robot from floating into space. And then, of course, there was another important due date: our next album.

With an immovable, already announced release date for early 1999—and not a single song written—we headed to L.A., grew mustaches, and got to work.

REINHOLD

AS WE EMBARKED ON OUR THIRD STUDIO ALBUM, *THE UNAUTHORIZED Biography of Reinhold Messner,* I arrived at Sound City in Burbank with a notebook full of song fragments. There's a world of difference between fragments, good ideas, and actual songs. It's called craft, and I'd brought little of it to the session. I was tired of *crafting* typical verse/chorus kinds of songs, so I did what songwriters typically do when trying to avoid being typical. I went *prog* (for the uninitiated, this refers to progressive rock, a genre of awesome self-indulgence that dates back to the mid-1960s). I began gluing these fragments together as one long song, loosely connected by a few common melodic and lyrical themes that weaved in and out. It was a revolutionary approach, except of course that the Beatles had done the same thing on *Abbey Road* thirty years before. Still, the fragments themselves had loads of soul.

The long string of fragments had its moments, but the band and Caleb were right when, after a few weeks of this expensive experimentation, they urged me to consider dividing the material into normal songs. You know, the usual four-minute ones with beginnings, middles, and ends. As I struggled to have new material to record each day, coming in hours before the band, tearing things down and rebuilding, rewriting, and adding new stuff, Robert and Darren became understandably frustrated. Most of these fragments had no words and no titles, so I referred to them by time signature and key. Like, "Let's go back and work on that 6/8 dirge in C."

But Darren gave us the shot in the arm we needed when he brought in a finished beautiful soft guitar song he'd written for our friend Stacy, a great musician who'd recently died of an accidental overdose. It was called "Magic." It was a completed melody with words that I could sink my teeth into, rearranging it for synth, timpani, and upright piano. The proper way around! *Oh! But of course!* Writing the song *first,* and *then* arranging it. I needed to be reminded of what it was like to just sing a simple great song, without faffing around with bits and pieces, composing and orchestrating it like it was an unfinished symphony. We recorded "Magic" mostly live, vocal and all, in the studio, and as we went on Christmas break, I knew that I needed to get back to the business of actual songwriting.

In the two weeks of holiday break I wrote "Mess," "Jane," and "Your Redneck Past" from scratch. I started another song called "Carrying Cathy," which I couldn't quite finish in time for our deadline, as well as two others, "Zak and Sara" and "Jesusland," both of which I finished later for solo albums. Those new songs that I finished over Christmas, plus Darren's brilliant "Magic," and the various reworkings of my abandoned frag-prog symphony got us to the thirty-eight minutes of music we needed for an album. Just under the wire. It was a short but somehow heartfelt and interesting album. The record is a snapshot that evokes the insanity of it all, my struggle not to be a robot, and how it felt when the three of us finally got to escape back into pure music. I'm proud of it, and however we got there, my fragments ended up being real songs.

As we were mixing our record in New York, Frally fell dangerously ill in her first trimester and ended up in the hospital on the Upper East Side. Being an Australian citizen who had booked a spontaneous ticket to the United States to hang out with a piano player, she was now within days of her visa deadline. She was half conscious, living on a drip, and in grave danger of losing the twins. I was never so despondent in my life as the night a nurse flippantly mentioned that "Yeah, you'll probably lose the babies." But in the morning, their little hearts were still beating. My nights during the *Reinhold* mix and mastering sessions were spent sleeping in a chair next to Frally's hospital bed and cabbing back down to the session when the sun came up. Those two weeks in the hospital cost us both our life's savings. Dear reader, always get traveler's insurance. Really.

Barely well enough to walk, Frally managed to catch her plane back to Australia the day before her visa expired. I finished the mix and the mastering with the band in New York and headed to Adelaide. *The Unauthorized Biography of Reinhold Messner* juuuust made the deadline for its release in April 1999.

Frally and I were married in June, and the twins arrived in July. As the first single, "Army," was struggling on the radio back in the States, I was eleven thousand miles away, sorting my passport and moving things into a small house in Hyde Park, a quiet suburb of Adelaide. I welcomed this new chapter of my life and took special joy in watching the twins as they learned to crawl, make noises and all kinds of faces, and finally to *get the fuck to sleep*! Being a new parent does little to help the sleep deprivation of rock touring, but I felt great relief in getting the spotlight off myself. I was happy tending to someone else for a change. Too much "me" had made Ben a dull boy.

The news of the album sales, the airplay numbers, and the reviews weren't particularly positive. It wasn't *awful*, but we weren't scoring big prizes anymore. And no wonder. It wasn't a big prize kind of album. It wasn't really a pop album at all, so what did we expect? I was relatively disconnected to the progress of the record, with baby

Adelaide, Australia, with twins, 1999

spew on each shoulder and a VHS of *Teletubbies* on repeat. I decided to tune it all out until I was called to tour duty again.

We began touring with some scheduled breaks in between gigs so that I could fly back to Australia, finally hitting the big venues we had always been aiming for. But with no real radio buzz to kick it off, we only half-sold most of them. And we had gone big this time, spending oodles on production, with official big-ass lights and a larger crew. I carried two baby grand pianos, one of them with tacks in the hammers for a different sound. I sometimes played both pianos at the same time. Robert had an array of synthesizers, and Darren had timpani and gong in his setup. Musically, it made for an interesting tour. We had grown more confident and could sit inside ballads and the introspective songs without having to make a joke every other moment. But with no radio hit, we had suddenly dipped back into unsustainable territory. The expense, the distance, my parental requirements, began to wear on all of us. The squeeze was immediate.

There's an insane video from that era that made the rounds. It's from a live nationally televised concert in Japan, in a sold-out five-thousand-seat arena. The video was dubbed the "Freaking Out DVD." Indeed, Ben Folds *was* Freaking Out, and doing so for a confused Japanese audience. Returning for our encore in official Japanese police uniforms, Robert, Darren, and I broke into faux Rage Against the Machine meets Black Sabbath meets Weird Al as I ran around the stage shouting and rapping like an idiot. That much had become routine, but this one went *way* over the mountain. Darren took part in the tantrum, beating the living fuck out of a gong as I screamed, "Thank you, sir, may I have another!" repeatedly. I mean, *way too many times*. It's damned uncomfortable to watch. I told a lot of very sweet Japanese fans that they were all going to prison to be "fucked up the ass."

But we love Ben Folds Five! Why would they want to hurt us?

I find it simultaneously funny and alarming. Because it's a real tantrum. It's profane, angry, and childish, and it was on mainstream Japanese TV. Our album was tanking. We had been told the only chance to get a video for "Magic" was on this filmed performance, and we'd just bungled that. The first two singles had broken the bank for Sony. Especially "Don't Change Your Plans," with its *three-hundred-thousand-dollar* video directed by the brilliant filmmaker Abel Ferrara. Making a cheap video for "Magic" might have persuaded the label to give that song a chance, because we all thought it was a hit. But that was it for *Reinhold's* promotion budget, and the door was shut. I was raising a family and needed this album to succeed more than ever. The arc of my marriage was also following a familiar pattern, in the shape of a spiral pointed downward.

When I'm struggling emotionally or I'm stressed, I act up, especially onstage. I go too far in nearly everything. It's the same thing I did when I was in school, except that instead of being sent home, I get paid. I throw childish tantrums, which I more or less pass off as humor. Hopefully they have provided someone with entertainment. They're certainly good for blowing off steam. But I knew *something* had to give soon, because inwardly I *was* freaking out. I was spinning way too many plates, and some of them were now hitting the floor.

STOP THE BUS!

THE EUROPEAN TOUR IN SUPPORT OF *REINHOLD* WAS THE BASEBALL BAT that broke the camel's back. The record was dead and we knew we were wasting our time.

This tour was particularly dark. It was a version of *This Is Spinal Tap* without the funny parts. The bus driver was on uppers to stay awake and he drove in a manner that kept the rest of us that way as well. He was morbidly obese and always left his pants unbuttoned while driving. I don't believe I ever even saw him stand. He certainly never got himself up to empty the bus toilet tank, which overflowed as he took excessively fast turns, wandering from lane to lane across the highway. The funk of forty thousand tours trickled from the toilet, oozing beneath the bunks. Not that it was easy to spot beneath the trash, beer cans, and excessive drug paraphernalia. We weren't a druggie bunch, but this tour was as close as we got to Mötley Crüe.

The bus driver thought he had a girlfriend, but she turned out to be a prostitute who was using him and the bus for a free ride. She would crawl around and knock on all our bunks during the night, ask-ing, "Do you want me to do your laundry?" I wasn't quite sure what that meant, but I had a feeling I was better off declining. There was one crew member who I imagine probably did let her do his laundry. Finally the bus driver did what I didn't think was possible and got a traffic ticket on the Autobahn. I mean, there's no speed limit on the Autobahn, right? I called Alan and insisted that we get another bus somehow, because I had to survive to be a good father. We fired the bus driver, who sued and won for unfair dismissal. Another pay-to-play tour. For some in my crew, like Leo, who'd been with us since near the beginning, the heaviness of the vibe on that tour, the awful and uncomfortable living conditions, and the toll of the past few years of grind were all too much. He took a break from my touring until well into my solo years and then returned once he'd recovered. He's still with me these days. In fact, he just showed me which Griswold pan to buy on eBay.

It was obvious the end was near. Robert, Darren, and I were on such different pages. We sat side by side on the bus, as they read cool biog-raphies of sixties' Beat poets and *On the Road* and I sat with my high-lighter and a book about child development. I was no fun. And how do you even get together for practice when you live eleven thousand miles away?

Cue the Phil Collins and Marilyn Martin classic, "Separate Lives."

I don't really recall much about our last gig, at the Summer Sonic Festival 2000 in Japan, except that Robert spent much of the time walking around the stage holding his bass up and not playing it, trying to get the attention of the crew. And I remember some big hairy Americans, who I figured worked on Green Day's or Weezer's crew, heckling us from the side of the stage.

The next two shows were canceled due to a typhoon in Okinawa and political unrest in South Korea, so the tour ended early and I got to come home and surprise my kids. I was excited for them to try Pop Rocks, which I hadn't seen since the seventies. Pop Rocks are a fizzy crackling packet of sugar candy that sort of explodes in your mouth. I was stoked to have procured two packs in Tokyo. The twins were not so stoked and there were tears. Wait until your kids are at least five before you give them exploding candy. #ProParentTips.

The twins were now walking, just well enough to get themselves in trouble. And they were now talking well enough to say all kinds of crazy shit. I was glad I wouldn't be missing any more of that for a while.

Getting back into my domestic life, a few days after the tour, the familiar old school AOL, "You've Got Mail!" summoned me to the office, which doubled as a baby-changing closet. It was an email from Darren, and it wasn't exactly a surprise. He had aspirations to write and sing his own material, and none of us was getting any younger. The email was a brief one, which just said he was done and out of the band. Before I could respond, my computer dinged again, "You've Got Mail!" This one was from Robert, who quickly replied that "It's only a band if it's the three of us. If Darren is out, then I'm out too."

I had one child over my right shoulder and the other playing with my shoestrings. I don't recall how I responded, but it was as brief as the two emails I'd just received. I just acknowledged that we would no longer be a band. I forwarded the emails to Alan, shut my phone off, took the twins for a stroll, and that was that.

ROCKIN' THE SUBURBS

I WAS A NEW PARENT, IN A NEW COUNTRY, AT THE DAWN OF A NEW century, and I thought that *Rockin' the Suburbs* should be a musical document of that moment. It should be memorialized with the musical stenographic equipment of the day, which meant using computers. *Ugh.* My comfort zone had always been the methods and sounds of good old-fashioned twentieth-century recording, but this was clean-slate time again, so I set my fears of twenty-first-century technology and all its evil editing ability aside. I wanted a time stamp on this one: *Class of 2001.*

> *Some producer with computers fixes all my shitty tracks*
> —From "Rockin' the Suburbs," *Rockin' the Suburbs,* 2001

I sent a demo of the song "Rockin' the Suburbs" to Ben Grosse when I asked him to produce my first solo record. He said, "About that line with the 'shitty track fixing,' you know that's what I do, right?

I record on a computer and fix everything. It's the way I work." I told him that's precisely why I wanted him. He was a virtuoso in computer recording, and his records sounded very "now." He had a few albums at the top of the modern-rock charts. It wasn't music I cared for, but he knew exactly how to present it, how to dress it. We set up a digital recording studio in a church in Adelaide and I played all the instruments, even electric guitar, with the exception of a few overdubs here and there. I had spent the previous six months writing these songs and had demo'd them already. I put in more time writing and preparing for this album than I ever had before. I knew I had to make a great first solo album, or perish.

One of the first songs we recorded was "Still Fighting It," the lyrical spark of which had come to me after witnessing the birth of my twins.

You're so much like me—I'm sorry . . .
—From "Still Fighting It," *Rockin' the Suburbs,* 2001

People say your life flashes before you when you think you're going to die, but that's never been true for me. The few times I've thought it was lights-out time, nothing really flashed before my eyes, except for weird thoughts like, *I wish I hadn't eaten, because I'd like to die on an empty stomach. That would be more dignified.* And *I hope this doesn't hurt for long.* I found myself on a plane once that seemed certain to crash, and there was no time for sentimentality. The pilot was obviously convinced we were going down, as hard as he tried to sound cool. CNN was even waiting when we miraculously landed! But nope. During that flight, with loose objects and unbuckled people being tossed over seats, I had no deep thoughts, no flashing of my life before my eyes. But the birth of my children? Seeing two new lives as they came into the world, struggling for breath, shocked by light and sound, crying and scared, *did* bring it all back in a flash. It was profound and I wanted it in a song.

It sucks to grow up
And everybody does
It's so weird to be back here
—From "Still Fighting It"

I suddenly saw life as a series of scary challenges in an exponential incline. One that never ends. You're always fighting against something, facing challenges, for which you're not quite prepared. Birth, then your first sickness, your first rejection, first humiliation, first breakup, first fight, first bad grade, first firing, a heart attack or cancer, and then you shit the bed and die. And who knows what lies beyond that. But once you've surmounted each new obstacle, you can live in some calm temporarily. Those problems become old hat, not so scary, until the next unknown storm. But still, life is wonderful, and I wanted that in my song too. It had never occurred to me that I would live my life a second time—its ups and downs, joys and fears—by having children. But my life has flashed before my eyes every day since.

I tried to hang on to the emotional weight of this as we recorded the first track of "Still Fighting It," late one night with just piano. We got into a vibe and laid something simple down that felt special. Listening to the piano track the next morning, I thought it sounded like a classic track but . . . it was too slow. Maybe I had been a little *too* into my midnight vibe. *No problem,* I thought. It would be easy enough to record again.

"No," Ben Grosse told me, "that piano track is magic. Let's keep it. We can speed it up on the computer. There's a program that will do that without also raising the pitch."

Fine. I went to lunch to let him do his tricks. Hours later it became obvious it wasn't going to be so simple. When Ben Grosse sped the track up but left the pitch the same, the piano suffered from what is known as "digital artifacts." Subtle but nasty ticks and flutter trashing up the sound. The piano lost its luster. Soon, Ben Grosse was auditioning various "pitch and time" plug-ins from the internet. The hours turned into days. He had put so much energy into this, and we were not going to give up now. I was desperately trying to hang on to the *feeling* of this song about the miracle of childbirth and the challenges of life, but I kept having to reach for my credit card repeatedly

During recording of Rockin' the Suburbs—*waiting for hours on edits*

as Ben downloaded trial versions of plug-ins and we compared the artifacts.

"Okay . . . which sounds better? This one . . . or . . . this one?" he asked, watching my expression for clues, his hand on a switch.

"God, it's hard to tell. They both sound weird. Play it back again?"

"No, no, listen to the upper harmonics. Here's choice A. . . . All right, now here's B. . . . What do you think?"

Where's the fucking stash of razor blades? That's what I thought.

I just don't know about these time-saving audio plug-ins. I'm not convinced they save time. I'm not quite convinced computers and cellphones save time in the end. But, hey, we got through. I wanted the Class of 2001, and the Class of 2001 is what I got. I'll admit that I was uncomfortable with recording on computer because I worried all those digital seams would show through. Recording that way often seemed like a series of dental appointments, and I came home each night threatening to quit. But the computer is just another process, our era's process. It's the music that matters. I believe the album truly holds up. Ben Grosse taught me some important lessons in music, performance, and arrangement. You can indeed teach an old pianist some new tricks.

The title *Rockin' the Suburbs* struck many as silly and uncool. Especially the "suburbs" part and that's exactly why I was attracted to it. Rock and roll was supposed to be about the darkest streets, not the cul-de-sacs with up-lighting. But I was interested in life in the suburbs, so why wasn't it okay to write about it? Everyone in the nineties was so taken with the freaks, the losers, the weirdos, and the creeps. But I figure if you wanna talk to a real weirdo, just open the phone book, put your finger down somewhere in the suburban pages (if you can find a phone book), and call them up.

I felt that rock music and popular culture took the middle class in the suburbs for granted. Stuck somewhere between the rural and the urban, just beyond the strip malls and before the pastures, the suburbanites were expected to buy all the CDs, but their stories weren't supposed to be featured in them. The suburbs were so uncool that there was even a book (a very good one) in 2001 called *Bomb the Suburbs*, by a graffiti artist named William Upski Wimsatt. (Interestingly, by 2010 Wimsatt had thought about it some more and followed it up with *Please Don't Bomb the Suburbs*, around the same time that Arcade Fire chimed in with their wonderful album, *The Suburbs*.)

On Rove in support of Rockin' the Suburbs, *with compulsory angry red backward baseball cap*

Y'all don't know what it's like, being male, middle class, and white
—From "Rockin' the Suburbs," *Rockin' the Suburbs*, 2001

I thought it was notable that what most of the music middle-class suburban kids were listening to, and making, was aggressive, loud, and angry. Modern-rock radio was 24/7 middle-class anger. No sad songs, no happy songs, no love songs, just pissed-off songs. So I wanted to write a song about it, but I wanted my song to sound annoyingly happy. As it happens, I saw a *Spin* magazine with some oddly familiar faces on the cover. Remember those hairy roadies I mentioned heckling us at the last Ben Folds Five gig? It turns out that was a famous rock band called Korn. According to *Spin,* they were "taking on the wusses." That sounded brave, so I read on, putting it all together when I saw Korn's quote, in massive type, beneath their photo:

BEN FOLDS FIVE ARE FUCKING PUSSIES. THEY PLAY FUCKING "CHEERS" MUSIC.

This was a reference to the theme song of the TV show *Cheers.* Awesome. *Good association,* I thought. *Good melody.*

It made me wonder, though. Why did the middle-class white suburbanites of that era consume so much anger rock? Why was Korn's main mission that day taking on musicians with pretty chords and not-so-angry music? Were things *really that* bad? What exactly was in the air? I seemed to know as little about Korn as they did about me. Checking out their music, I had to admit it was pretty damn good. But it was striking how one-tracked it was emotionally, like the rest of the successful bands you heard pumping out of cars in the 'burbs. Something was definitely afoot.

While writing the song "Rockin' the Suburbs," I thought a lot about Stevie Wonder, who grew up black and blind in the turbulence prior to the civil-rights movement. One can't imagine that challenge. Don't you think he had more to be pissed off about than the majority of white middle-class suburbanites? And yet, alongside some rightfully edgy songs like "Living for the City," Stevie wrote songs about the full range of the human experience. All the emotions—sadness, happiness, empathy, despair. Why was the popular music of the suburban youth so "one-holler-fits-all"? Is there a line connecting all of this to the political landscape of 2016, when the now-grown-up consumers of this music decided a world-changing election? "Rockin' the Suburbs" is just a fun observation—more a question mark than an answer, but it was something I was compelled to think about.

And speaking of Stevie Wonder, whatever happened to love songs? It didn't seem anyone of my generation had dared touch the "Love Song" with a ten-foot pole. It wasn't *cool*. There were some cheesy love songs on pop radio, as always, but more-serious songwriters didn't seem to want to broach that genre anymore. From R.E.M. to Nirvana, it just wasn't the "Decade of Love" for rock dudes. I'd never considered writing a damn love song either, until I was approached in 1999 by moviemaker Amy Heckerling, who'd made *Fast Times at Ridgemont High* and *Clueless*. She had this glorious final long one-shot nerd-kissing scene in her new movie, *Loser,* which required a love song, so I took the plunge. I watched the scene over and over, taking in the camera pacing, and considered the lives of these two nerds embraced in a kiss in a final bold scene. I delivered the song to the movie studio kind of assuming I'd get some kind of award for it. But the whole scene was cut from the movie after a focus group didn't like it.

As the song sat for a year, I came to realize it was incomplete. The third verse wasn't right. It was a crayon scribbling of the concept of love, not the real thing. That's the danger of writing a love song. Love is so hard to describe. It's complex, and it's easy to oversimplify and end up with dross. I suppose that's why my peers had avoided it. When I was recording *Suburbs,* the ninety-year-old man next door to me died in his sleep, and his wife passed away days later. A lifelong partnership, like the one my elderly next-door neighbors had, was something we'd all be lucky to experience. It's what I wanted so badly in my life, which, along with my wild impulsiveness, had led to my many stumbles and falls. And so *that* would be the third verse.

The movie rejection had given me time to finish it properly, and now "The Luckiest" could be on my album. It would also be free years later to find its proper home in the Richard Curtis movie *About Time,* placed in such a dignified and poetic way as to give me the unique experience of hearing my music and forgetting I was the one who wrote it.

Completed just in time to be on *Rockin' the Suburbs,* "The Lucki-est" was recorded with the assistant engineer while Ben Grosse was busy mixing the rest of the album. Grosse had yet to hear the song and I was nervous he wouldn't dig it. It was the last track he mixed, finishing as the sun came up. I had passed out on the sofa in the other room and he woke me up with teary eyes—a wonderful compliment. Wow, I thought, if I could make *this* tough motherfucker cry, I just might have written a good love song. He said he hoped he'd done it justice with the mix. If there's a song I've written that will outlive me, it's "The Luckiest." Not a week goes by without someone telling me they were married to this song (I never tire of hearing that). Yes, Ben Grosse, you did it justice!

Everyone had seemed so gratuitously edgy in the nineties. All that rock "edge" seemed silly. Fashion-magazine silly. Not tough. In truth, the nineties was a decade of relatively smooth sailing, cultur-ally and politically. We rock stars were actually a softer breed than those who came before us, despite all the shouting and snarking. So were our audiences. The economy was relatively stable and most of us were growing up better off than our parents. There had been no major wars, at least not in our neck of the woods. Hunger mortality in the entire world was declining; death by infectious diseases was being beaten down like never before. I'm not saying there wasn't anything to complain about and that some didn't have it unbeliev-ably rough, but it's notable that our music got more pissed off as things got cushier.

Alas, the tides would soon change, and the waters would become a lot choppier in 2001. It's worth noting that with the increased tur-bulence, the music actually got *sweeter* in the 2000s—"the aughts," as they are often called. There were more harmonies in pop music, more pianos, more love songs, more smiling. Anger and distortion became a little less welcome, almost passé.

Rockin' the Suburbs was tracked back during President Bill Clinton's last months in office, when life was more innocent and music was angrier. My overdubs were recorded as we learned the term "hanging chads." We were mixing the tracks as the Supreme Court chose George W. Bush as our next president. The mastering took place during his inauguration. *Rockin' the Suburbs* was released on September 11. Class of 2001.

September 2001
Monthly Planner

Sunday	Monday	Tuesday	Wednesday	Thursday	Friday	Saturday
						1
2	*3*	*4*	*5* Full CD release (Australia)	*6*	*7* Chapel Hill - Cats Cradle	*8* Chapel Hill - Cats Cradle
9 Pittsburgh - Metropol	*10*	*11* AFT- WHFS (?) AM - DC101 morning show Washington DC - 9.30 Club Worldwide full CD release	*12* Philadelphia - Theatre of the Living Arts	*13* AM - Y100 Sonic Session - Phila New York City - Irving Plaza (CMJ)	*14* Conan O'Brien Show	*15* Boston - Avalon
16 DCN webcast (?) Providence (w/ Built to Spill) - Lupo's	*17*	*18* Charlestown SC - Music Farm	*19* Atlanta - Roxy Theatre	*20* Nashville - 328 Performance Hall	*21* New Orleans - House of Blues	*22* Austin - La Zona Rosa
23	*24* Dallas - The Red Jacket	*25*	*26* Lawrence KS - Granada Theatre	*27* Cincinnati - Bogart's	*28* Nashville radio show (WZPC)	*29* 96X - Salt Lake City radio show - State FairPark
30 Detroit - Clutch Cargo						

Printed by Calendar Creator for Windows on 8/15/2001

Tour calendar from September 2001

GOING IT ALONE

ON THE MORNING OF THE RELEASE OF *ROCKIN' THE SUBURBS*, I WAS
seated at an upright piano on live radio in Washington, D.C., pounding out a ridiculous comedy song called "Hiro's Song." It's about a
businessman in midlife crisis, dating his daughter's best friend and
trying on low-riding jeans at the mall that reveal his ass crack. The
DJs were politely chuckling at this ridiculous ditty when their attention drifted to the TV screens above my head. There was obviously
something very heavy happening. Planes were crashing into the World
Trade Center. "Hiro's Song" suddenly seemed really inappropriate and
long. I struggled to find an early ending so we wouldn't have to yuck
it up anymore as this tragedy was unfolding.

The DJ tried to get me to speculate on air what kind of plane had just
hit the building. Like the piano player knew? It was a cargo plane, he
thought; what did I think? Well, I thought it was time to go. Washington
and the rest of the world had way bigger things to think about now. Our
driver had to take a detour on the way back to the hotel. He told us that

there were reports that the Pentagon was on fire and the highway was being shut down. Obviously, there would be no show in D.C. that night. Release day of *Rockin' the Suburbs* was officially over. In fact, the record was commercially DOA, like all other releases on that day (with the exceptions of every record Lee Greenwood ever made). Still, a failing album was *not* a big deal in the big picture on that terrible day.

On the night of 9/11, we decided to drive out to find a hotel in the sticks somewhere in New Jersey or Pennsylvania, away from the big city centers, to call home to our families and make some decisions. Alan read me a list of artists who would be canceling their tours for the foreseeable future. "Let's not add me to that list," I told him. If there ever was a need for music, wasn't it now? Band and crew, who were free to go home, agreed with me and elected to stay on. We would finish our tour, starting in Philadelphia the next day—my birthday.

It was tough to focus on music in that atmosphere, but I felt that when people came in off the street and into a concert, they should have a momentary respite from the tragedy and the uncertainty that had enveloped the world so quickly. Indeed, I spoke to a group of fans behind the venue who, just the day before, had been running from falling debris and a plume of smoke. A moment of music meant the world to them, and to me. Soon, as the sun rose on September 13, I would see the poor smoking island of Manhattan with my own eyes, as we passed on the Jersey Turnpike—the reflection of the teary faces of musicians and crew in the front lounge window is permanently etched in my memory.

In October 2001, as soon as Lower Manhattan was open, I performed alone at a piano for the first time in my career, at the Bowery Ballroom. It was scary as hell, but by the middle of the set, it felt right. I came offstage and told my booking agent that this would be my touring method for the foreseeable future—we could call it "Ben Folds and a Piano." It would be a sustainable way to tour, given that

the album was dead and the touring band was expensive. I told her I wanted to ditch the bus and scale down to a van, a soundman, and my trusty tour manager, Doug. We'd share the driving and do it *old school*. She warned me my career might never recover if I made such a move. I was nearly back to square one with unconvinced promoters, who'd just taken a bath on the last Ben Folds Five tour. Now was the time to prove myself again, she insisted. I needed a band. I could take risks later when I was back on my feet. She's one of the best in the business because she's nearly always right. But somehow, in these uncertain times, a sing-along solo piano tour felt like the "Church on Wheels" of rock clubs. Which is to say, it was a hit. Solo piano was what the doctor ordered. A loud band on tour in this tender environment would have felt like an assault, less intimate and less real.

Anyone who was in the United States in the wake of 9/11 might recall that, rising from the ashes of the tragedy, something magical was also happening. People suddenly acknowledged one another in the streets, smiled, opened doors, and helped with groceries. Everywhere. I think this is often overlooked. As I toured the country I saw a sense of community and humanity expressed that I hadn't seen in my lifetime. Back at "square one" of my career, back in the small clubs, I discovered the storytelling inside my old songs and found the organic kernels hiding inside the large production of the recent *Rockin' the Suburbs* material. I was reminded of the necessity of gatherings with singing and stories. Music's healing power was on display for me nightly. I'd never heard people sing together quite like that. Remember when members of Congress spontaneously began singing together on the East Front steps of the Capitol? That actually happened on 9/11. Imagine that. My interest in group singing, college a cappella, and advocacy of music education was born out of all of this.

One night in Champaign, Illinois, I was in the middle of the song "Not the Same" when I heard what sounded like a professional choir filling the venue. I looked up to see the choir, and it was the audience!

They were singing perfect three-part harmony spontaneously. Each night after that, the audiences would sing those parts, unprompted, with varying degrees of success. I began helping that along, showing them the parts and conducting. It never gets old, hearing people sing like that, which is why it's still a part of my show. I'd never imagined having audience participation as a staple of my act. I'd never been a fan of that overzealous singer shtick: "Sing, people! Come on! I can't hear you! *Sing!*" I mean, you've paid for a show and now the performer up onstage wants you to do the work? But now I understood what the audience participation bit was all about. People wanted—and needed—to sing together. It was a brief moment in American history when people didn't need to be reminded of basic kindness and humanity or to be *prompted* to sing in harmony together. Unfortunately, a little "shock and awe" later and that moment had passed. But I was in small rooms in every town across the land, and I will tell you that the intensity and warmth of people singing together is what I'll *never forget* about 9/11.

ROCK THIS BITCH!

AT THE END OF MY SHOWS ON THE BEN FOLDS AND A PIANO TOUR, HALF of the audience would often reconvene behind the venue. They knew I'd be there, loading up the van with my soundman or warming up our rental car. We'd all hang, snap a few pictures, and I'd sign stuff before we drove off, waving goodbye. It was a pretty informal affair, especially the signing of burned CDs of *Rockin' the Suburbs*. I'd never signed blank CDs before, a technological sign of the times, but what the hell. My audience had always been particularly computer savvy, and I was philosophical (or maybe just lazy), about piracy.

There's no telling what the impact of the internet was on sales of that album. This was at the very beginning of the whole downloading thing. But this was not my battle. To be honest, aside from feeling badly for my friends who lost jobs in the music business, it seemed to me that the music business was just paying the piper for years of gluttony. Album and video budgets had been bloated for years, and execs had gaudy expense accounts. CD prices were particularly overblown, and kids knew it. Kids with computers. That's who cut the business down to size.

Anyway, the music business had had a pretty damn good run for a good fifty years. Technological advances had always been our friend before the internet. And the music biz had milked each new format to repackage and sell the same old classic records, over and over. Vinyl LPs, then 8-track tapes, then cassettes, CDs—they even took a swipe at selling it all again on mini-disc. How many formats of *Dark Side of the Moon* and *The Eagles Greatest Hits* did we all need? Indeed, the music business had come to believe that new technology = more prizes.

But the newest format was a technological development that wasn't quite so kind to the music business. Downloading, MP3, the elimination of physical distribution, was the end of the music business as we had known it. In truth, most artists didn't actually profit directly from physical record sales back in "the music business as we had known it" era. I'm not sure that most of them who went to bat for their labels, lecturing fans about piracy, understood that. That doesn't make it okay to steal music, but I wasn't going to stick my neck out for the labels by chastising music fans. Especially when those music fans were spreading excitement about my music and coming to shows. It was a mixed bag.

I don't want to get too technical about the music industry, but just know that there are plenty of ways to make a buck in this business. Publishing, merchandising, touring, licensing, and, of course, selling your body to the night. But profit for *the artist* from actual direct record sales? Not so much. It was never the main way the artist made a living. Records cost so much to make and promote, and whether you agreed with label practices or not, it simply wasn't where the money was, at least not for the artist. The labels were, after all, taking the risk.

I didn't want to spend time fighting when I could be creating, so I accepted what seemed to be an established fact. I'd just make my living on tour. *Me work, me get paid.* Liberated of all concerns related to the bottom line of album sales, I could deliver albums to the label that weren't even in my contract, like EPs, specialty albums, and live albums. No need to fuss over recoupment. I could get on with my dream of littering the planet with my music, starting with a live solo piano record, *Ben Folds Live*.

My new soundman, Marc Chevalier, captured as many shows as he could in early 2002 for the *Ben Folds Live* LP. We brought some fantastic tube pre-amps and compressors on tour. All that fancy fragile vintage equipment is not normal for live recording, but we only needed a few channels for a piano and a voice. Audio nerds might be interested to know that the front-of-house sound at these shows actually came through all of this exotic tube gear. We mic'd the audience as well, to document the singing on "Not the Same." Of course, those mics picked up everything the audience said or did during the whole show.

Ben Folds and a Piano tour, 2002

"Rock this bitch!" someone shouted from the front of the audience as we were recording at the Vic Theatre in Chicago. I told this young man that I didn't know the song "Rock This Bitch," and I proceeded to make one up on the spot. The song was good enough to make it onto the album. This excited heckler had unwittingly launched a new tradition, because from that night on, someone always shouted, "Rock this bitch!" at my concerts, a cue for me to improvise a song. The rules developed spontaneously. Each "Rock This Bitch" (RTB) would be completely new, musically and lyrically, as long as somewhere in the song I sang, "Rock this bitch." I have improvised an RTB at most shows since 2002.

I've Rocked This Bitch solo; I've Rocked This Bitch with various touring bands and even with symphony orchestras. With orchestras I come up with the bones of a song quickly and then dictate some simple orchestration. It usually takes about ten minutes to get it together, but the process itself is of interest to the audience. They like hearing how the different parts of an orchestra function and how they come together. It also humanizes the symphony orchestra for pop audiences, seeing the players work through this unusual exercise.

Thanks to that random dude who immortalized himself on my live album, I've gotten some unique on-the-job lessons in songwriting. Improvising RTBs at my concerts has given me a healthy new perspective on songs and how they are made, and what music is for. Freestyling in groups and making up songs, whether it's on banjos or bongos, is ancient stuff. Temporary music. A celebration of the moment.

We're all here now! Yay! We had a day and it was tough, and it was wonderful, and here's what the day sounds like. An interpretative dance of what now feels like. Our song will evaporate and expire like the day did, and there will be another tomorrow—another song. Let us then jam, motherfuckers!

An RTB, like any freestyling, is an event, not a final product. Music that is highly crafted, considered, professionally performed and packaged is, of course, the norm—it's modern music. We love that. But you can hijack this modern apparatus, the musicians, the technology, even a large audience, to celebrate a spontaneous moment and take a detour from the regularly scheduled program, to make up a song on the spot. Now, that's exciting. It's *off-book,* unplanned, unrehearsed, with no guarantees or safety net. It's *breaking the law!*

Rap musicians understand the power of spontaneous songwriting. Freestyling is still essential to the art form of rap, while classical music has left freestyling behind for the most part. But it used to be the way a classical musician earned his stripes. Nineteenth-century composers regularly dueled with other pianists at what were called "salons." They created pieces from thin air on the spot, as they tried to outdo one another creatively and technically. The jazzers have taken improvisation to a high art, but I wouldn't quite call it freestyling. Jazz musicians generally improvise over already existing song structures, which they call "the head." They might play one pass of "Someday My Prince Will Come" and then continue the chord structure as they take turns improvising over it. But the kind of freestyling that connects Biggie to Beethoven requires creating the whole ball of wax in the moment. When it's over, *poof,* it's gone. Next.

Freestyling an RTB with orchestras is a nightly lesson in orchestration for me. I can hear the result immediately as I dictate my spontaneous ideas to musicians. Few budding orchestrators like myself get to hear their ideas on the spot, to determine if, for instance, the flute might be heard in unison with all the violins, or if the French horns would be better in tighter harmonies or broader intervals. A computer simulation only gets you so close. You have to actually hear it with real players. Oddly, I find that my riskier, more audacious on-the-spot ideas often play better in an orchestra than some of the more considered ones that were auditioned with the computer beforehand. A good reminder when composing: Imagine big. Imagine beyond those tools.

I've mined the recordings of hundreds of RTBs and completed some of them, like "Effington," "Cologne," and "Hiroshima," for albums. All of these songs were surprisingly complete the moment they were improvised, as a quick YouTube search would corroborate. They had verses, choruses, and sometimes complete forms, all done on the spot. I just needed to give them a little help to get them polished enough for a record. But, like most freestyling, most RTBs were meant for the people in the room. This was the spirit in which they were improvised. As badly as I might want to make songs out of all of them, we can't be too greedy. There's always another idea. You *can* turn the faucet on anytime you like.

I recently taught a class in songwriting at a music retreat, and I had each songwriter do an RTB in front of the class. I'd throw the songwriters a title and say, "Go!" They did great! It is not a matter of genius to do this, as I prove each night at my own concerts. Something just kicks in. It's intuitive, natural. You just need to be in front of an audience, with no way out, with the intention of saying something, anything. It can begin by the repeating of the phrase "I'm scared of improvising," over two changing chords. You'll get tired of singing that over and over, and you'll naturally discover and explain more of what you mean, and in doing so will develop your song. Who knows where it will go? We find out together, which is the way any song should feel.

And nobody expects an improvised song to be a masterpiece, so keep that in mind and maybe you'll relax a little. You and the audience will live in that moment together for the ups and downs. And since you can't edit those lulls out, you will have to own those lulls and find your way up. This is a gift. It teaches us that dynamics don't always have to be about literal sonic loud and soft. Dynamics can be about the tone of the content musically *and* lyrically. Anyway, a song can't actually be "all killer no filler." That's not the way life works. We can't just edit out the boring bits of our lives—the ones that led to the exciting ones. Those were necessary. When freestyling, you have to accept that you have found yourself down in the valley, own it, and do what's necessary to get to the peak. As an audience, we appreciate being in on the journey.

Then there's form, something we take for granted in songwriting.

Where did that come from? How can it be that while freestyling intuitively I keep stumbling into *intro-verse-chorus-verse-chorus-bridge* and so on, which is textbook form? It could be that I'm trained that way, but I can feel something else going on. Form has evolved because it's intuitive to organize your thoughts in real time when you're communicating. This is more obvious when you're forced to create onstage. It all suddenly makes sense. For instance, if you're the one onstage, and I shout at you, "Rock this bitch!" you'll most likely instinctively go for a simple repeated riff on your instrument. It's what we normally do to get it going. To the listener, this riff sets the backdrop and tone. We assume the artist knows what's next. But for the freestyler, that riff is just buying time to figure out what to do. The jazzers call this a "vamp." The classical musicians call it "ostinato." Form and proper song development, as you discover when you improvise a song before an audience, is not only for the benefit of the listener; it happens to be the natural way an idea rolls off the tongue, as it comes from the heart, filtered through the brain, when you're just trying to discover and communicate a point musically.

I've been Rocking This Bitch for more than fifteen years now, and I imagine I'll keep that up until I shit the bed one day—if for no other reason than I keep learning. I know it's what all the cool old men say, but, really, we're all students for life. It's important to try new things. What's newer than performing a song that didn't exist until that moment?

FOLLOW THE BROWN

DON'T THINK FOR A MOMENT THAT I BELIEVE A SONG THAT'S BLURTED out onstage is the best we can do. I'm actually an impossible stickler, and a painfully slow songwriter. I sometimes sit on an unfinished song for years. Like "The Luckiest," or the title track from my most recent studio album, *So There*. I had originally planned for "So There" to be a centerpiece on the 2005 record *Songs for Silverman*. At the time I was going to call that album *Death of the Cool,* in response to Miles Davis's *Birth of the Cool.* The vamp of the song "So There" was going to open *Death of the Cool* with an overt tip of the hat to Miles's "Someday My Prince Will Come." But *Songs for Silverman* ended up going in a different direction, and I didn't get "So There" finished anyway. Albums and years went by and I kept not finishing that damn song—until I finally did. That's a whole decade on a song—about as far from freestyling as it gets.

The most common question I'm asked about songwriting is whether the words or lyrics come first. And that's a reasonable question. Hell, I ask my songwriter friends the same thing. We all want to know what the spark was. What was the first syllable the writer uttered before the musical sentence was complete? What stuck to the page first? For me, it's almost always music. I believe my subconscious clues me in to my feelings by expressing them abstractly through music—a few notes, a musical sentence, that I don't yet understand. I will follow the music to the edge of my lyrical comfort zone, because I firmly believe the music is about something and that's for me to decipher. Often, the music fools me into writing something I'd rather not have revealed lyrically.

The spark of a song can come at the oddest time. Maybe at a stoplight, a meeting, or in bed at 4 A.M. For me, there's usually a subtle glow in the air just before the notes start to come. A sense that something is around the corner. Like the farm animals in a disaster movie right before an earthquake, who seem to know what's coming before the humans do. It feels the way light often looks at "magic hour," before sunset, when it suddenly seems that anywhere you point the camera will make a good picture. That's the kind of feeling that tells me to watch for some music. It's coming soon.

If freestyling onstage teaches us that you can always turn on the faucet and that some kind of music will always flow, then songwriting in solitude confirms that the water can sometimes flow muddy brown. Non-potable melody. You have to let it run for a while, until it begins to run clear. Yes, it hurts to hear the brown ideas coming from the center of your soul, but you don't have to show them to anybody. Don't let brown get you down. Here's a common bit of advice I've heard from every songwriter I've ever met: *Just keep moving.*

I personally do not believe there's such a thing as writer's block. It's just that we don't like everything that comes out. When our self-judgment takes over, it shames us into submission and we shut off the faucet. We *say* we have no ideas. No. We have ideas, but we aren't willing to fess up to how bad they might be. But, really, who gives a damn? Own them. They suck, and they came from you. Fine. That's not a crime, that's normal. Take it easy on yourself. Remember that you can always write something, it's just that sometimes it's shitty! Let it be so! And then follow that brown until it runs clear.

A great musician and producer named Pat Leonard told me that it's important to know when to send your inner editor away. His advice is another version of my faucet metaphor. Maybe it works better for you. When you're creating, make a deal with your inner editor— that judgmental but necessary part of your psyche that keeps telling you what sucks. Tell this trigger-happy editor in your mind that you need them to step out of the room while you create. You need to be free to follow all ideas, bad and good. You need to create with impunity—alone. However! The other half of the deal is that the editor gets to come back the next day—*with a chain saw*. Your editor will get to go to town on what you've written. The editor may even throw the whole song in the trash. But not now. Now you must create.

I consider myself a *part-time* artist. I'm not always all that damn creative, so when I'm not in artist mode I store up observations like a squirrel for the winter. I try and keep my antennae up so that I have a lot of extra pieces with which to complete a song when I'm an artist again. There's a time to collect data, a time to run on the fuel of inspiration, and then there's the heavy lifting at the end—the craft.

The craft might not seem all that damn sexy, but you need compositional tricks, and some understanding of music theory, formal or informal, to knock a song together. I cannot accept the notion that knowing less about music can be a good thing, though I recognize everyone has their own capacity for the technical stuff. Some of us stick with three chords, while others go full Schoenberg on it. You should learn as much music as *you* can stand. You'll know when cramming in one more scale will break your brain. And until your brain is broken, keep cramming, keep learning, keep storing up for winter.

Some songwriters like to say it's all about feel and that too much musical vocabulary or time spent in craft will kill the emotion. To them, it's about smoking a joint and telling the truth in three chords. At times I agree. Others feel it's a process of consideration and requires technique and a grand palette from which to paint, because big feelings require a big vocabulary. I've found that to be true as well. I've often sat on these funny songwriting panels where I wondered if the two camps might come to blows over how a song is best written. What we can all agree on is that songwriting is about communicating. In real life, we might find the best way to communicate something difficult to a friend is doing it while drunk at a bar, in a single blurt. *I fuckin' love you, brah!* Other times it requires deleting and revising an important email for days on end, while quoting Voltaire or *The Bridges of Madison County* to get the point across. It's whatever it takes to just *say it*. How you feel, what you saw, what life is about. My experience is that if I continue to stubbornly swing into the dark, if I just follow the brown until it runs clear, any feeling will eventually find its corresponding notes and words, and be set free.

VINCIBILITY

AT THE END OF MY LAST SOLO PIANO SHOW OF 2002, NOT A DROP LEFT IN the tank, I found myself struggling to walk in a straight line just to make it offstage. Post-show applause ringing in my ears, my peripheral vision began to darken and the horizon spun. I did not—*did not*—want to wobble and fall down in front of people. Fuck that. *Steady, Folds!* I ordered my knees to get me a few more steps. And they did—just.

I collapsed into the arms of a nice security man backstage. I remember him telling me I was "one tough motherfucker"—a kind thing to say to someone who doesn't even have the strength to walk. He'd been aware of my 104 fever when he'd told me "good luck" as I'd walked out onstage at the beginning of the show. He'd seen me with ice-water towels on my forehead, inching the fever down one degree from 105 before stubbornly bounding out for a two-and-a-half-hour set. After all, I was invincible.

. . .

The previous night in Detroit my fever had been just as high, but damned if I was going to cancel a sold-out State Theatre show. I muscled through and even signed autographs in the freezing cold for forty-five minutes before driving to Chicago. Now here I was at Chicago's Vic Theatre, being carried down the stairs like a limp rag by a 250-pound stranger with a shaved head. Tour over and done.

Self-portrait, just before pneumonia, late 2002

I was devastated and humiliated that I was being sent home. *Goddamn it, I sold out next week's New York's Beacon Theatre show with just a piano, y'all!* It was to have been my big "I told you so" gig. Only a year prior I had accepted the professional prognosis that a solo piano tour would be the nail in the career coffin. But I *did it anyway*—no band, no production, very little press. The Beacon! Six times the size of the venues I'd played when I'd started the tour. Sorry to gloat, but, Christ, it was an uphill battle of a year, and I do love to prove naysayers wrong, even if I had been heard to say a few nays myself in moments of uncertainty.

How do some musical artists become "career artists," artists that survive the changing trends and generations, that stick around for decades? Who knows? Aside from talent, it's probably mostly luck, and a dash of unreasonable stubbornness. I probably should have been dropped from my label in 2002, because commercial radio pretty much dried up for me that year, and everyone around me was getting dropped. But as *Rockin' the Suburbs* seemed over and done, some noncommercial under-the-radar radio stations, like WFUV at Fordham University in New York City, kept my career going. Sometimes when you persist past the expiry date, if you're lucky, you can catch an unlikely break.

During my 2002 piano tour, whenever I had a week off, I flew back home to Australia to be with my kids. It was usually a twenty-hour plane trip each way. When that proved impossible to maintain, I decided to move the whole family to Nashville, where I also took on a major studio business I had stumbled upon while mixing the *Ben Folds Live* album. I assumed the lease at the historic RCA Studio—it had been sitting empty for quite a while. Large studio spaces were less in demand as home recording and plug-ins, which simulated big rooms, became common. Moving a family from one country to another and taking over a new business put a few more boulders in my backpack. But it was all exciting stuff.

I might have made it through this incredibly jam-packed year if only I hadn't put myself on a rigid cleanse diet early in the fall of 2002, just as we were moving to the new place in Nashville. I thought maybe I'd purify myself, like all the cool kids were doing, and I went all in —as I do. The peak of the cleanse was a one-week fast of water, carrot juice, and raw almonds. That's it. I was down to 120 pounds. Upon returning to tour, with its shared van drives of hundreds of miles a night, I stubbornly stuck to only raw vegan food. And if I couldn't find that while traveling, I just had water or a piece of fruit and got on with it. Now, recovering in Nashville after my dramatic made-for-television movie collapse in Chicago, I lay in bed with a dangerously high fever and reflected on the idiocy of dietary extremism.

For my first few days in bed, I felt like an otherwise healthy person dealing with an annoying infection. That's the way sickness had always felt to me before—like something in the way. But this became something else, something I'd never felt before. I was struck with total lack of confidence that I would ever recover on my own. And at that point I submitted to a visit to the doctor, who confirmed that I had advanced pneumonia.

It turns out there are some things that just can't be outrun or buried beneath work. Cheap lessons weren't sinking in, so the cost was rising. I bent over for shots of antibiotics fit for a horse and followed doctor's orders. And I actually stopped everything I was doing. I surrendered. Something I hadn't done before. But now I had to. I was now officially Vincible.

Oddly, I file this month in bed under "pleasant times." It was probably the first quiet time I'd had since that month spent on Australian cliffs with a notebook in 1998. The doctor warned of seizures that might occur because of the sustained high fever, but luckily that didn't happen. However, fevered and weak, I *did* find myself a bit emotionally vulnerable. I'm ashamed to say I shed tears at a fucking life-insurance commercial, there alone in my room. I also cried at two points during a Ronald Reagan biography. Especially when the horse trainer had to tell the Gipper his horse-riding days were over. I should have just had the seizure. It would have been more dignified.

I had time to read while I lay helplessly in bed waiting for good antibiotics to prevail over evil biotics. I had time to stare at the ceiling and shudder as I reflected on a couple of times we damn near died in that touring van, driving through snow in the mountains too many late nights. I had time to write letters and call family and friends. I even had a moment to clear up some confusion I'd caused over a practical joke I staged earlier in the tour.

I'd pulled my best modern Andy Kaufman and gotten audiences to post some tall tales to the internet, including that I'd once floated above my piano. We had many people online convinced that I had actually levitated. At another gig, I instructed the audience to post that Bill Clinton had sat in on saxophone. He hadn't, of course, but the myth got traction. I also suggested that the audience add on forums that Clinton had snuck away with my wife and that this was easily seen happening just offstage as I played on. Finally, I asked a crowd to start a rumor online that I had been arrested. Each audience did such a creative job and kept it secret, like the Manhattan Project of bad practical jokes.

The trouble was, I wasn't Andy Kaufman. He always let it all hang in the air and let people wonder, and that was part of his genius. I couldn't quite live with that discomfort. Rock promoters from around the world had called my management, concerned that my arrest would mean a cancellation. So I felt the need to explain it afterward and clear the air. While recovering, I joined some fan conversations and explained what I'd done. We had a good laugh, which probably sent me into a severe, painful coughing fit.

But all of this stuff, the going-too-far jokes, the self-destructive diet, and the physical crashes were all expressions of things I needed to address personally. Some of us aren't as good at looking at ourselves and taking the time to process, much less sleep. It took my believing I would die from pneumonia to give me appreciation for my health. The warning bells had been sounding for a few years. Back in the last days of Ben Folds Five, I'd shuffled some excessive bleeding and a few other symptoms under the rug until I finally had to take a couple of days from recording *Rockin' the Suburbs* for a simple operation. I'd also had panic attacks, which I'd been blowing off for some time. While playing that fateful radio show on 9/11, I'd had a bottle of antidepressants rattling in my pocket. They had been prescribed the day before in the emergency room, after I'd had a hyperventilation fit. And I'd decided not to take them. I figured I'd just move along and not think about it. All of these variations of nervous-system crashes are meant as speed bumps, but I ignored them until I was persuaded of my vincibility. Vincibility 101: a class that some of us have to repeat a few times. Really, it's best to pass it the first time around. Take the lessons while they're cheap.

BENNY! WHAT *IS* COOL??

WILLIAM SHATNER PUT A SEEMINGLY SIMPLE QUESTION TO ME ONE night in 2004 over dinner at my studio, during our sessions for his album *Has Been*. This record, which I produced and co-wrote, is one of my proudest moments. It wasn't a massive seller, but it's certainly achieved cult-record status. Nearly fifteen years later, I still find it moving and funny. And it was a lesson in creative courage. Shatner never does a take the same way twice. He commits and puts equal energy into ideas both in and out of his comfort zone. Many a rocker could learn from his fearless attitude.

William Shatner's energy seems boundless. I was once staying at his guest house when he knocked at the door, balancing a two-hundred-pound oak table on his back. I glanced up the steep hill from which he'd hauled the damn thing and shook my head. He plopped it on the floor. "There, Benny, you'll need a table." This was a man of seventy-two years.

· · ·

Bill and me

Shatner and I had first met when he guested on my experimental solo album *Fear of Pop* back in 1997. A few of his friends had pulled me aside to warn me that Bill didn't take direction easily. "He eats directors for breakfast!" said one. If you'd ever seen Bill at breakfast, this took on a whole new dimension. But we hit it off and I escaped being eaten. He became "Bill" to me, I became "Benny" to him. I should add there's only one motherfucker for whom I'll be "Benny," so don't even think about it.

Despite his friends' warnings, I found that Bill took musical direction well. I never felt I needed to sugarcoat anything while working with him. I was blunt as I needed to be, and he only ever snapped at me twice. Once was near the end of the entire *Has Been* session, when he suddenly barked, "BENNY! You've been pecking at me like a chicken!" I had been pushing him hard for weeks to improve the lyrics of the second verse to his song "It Hasn't Happened Yet." He'd tried draft after draft and I just wouldn't give him the thumbs-up. I'd just told him his first verse was about his life and the second verse sounded like the high school play about his life, and he had a very minor but understandable conniption.

. . .

The other bark was the question I mentioned. The one over dinner in the studio.

While laying waste to a black-bean burrito (he always had coupons for Baja Fresh, for some reason), Bill, out of nowhere, charged me with overuse of the word "cool." His distaste for this word had been building for a while.

"BENNY! WHAT *IS* COOL??" he shouted across the table.

I had used "cool" a good one hundred times during the day's recording session, he estimated. For instance, he said, if anyone had asked the question "Could we try bongos on this?" or suggested "Maybe it's time for a break," I would always respond with "That's cool." While listening to a handful of vocal takes, I might proclaim one to be "cooler" than the others. Bill felt that I didn't even use the word "yes" much anymore and fell back on "cool" for that too. He thought I should expand my vocabulary to be more precise. There's a big difference between "acceptable" and "transcendent." How could they both just be lumped in together as "cool"? Simply put, this word was used in more ways than Bill thought necessary.

In an attempt to answer what seemed a rhetorical question about a word that certainly Bill had used himself since the sixties, the best I could do was to give him some examples of things that I thought were cool.

"You know, Bill. Cool. Like when you don't care what anyone else thinks. Or . . . cool . . . like, like, when something's *just right*. Or . . ." But Bill actually wanted a definition.

"No, Benny. Listen to me. What is . . . cool?" he repeated, now sounding uncannily like William Shatner.

"Okay, I'll tell you something cool," I said. "*Cool* is that story you told just moments ago about you, Larry Hagman, and, as you called him, 'some guy who drummed in that rock band . . . Oh, what was his name? Oh, right. Keith. The band was called The Who, I *think*?' *The three of you on a motorcycle trip across the States in the late sixties?*

Keith Fucking Moon, Bill . . . and it makes it double cool that you couldn't remember his name!"

But that.

Was not.

What he was looking for.

Bill wanted a very specific definition for this word I'd used a hundred times and he was in the middle of playing a lawyer on the popular TV show *Boston Legal,* and so his cross-examination technique was at its peak, and I found myself crumbling on the witness stand. He was starting to scare me. Here's a play, or a score, of the conversation. So that you can perform it at home with the help of a friend. You will certainly know someone who thinks they can do Shatner:

DEATH OF THE COOL—A One-Act Play

WILLIAM SHATNER [*con appassionato*]: "NO, NO, BENNY! You haven't answered my question!"
[*The dropping of a single spoon cuts through the stunned silence. Band and engineers cease any food-chewing. Some pause with lips to cup mid-drink, and the room falls still.*]
BEN FOLDS: "Well . . ." [gulps]
WILLIAM SHATNER: ". . . What IS cool?? [*molto accelerando*] How can I be cool or make coooool music if I don't . . . even know . . . WHAT [*pausa . . . wait for it . . . subito furioso ff*] . . . IT IS!!!"

[*Shatner stabs his fork into table with a* doinnng! *à la a 1970s' cartoon spear-stick-in-ground foley. His eyes widen, and he sits back, mouthing a silent "aaaah," and gazes through the tops of our heads. He's frozen in a masterful thespian quake, hands positioned just above his forehead, as if holding an imaginary volleyball for all to see. Then. He collapses back into his usual shape. The trance has passed. He blinks a few times, subtly shakes his head, and then makes eye contact with everyone*]

*around the room to confirm that nobody beyond these walls will
ever understand. But us.]*

The End.

Obviously, it didn't quite happen this way. I'm sorry I got carried
away. It's too easy to make things great by just adding Shatner. But as
for the question "What is cool?" and his insistence that I answer it?
For me, it was helpful, if not profound.

What Professor Shatner was doing, as he spat black beans
across the studio table, was pushing back against something that
seemed creatively oppressive to him. I think he's dead-on. It *is*
oppressive—judging music *as* you create it, on how *cool* it is? On
how every little idea might conform to what we consider some current cultural and probably unachievable ideal? He was right. Let's
make music and be creative. And let's be specific about our language as we describe what we're doing. We can worry about that
cool shit later, if at all.

By going full Buddha on us, William Shatner was really asking
these broader questions:

- Shouldn't we avoid language that invites self-awareness into the
  process?
- Shouldn't we try and be more precise when talking about music?
- Isn't making good music in and of itself *cool* enough?

Looking back on my songwriting, I can see that I had a fraught
relationship with this idea of being cool. It's probably because I never
felt cool myself. But also because I've always suspected nobody else
does either. We all want to be cool. We can't all be cool. And we don't
even really know what it means in the first place.

*I was never cool in school
I'm sure you don't remember me*

These are the opening lines from my song "Underground" (*Ben Folds Five*, 1995). I felt terminally uncool and so I was honest about it.

On *Whatever and Ever Amen*, I was still grappling with this cool business:

I know it's not your thing to care
I know it's cool to be so bored
It sucks me in when you're aloof
It sucks me in
It sucks it works
I guess it's cool to be alone

My character in "Battle of Who Could Care Less" felt oppressed by the culture of apathy. It was, after all, cool to be bored in the nineties. Apathy, like the beautiful feathers of an exotic male bird, is what attracted a mate in that era. Back then, we rockers worshipped the slacker above everyone else, except maybe for the suicidal. (Talking about killing yourself would definitely get you laid in the nineties.) So I imagined a battle between two great forces of don't-give-a-shit-ness: the characters General Apathy and Major Boredom. And though I poked fun at it, I secretly thought all this apathy business was, well . . . cool. The last line of "Battle of Who Could Care Less" is, after all:

You're my hero I confess.

But I wasn't done with the theme. A few years into my solo year, and right before recording William Shatner's record, I had written a song called "There's Always Someone Cooler Than You." It's on my solo album *Supersunnyspeedgraphic, the LP*, released in 2006:

Make me feel tiny if it makes you feel tall
But there's always someone cooler than you
Yeah, you're the shit but you won't be it for long
Oh, there's always someone cooler than you

As it happens, after the night Bill asked, "Benny! What is cool?" my songs didn't revisit the subject. Having just learned a great lesson in vincibility, did I really want to be spending my limited time and energy worrying about stuff like being cool? I was sitting across the table from an incredibly healthy man in his seventies who didn't seem to think so. Maybe he'd learned a thing or two. That, for me, was the *Death of the Cool.*

It's hard for a man to stay cool
—From "Silver Street," first released on *Ben Folds Live,* 2002, but written in 1991

TIME TO GROW UP . . . WAIT.
WHAT? AGAIN?

I'VE NEVER FOUND GROWING UP TO BE STRAIGHT AND LINEAR. IN MY case, anyway, it's been quite a zigzag, fixing one hole and then springing another leak somewhere else. Overcorrecting from the ditch on one side of the road, only to find myself crashed in the opposite. I had dialed back my touring *some* in 2002 after my pneumonia, but rather than actually slowing down, I had filled my schedule with more work.

I built a studio from the ground up, and by the end of that year, 2003, I had written and recorded four separate studio EPs—three of my own (all of which debuted at number one on iTunes, before iTunes was a big deal), and one with Ben Lee and Ben Kweller, called *The Bens*. As the lesson of my vincibility faded, I got cocky again in 2004 and slipped back into my habit of heavy touring, while maintaining the pace of studio work. There was, of course, *Has Been* with Shatner, which had been a massive undertaking, writing the music, producing the recording, and flying in new guests every day. Before taking a breath, I undertook a complete reimagining of my catalog for the release of *Ben Folds and WASO Live in Perth* (the West Australian Orchestra). And I still managed to get another full-length studio album, *Songs for Silverman,* released by 2005. Unwilling to miss out on the twins' childhood, I found myself manically running back and forth from the studio to home or school. Or I'd take them with me to the studio, or on tour, the way my parents would drag me to the construction sites. Their presence, despite the challenge of fitting parenthood into a rock career, is probably what kept me sane.

> *You nodded off in my arms watching T.V.*
> *I won't move you an inch even though my arm's asleep*
> —From "Gracie," *Songs for Silverman,* 2005

To add to the mix—just because—I spent an average morning from 5 A.M. to noon in a darkroom, making countless prints, before my late nights in the studio. This is all doable if you just cut sleep in half. The pace continued through 2007, as I unsurprisingly found myself headed for another divorce and hopping on the tour bus that summer to support John Mayer.

I was supposed to be the adult on the John Mayer tour. In terms of years, at least, I was the elder statesman. But as I stretched myself thin with work, my life outside of work paid the price and my typical symptoms once again surfaced. The childish *what-the-fuck-is-he-doing-now* onstage antics, along with the physical and nervous-system breakdowns. A quick Google search, like I've just done at the time of this writing, turns up articles about the Continuum Tour 2007 that pretty well paint the picture: "Folds was profane"; "Folds told tall tales"; he "outraged parents"; he "dropped his pants and flipped off the audience." Yup, that's how I remember it too.

I'd first met John in the late nineties, when he was just some kid at Berklee College of Music who was bootlegging Ben Folds Five concerts and selling them online. My manager, Alan, had noticed he was selling these recordings of our shows online and wanted to bust his ass for profiting off our music. Alan often warned of the peril ahead in the new frontier of digital music distribution, and he was ready to make an example of someone. But I told Alan to call off the dogs and leave the kid alone. I didn't see anything wrong with someone being excited about our music and sharing it with others.

I didn't think about this John Mayer for a couple years, until he popped up backstage at a solo show in Athens, Georgia, in 2000. Soon after, as Weird Al Yankovic and I filmed the video for the song "Rockin' the Suburbs," there was young John Mayer again. Just hanging around, I guess, to see how it was done. Seven years, millions of records, a handful of Grammys, and countless tabloid covers later, he had pretty well figured out how it was done. It turns out this kid was an absolutely brilliant guitarist and songwriter. And so now we were touring together, a newly world-famous John Mayer taking out the old dude he looked up to when he was younger.

John's tour was much more of a mainstream affair than I was accustomed to, and I was definitely causing problems. But the biggest problem was one particular song, which was becoming a very successful single for me. I don't mean "Landed," from the album *Songs for Silverman*, the single that had been released and highly promoted by Sony. I mean its B side, "Bitches Ain't Shit," which had spread by word of mouth and was now doubling my audiences. Its title is the cleanest part of the song. You may know the Dr. Dre original from "The Chronic." I just added pretty chords and one of my best melodies to it and it became a thing.

Since I was in college I had always wanted to make a melody to "Can't Do Nuttin' for Ya Man" by Public Enemy. I loved that song and wanted to hear it on the piano. But when I actually sat down to work on it, I found it too symmetrical for a good melody. It had too much of a *Cat in the Hat* vibe to sound serious with sad chords. Needing a B side at that moment, I searched my record collection in the studio for another spoken or rapped song that might be less iambic-pentameter driven—so I could experiment with music that might highlight a different side of a lyric. And there, glowing out of my stack of records, was Dr. Dre's classic.

I'd always thought the lyrics of "Bitches Ain't Shit" painted a sad picture. Or, rather, the part that I chose to excerpt skewed sad. I actually didn't use the entirety of the lyric. I decided to concentrate on the parts where the main character is released from prison and is excited to see his girlfriend, only to discover her having sex with his cousin on the floor. It's like a sad Johnny Cash song with a lot more vulgarity. Slowing these words down from their gangsta-rap presentation and adding melody creates an absurd effect, both sad and funny. Sung this way, the misogyny in the original lyrics, no matter how wrong, *could* be explained by how badly the narrator was hurt. I consider the melody for "Bitches Ain't Shit" to be as good as any melody I've written. It's no throwaway. It was a joke only to the extent that the comedy I loved from the seventies was a joke. It was based on something real.

"Bitches Ain't Shit" in ballad form was expanding my audiences much like "Brick" had done for Ben Folds Five in the decade before. I can't say I was completely thrilled with this new demographic, but that's the way it is with hits. The song brought in more drunken college boys with ironic (I guess?) backward baseball caps. And YouTube was full of *children* lip-synching along to this vulgar song—something I wasn't expecting. I can't say I was comfortable with all of this. In fact, the song never got easier for me to sing. It always felt so very wrong, but, then, that was also part of what made it interesting. At the time of the John Mayer tour, this crude and melancholy tune was undoubtedly my hit. And when you're on tour with a major recording artist, you *must* play the hit. Needless to say, "Bitches Ain't Shit" wasn't very well received at John Mayer's general-audiences-rated concerts.

The song, which I sang completely earnestly, got me booed regularly. And in response to that, my inner punk took over and I began flipping off the audience with one hand while playing with the other. Thirty-something parents with respectable jobs had brought their children to this concert for an evening of polite rock, not to hear a foul-mouthed pianist as he gave them the finger. As they hissed and hollered in disgust, covering their children's ears, I would finish the song, pretending to be flustered by the negative response. "People, I'm sorry. I'm here to have a good time and I don't understand why all the booing." (Straight out of Kaufman more than Compton.) "That's just rude of you. I'm so nervous now—all this bad energy and angry vibes. I'm really sorry. I'm sorry if I upset you. But can you see my children just off the stage there? Do you think they want to witness their father being booed like this?" (Never mind that they just witnessed their father singing about dick-sucking.)

There would be a palpable forgiveness in the air. They weren't a cruel audience.

"I'm a little lost now. . . ." I would pause and then continue, "Let me look at this set list. I don't even know where I am now, or what I just played. Hmmm . . . Okay, I don't think I played *this* one—I have to say, your booing has really thrown me off. Okay. Ladies and gentlemen, the next song is called 'Bitches Ain't Shit'!"

The audience groaned.

Then I'd play it again. *All the way through.* Sometimes even slower, savoring every word. I often told them to sing along or I'd play it yet again, which I did on a couple of occasions. Thrice. Sometimes I'd break their will and the booing would stop, and a few would even indulge in a sing-along. They must have thought if that was what it would take to shut me up, then fine.

"Would you please just not play *that* song?" Michael McDonald (not the singer, but John's manager) asked me after having been pummeled with audience complaints.

We had a very earnest long conversation about it on the tour bus. I told Michael that he was asking me not to play something my audience expected me to play. Further, I pointed out that Michael and I had toured together before, and he was surely aware of the kind of language I used at my shows before this tour was booked.

"No, Michael," I said, "this is censorship." And I stuck with that line.

I told him that I wouldn't hold a grudge if he fired me. But he knew John wanted me on the tour, and so I was kept on. It probably was unfair of me to be so stubborn, but I was a child that year, at least onstage.

Offstage I was buried in grown-up problems, many springing from what was shaping up as an awful divorce—if, in fact, there's such a thing as a good divorce. The legal and financial issues of divorce can certainly take their toll, especially when you're trying to keep the children safe and stable through the mess you've created. I was filled with dread the entire waking day, except when I was onstage. My ears rang from high blood pressure most mornings. I often wished I'd just go to sleep and never wake up. But sleep itself was rare, as I endured bouts of a condition called "Restless Legs Syndrome," involving a sensation in your legs and lower back that gives you the overwhelming urge to jump out of bed and sprint. It's awful, and I was in agony. RLS is something I've often had during periods of high stress.

Maybe I should have tended to myself rather than going out on tour, but here I was, on the move from city to city, with voicemail and inboxes full of drama—a disaster of my own making, indeed. We all encounter rough patches, and we each find a way to power through. Luckily, I could still have a laugh, something that's gotten me through my toughest chapters. But these were times that made me wonder how much longer I could even hang on to that.

"How about you work with me on this, Ben," Michael asked, "and just don't play that nasty song *twice*? Can you do that much? Just don't play it twice? Please?"

I agreed. I would not play it twice. And that night as I passed him going on for my set, he kindly reminded me, "Not twice, right?"

I assured him, "I won't play it twice, Mike." And I turned around to him, nearly seated at my piano, and mouthed, "Thrice!" holding up three fingers. He had forgotten to say anything about playing it three times.

These days I've stopped playing "Bitches Ain't Shit" and I ignore requests for it. Music should work to ease social tensions, not throw gasoline on the fire, even inadvertently. I don't want non-white people in my audience subjected to large numbers of white people gleefully singing a racial slur that had never been the point.

We had our Dre moment. Moving on.

My most childish episode during that tour was in Indianapolis, one of the biggest shows on the tour, and it had nothing to do with Dr. Dre. Before an audience of ten thousand devoted John Mayer fans, I spent my whole forty-five-minute set meticulously developing a huge absurd whopper of a story. In banter between songs, I made myself out to be the son of some mystery famous songwriter whose career had tragically ended on the very stage on which I performed that evening. For much of the set, I didn't let on whose son I was. I spoke as if they were, of course, supposed to know who my dad was.

Early on in the set I said things like, "This next song was the first record that ever sold as many copies as my father's biggest hit," or "I never wanted to be compared to my old man. I wanted to be my own songwriter, but this one is a nod to my father's style." Nobody in the audience seemed to know who I was anyway, so I figured I was free to spin tall tales with impunity. I set it all up so that near the last song I could tell a story that went something like this:

"Ladies and gentlemen: This is, as many of you know, a very emotional show for me. I was eight years old the last time I was here. Sitting right over there, just offstage, watching my dad. It was one of those nights, and I knew how he could be when his drinking started. I knew something was going to happen that night. Everyone did. I know some of you are old enough to know what happened, right?"

There was a muted and confused response, but I had their attention. I continued.

"It changed my life. It changed his life and the life of the woman who lost her sight in the incident. It's painful, but I'll recount what

followed for those who don't know: My father, of course, was the lead singer of 38 Special"—crowd goes *wild*—"and that night, the last night he took the stage, ended his career in shame. Someone in the audience, front row, as many of you will remember, had thrown a whisky bottle at my father, who was slur-singing out of tune. Dad picked the bottle up, threw it back as hard as he could, missed the guy who had thrown it at him, but blinded his girlfriend. . . .'"

The audience gasped, of course.

"But he's spent his life being sorry. He's done wonderful things for those people, and they've forgiven him. She has her eyesight back because my dad spent every last penny on that experimental surgery. And she's here tonight, friends, with my mom. In fact, they're just offstage together! Hi, Mom! Hi, Lisa!" Applause for Mom. "And my dad: He's! Here! *Tonight!*"—thunderous applause—"And I talked him into coming out here. Onstage, for everyone to see! It's about healing! Dad, wanna come on out?"

On cue, my stepmother then rolled my father out in a *wheelchair*. Why did it need to be a wheelchair? I don't know. It just seemed comically sadder, as if something about the tragedy had rendered Papa unable to walk. I'd seen the wheelchair sitting unused backstage when I was cooking up this whole scene prior to the show.

Papa hadn't been sure if he wanted to be involved in this scheme, but my then-seven-year-old daughter had been very excited about seeing her grandfather onstage. She talked him into it—granddaughters have their granddads around their pinkies, you know.

So Papa was rolled out onstage, with a local crew helping lift him over various cables. Those in the seated section rose to their feet at the sight. My band swears there were tears in the audience. I didn't see that. I was too busy taking in the beauty of my father's form as he so artfully and painfully struggled to slowly raise one twisted fist in the air. He milked that. When he'd accomplished the feat of nearly extending his quivering arm, the place went nuts. There was no roof to blow off the motherfucker, it was outside. No, Dean Folds blew the *sky* off the motherfucker. Our last song—God knows or even cares what it was—was massive. It was my first actual positive response of the summer tour.

As we exited the stage, my tour manager anxiously announced, "Everyone's stuff is on the bus. There's press that wants to talk to you about this and I can't let you talk to them!. Move quickly to the bus. Let's get the fuck out." And we took off.

The next day in catering, John made a beeline to me.

"Please tell me that at least that was your real father?"

I nodded yes, sinking into my chair like a scolded child.

John shook his head like a disappointed dad and went to the catering line. It seems that at forty I was still getting paid to throw childish tantrums and mitigate my anxiety onstage. Who else gets to do that?

WAY TO NORMAL

THERE'S SOMETHING ABOUT TIME THAT WE JUST DON'T UNDERSTAND. Depending upon our perceptions and moods, time can feel as if it has accelerated or slowed. Sometimes it can feel as though it stands still. I don't sit around trying to understand Einstein, but I know he sat around trying to understand time. And if *that* guy had to dedicate his entire life to time, and died uncertain about the whole thing, then what chance do the rest of us have? But time—or, rather, our sense of time—has an important place in music, and I can speak to that from my experience as a musician.

Any musician will know that our perception of tempo, music's way of keeping time, can be quite elastic. We musicians practice like hell in private with metronomes, but the moment we get excited at a show, our sense of tempo can go out the window and we're off to the races! And we usually have no idea how badly we rushed until we hear the recording later. *Ugh*. It takes a lifetime for musicians to get a handle on this. Because humans are time-dumb.

Our time-challenged nature is what music therapists take advantage of to increase the gait of rehabilitation patients, who, by the end of a session, can routinely walk at a clip not thought possible at the beginning. Using music and tempo, the therapist plays with the patient's sense of time, which fools the mind *and* the body into doing something it couldn't previously do. This method is standard practice, proven and effective. Indeed, our shitty inner clock is no match for the mysterious persuasiveness of music. And this gives us a lot of opportunity to have fun with tempo, expression, and even the content of a song.

I think that manipulation of time, musically and lyrically, is part of what makes songwriting so interesting. Because what four-minute song has ever been about exactly four minutes of someone's life? Within the structure of a simple four-minute song, you can play with what happens between the beginning and the end and warp the sense of time. A four-minute song might dwell on one special second in our life. And that one second might represent a turning point, something that implies a whole lifetime. *Whoa, dude!* I know, it may be a fairly pedestrian concept to philosophers and scientists, but it's worth considering that songwriting, like any time/performance-based art like movies, plays, or symphonies, wouldn't be possible if we didn't have such gullible inner clocks.

I read somewhere that when teenagers are asked to stand and reel off their life stories in front of an audience, they tend to go on for ages about what seems to them to have been a very long life. But when you ask someone in their forties to step up and recount their life, it's usually over in a few minutes.

The metaphoric language around time illustrates how much poetic license we're willing to take with time on a regular basis: *It took forever to get my coffee. The summer was over in a second.*

I thought it was pretty damn deep when I wrote this line from "Jackson Cannery":

When seconds pass slowly, and years go flying by

That sentiment feels a little less revelatory to me now, but it's still true. It ain't a bad line. I wrote it on a napkin while doing my "side work" waiting tables at the Dogwood Room Restaurant at UNC–G in 1988. A decade later, audiences were singing along with it in places I never dreamed I'd travel. And then a decade after that, Robert, Darren, and I found ourselves together sound-checking that same song for our reunion concert in Chapel Hill in 2008. *2008!* Boom, just like that! It had been *years* since we'd seen one another. But as soon as we hit the first note together, it felt like no time had passed at all. We broke for lunch and the present elastically snapped back into place.

While not in our time machine, playing music as we had done so many times before, it was obvious we were all changed and older. Time *had* passed after all. And it was striking that we all stepped away to check our cellphones, something that had never been part of our band back in the day. The broadcast of the Ben Folds Five reunion concert that night was for Myspace, which was king of the internet in 2008, (though its days were numbered). I remember it all even more clearly because it was September, right in the middle of the massive bank crisis, and the world was shifting. An historic week.

After our rehearsal, I downloaded the artwork proposals for my soon-to-be-released third studio album, *Way to Normal*. I was considering using my brain scans for the cover. They had been taken the night I fell offstage and suffered a concussion in Hiroshima a couple years before, the story of which starts the album. (I don't recall much of the Hiroshima concert, other than bleeding on the piano a lot and joking to the audience that I'd cut myself shaving.)

In the end I decided against the brain scan. Instead, I thought the art should reflect a sense of loneliness and feeling lost. After the reunion show, I went back to Nashville and we shot a series of photos of me wandering what was supposed to be my lonely mansion (I actually lived in a 1,600-square-foot house), pondering my sad life. The cover shows me in silk pajamas, with two butlers (played by my band, Jared Reynolds and Sam Smith) protecting me from the rain with an umbrella as I meditate at my pool. It seemed to capture the time better. At least it made me laugh, which is important to me.

From series of me wandering my imaginary sad mansion with butlers (my bandmates)

Finalizing my third divorce during *Way to Normal,* I should have taken an opportunity to rethink my life. To slow the tempo down and take a pause. But, instead, I immediately launched into a new relationship, soon to be married once again, soon to become what I now consider the worst version of myself. Of course, everyone around me could see that it was all a fast track to yet another divorce. How many times would I set the needle back to the top or count my life's repetitive song over again? I was beginning to resemble the character in my decade-old song:

I have made the same mistakes over and over again
—From "Mess," *The Unauthorized Biography of Reinhold Messner,* 1999

I think *Way to Normal* is a fine record. I can't imagine not having songs like "You Don't Know Me," "Cologne," or "Kylie From Connecticut" in my catalog. And it came in at number 13 on the Billboard album chart, my highest chart position to date. Not bad at all. But something was starting to feel wrong. Something about making *Way to Normal* seemed overly heavy and effortful. It was like straining to squeeze the last bit of toothpaste out of the tube, as Bill Bryson likes to say. But I think it's a good thing to get that last bit out. I needed to make that record, and then I needed to move on. After we mixed *Way to Normal,* it was time to finally toss the old worn-out empty toothpaste tube.

Honesty, humor, and vulnerability are all important to my songwriting. But equally as important is an element of discovery, a sense that time has passed. If the third chorus of a song hasn't time-traveled and unveiled a subtly changed perspective, or a third album hasn't evolved from the first, it's not going to be very damn convincing. In fact, it gets a little boring when a songwriter keeps messing up the same things and tries to sell essentially the same thing over and over again, honest and vulnerable as it all may be. The same goes for the human being behind the song. If he can't learn from a cheap lesson, or two or three, then what? I was starting to suspect that:

What was bad for the life might actually be bad for the music as well.

At the time, I thought that *Way to Normal* was a random title with a random album cover. The phrase "way to normal" was snatched from one of the album tracks, "Effington," which I had freestyled at a show in Normal, Illinois. I just thought it sounded good. But in retrospect I see it as representing my desire to find *my* way to "normal." I was trying to find the answers in well-lit and well-traveled corners, when what I really needed to do was muster the courage to head into the unknown. The same mistakes, lived the same way, sung the same way, weren't going to keep making good songs.

THE FAKE ALBUM

DESPITE MY ENNUI, I WAS STILL FINDING WAYS TO MAKE MUSIC THAT did make me happy. Music that was off the beaten path and interesting. Such was the case with the making of *The Fake Album,* which is something I file under "wicked awesome times." What is *The Fake Album,* you ask?

Well, dear reader, *The Fake Album* is a lesser-known joke version of *Way to Normal,* recorded and self-leaked just before *Way to Normal.* Back in the era when labels were grappling with methods to combat music piracy, I had an idea: Why not make a version of *Way to Normal* where the song titles are all the same but the music and words are completely different? Then leak that out to the internet to muddy the waters and confuse bootleggers. While on tour in Europe, we got word that our master had been leaked and would soon be available for download ahead of the release, and so this is exactly what we did.

I hit my bandmates up to write the most numbskulled lyrics they could manage, based on the original titles. Sam Smith, my drummer, turned out to be a genius at this. His spoofs on tired social and political commentary were particularly amazing. In his version of "The Frown Song" from *Way to Normal,* he lays down shit like:

A piano's all I got
And I know that ain't a lot
But music has the power
To change the future

I'd never be caught dead putting something like that on a real album, but it was perfect for confusing downloaders.

It took us a few attempts to properly leak *The Fake Album,* which is interesting. Some of the folks who regularly facilitated the leaking of music onto various sites were reluctant to leak mine, because they were concerned fans. (I have the most considerate fans, I have to say.) But we eventually got the tracks leaked. We, of course, just called it *Way to Normal* (it was only called *The Fake Album* later), and it was spread widely enough that some outlets even reviewed it as if it were the real *Way to Normal.* Sadly, upon hearing the real album, they said they actually preferred *The Fake Album.* Ouch! I recently did a *Way to Normal* tenth-anniversary interview for *Paste* magazine, and the writer only wanted to talk about *The Fake Album.*

I too have a special place in my heart for *The Fake Album,* but, then, I'm no judge. The entire thing was written, recorded, and mixed in an incredibly fun twenty-four-hour session, while *Way to Normal* was a long haul, with days spent on each song, and seemed like it took forever. Being time-dumb, maybe that's why I love *The Fake Album.*

MUSIC FOR THE MATING AGE

"YOUR DAD'S TIRED-ASS ROCK MUSIC FUCKIN' SUCKS!" AN OVERGROWN high school bully with a mustache said as he shoved my sixteen-year-old son against a cold locker.

"You got that lunch money you owe me, li'l bitch? Or has your daddy gotta go play 'Brick' at weddings to get paid first? Chump!" he sneered as his minions laughed. My son, who was left to fish his schoolbooks out of the trash, watched as the bully and his two side-kicks did a few chest bumps and headed to the bathroom for some smokes.

Sorry. This never happened. Obviously even my imagined school-bully scene is dated. Chest bump? I'll bet nobody even does that anymore.

It's a legitimate worry for an aging rocker that your music will become so out of date and toxically uncool, it will get your kids beaten up at school. But, hey, it's your job. I used to see all those old guys with stringy long hair, pouring their fat asses into leather pants year after year, and think to myself, *That'll never be me! That'll never be me!* But it's really understandable. How fair is it that, like in dance or sports, a rock-and-roll artist can expect to have to retire in his or her mid-thirties? That's just the way it is. But there's another world out there for them, if they're so lucky. They can become a Heritage Artist™ and keep reliving the magic, make the house payments, and send their kids to private schools with a security guard. This was the thought that began to wake me in a cold sweat each night! (Not really, I just wanted to make the point.)

It's important to remember that after an artist has made a few records, the entire music business and its audience must decide whether there's really any space on the shelf for this artist anymore. Any new record you release after your first few albums can be used as evidence that it's time for you to go. It's not evil, or personal. It's that there's so much new music and so little time and space. We all have to make room in our lives for new artists and new ideas. But an artist like me, in his second decade of making records, better not get stuck in any ruts.

As satisfying and safe as it can feel to have mastered a craft, it also can be a sign that it's time to learn a new trick. It's the known that the artist should fear, not the unknown. All that terrain that's been well illuminated should scare the piss out of you artistically. Because the known is where boredom takes root. Staying in the well-lit areas is what gets you stuck. I felt a strong urge to lurch into the dark and leave pop music behind, but of course we all resist change, we all want to keep our job.

So what about the middle-aged making pop music? Sure, it's allowed. But let's be honest about what pop, or *pop*ular, music is. It's music for the mating age. It's a soundtrack for that yearning, that youthful anger, those ideals and inside jokes of the teenagers and young adults as they experience the rough ride together. It fills an important need. It helps get us through to adulthood. Pop music can be a life jacket, a sexy security blanket, a hipster Hallmark card. And it communicates very real things. It also requires serious craft and is a competitive business, worthy of great respect. Pop music saved my ass as a kid, paid the bills in my earlier career. And I *love* to make fun of it.

Good pop music, truly of its moment, should throw older adults off its scent. It should clear the room of boring adults and give the kids some space. If you're post–mating age, you might enjoy new pop music to a degree, but it's not *really* for you. Post-mating-age adults have a whole other heap of problems, the likes of which the sickest beat and saddest rhyme are woefully unequipped to solve. You don't need an earful of sexy when navigating your aging parents into an old folks' home or when you're worried your kids might be trying drugs at their delinquent friend's house. There is music that speaks to grown-ass adults, but it probably ain't mating beats. And the grown-ass adults, when *they're* in heat, usually reach for music of their own era, the stuff they consumed back when they were mating age. They spring for high ticket prices for a magical night with their favorite Heritage Artist™.

I, for one, don't feel the need to try and relate to younger music that's not for me anymore. I appreciate it, but I don't try to like it or relate to it. Why should I? I view pop music the way I do a children's television show, with its cartoons and bright colors—it's for kids. I'm no more riveted by a grumpy puppet who lives in a garbage can than I am by a horny auto-tuned journal entry edited over a lonesome computer loop. I don't hang around playgrounds, so why, at my age, should I be wandering around Burning Man shirtless, tripping on ecstasy? Or speaking in vocal fry like middle-aged men and women I overhear every day in the coffee shop down the block?

If I'm being really honest? Really feeling my age and unafraid to admit it? Here we go: I'm actually repulsed by overly computerized music, which dominates pop music now. It makes me feel ill. Canned bass drum that dry-humps my eardrums four-on-the-floor in the back seat of an Uber while an overly gymnastic auto-tuned vocal holds me down . . . It just isn't my cup of tea. There's something sad about a singer pouring his heart out over a quantized machine. That heartless machine would keep playing out for days in an empty room, long after the singer keeled over. *Hey, kid! That loop doesn't love you!* I want to tell the singer. I'm reminded of those horse insemination machines where the poor stud is humping away into a horsey robot. It's just sad. Now, that's some old-man shit I just laid down, but it's about being honest, because I know that I cannot grow artistically if I am beholden to the opinions of an industry I've outgrown. If I require the approval of children.

I have equal respect for and interest in Cardi B and Teletubbies, which is to say I have *incredible* respect for both, because they're both brilliant, and little interest in either, because I've aged out of that shit. I too made my mark in the business of mating music of a now-bygone era but I wasn't nearly as good at it as the two examples I just mentioned. Still, my music was peddled by purveyors of fine procreation hullabaloo, and I happily signed on the dotted line. It was a pretty good run.

Back when we started, there were sometimes a few middle-aged people in attendance for the early Ben Folds Five shows. They came hoping to see some younger musicians doing "real music," but they often walked away disappointed. They came for those seventies' chords and mannerisms that warmed their hearts, only to find we used them all wrong. I recall one lone fortysomething man who pulled me aside after some gig in the early days and told me, "I saw Elton back in 1971, and the big difference was that everything wasn't some kind of inside joke to him. It was real music. He *meant* it. When he stood on the piano it was a celebration, it was triumphant. You do it and it has to be so ironic and clever. You boys need to tighten up. What was all that distortion? I had high hopes before tonight." I told him I was sorry he didn't enjoy it. But, honestly, mission accomplished. We threw him off the scent. It's what kids do. Ben Folds Five happily

made glaring mistakes, approaching great craft with the attitude of the drunkest two-chord punk band. We sounded our mutant mating call. No different from any generation before.

So as I approached Heritage Artist™ age, I had to decide: Did I want to adopt the affectations of the new generation in hopes of remaining relevant, begging for attention with each new release? Or did I want to get out of that business, head to Vegas, and just keep reliving my old shit? Well, somehow neither of those binary options seemed very attractive. So, then what? What to do with the Script™? The answer was in the dark somewhere, where it always is. After all, the dark is where we mated for the first time.

AFTER THE FLOOD

ON APRIL 30, 2010, I HAD A ONE-OFF GIG WITH WEEZER AT THE UNIVER-sity of Maryland, which I did solo at the piano in a football stadium. May 1 had been randomly chosen for an early mutual birthday party for the twins and their stepsister, all of whose real birthdays were later in July, when the twins would be with their mother. Somehow, this randomly chosen substitute birthday had become immovable—quite the production with RSVPs, blow-up waterslides, and extra parking. The only way I could do the afternoon Weezer gig and be back in time for the party was to book a private jet.

As large bouncy castles were being delivered and inflated back in Nashville, I was finishing my set in Maryland. Hopping into the car, which was idling just next to the stage, I could hear the opening riff of "Hash Pipe" and I felt my phone vibrating in my pocket. It was my old friend Millard, who told me a close mutual friend of ours had just died—suicide. I don't remember the fancy plane trip at all.

I arrived home in Franklin, Tennessee, to a backyard full of colorful inflatable structures, a handful of early arriving children, and a team of adults talking weather and pointing at some threatening skies. I wasn't sure how I was going to bear a couple hours of small talk with parents or being fun for the kids at that very moment. The news had stricken me near mute. But the skies spoke instead, and the party was over in minutes. A "hundred-year flood," as it was called, sank much of the neighborhood under water by nightfall and continued all the next day. Our dearly departed friend was always quite the performer, with a penchant for the dramatic. And his storm did not disappoint. It dumped a year's worth of rain in a weekend. Levees broke, fields became lakes, and sirens blared through the night. That was his style.

The next morning, people were paddling around the streets in boats, roofs were poking out of new lakes, but there was no national coverage yet. I assumed there would at least be some information online about this flood, but I saw nearly nothing, aside from a few local forums posting information and pictures. But these photographs that were posted just didn't tell the story, so I rolled my pants up and waded into the mess to take some photos to post online. I used my old Nokia phone instead of my fancy vintage cameras—that's all that was needed to tell this story. I accompanied my images with warnings like "Folks! There's poo in this water!" For a few hours they were some of the only decent pictures that could be seen of this flood, so they were getting tens of thousands of views a minute. *National Geographic* got wind of my posts and created a quick online story using my photos. By the next day, the professional reporters and photographers kicked in and we had a better view of the situation. I was invited a few months later to *National Geographic* to give a talk about my photography.

When there's a disaster, big or small, we all have to pick up a shovel and chip in. It's best to reach for the biggest one you have at

Franklin, TN, after the 2010 flood. Photos taken with old Nokia phone, used for National Geographic *piece online.*

your disposal. In my case, I decided to raise money for Nashville's beautiful symphony hall, the Schermerhorn, which was under water and had sustained incredible damage and lost many instruments. Conductor Francisco Noya was kind enough to fly from Providence, Rhode Island, on his own dime to conduct an orchestra fundraiser we put together. It was the first event of this kind I had ever initiated and we raised nearly a quarter of a million dollars, which was a small—very small—contribution. But it was the biggest shovel I had in the shed. I soon accepted a seat on the board at the Nashville Symphony Orchestra, where I served on the education committee.

My main recording/touring piano was destroyed in the flooding, so I decided to strip all eighty-eight keys off the ruined piano, autograph them, and sell them for eighty-eight dollars apiece to raise money for musical instruments in local schools. Nashville Symphony Orchestra had a program that located broken instruments and hired volunteers to repair them, so that is where the money went. We called the program "Keys to Music City." All eighty-eight keys sold in a few days and so Steinway began to chip in piano keys too, and we kept going. We found other artists to do some signing and at the end of the program we had raised eighty thousand dollars for countless instruments, which were distributed to kids who would otherwise never have had access to them.

This was quite a development for me. It was a long time coming. I was emotionally charged by the death of my friend and the incredible perspective that such a tragedy can give. I think I felt the need to start turning the negatives into positives rather than trying to outrun it all. I was ready to face the music, *and* the life.

THE EVER-POPULAR VH1 *BEHIND THE MUSIC* ARTIST-HITS-BOTTOM ACT

I KNEW I HAD TO SEE SOMEONE. IT WAS BECOMING OBVIOUS THAT I needed help.

My first session with Dr. McLeod was the most painful, but I learned a lot. It required me to open up. Immediately. And to trust. That's the hard part.

In a glance, Dr. McLeod was able to identify the contours of my anxiety, like an archaeologist or a psychic might. How I'd neglected myself, even down to my diet and my sleep. He laid it all out for me. And I didn't have to say a word. It's rare that I'm required to just shut up and listen, but in this kind of session you have no choice.

"Open widey!" he said cheerfully as he put gloves and mask on.

Dr. McLeod is, of course, my dentist. A poetic and wise one. Stuffing my mouth full of gauze and medieval equipment, he began his examination. It all seemed pretty routine for a dental appointment until he said, "Everyone has a black box, Ben."

I nodded with a light grunt and a slight shift of an eyebrow.

"It's where we lock up our secrets. The little black box. It's ours and ours alone, to the grave. Whatever is in yours, Ben, it's okay."

He reached for a pointy metal thing. "My good man, you've been quite the grinder and gnasher, haven't you? Your diet, the pattern of this wear right here, no sleep, lots of fretting . . . Look at this, Sandy." His eyes showed some concern as he peered over his mask. Sandy shook her head and lined up some more tools for what was going to be a long night. I hadn't been to the dentist in a decade and I was paying the price. I had a series of teeth I needed to lose, replace, crown, and cap, due to an old, failed root canal. It had all exploded in incredible pain and fever as I'd landed from a Japanese concert tour. My tooth emergency ended up being a two-year process all in all.

My dental situation was just one of the many signs of how I'd neglected myself over the years. I'd also been denying the incredible pain my left hand was in—I didn't want to know, and I didn't want to stop touring for a moment. But, yes, the cartilage in my left thumb turned out to be trashed from beating the crap out of pianos, and al-

My dentist, Dr. McLeod

though I can play piano just fine (for now), there are days when getting my hand into my pocket or turning a key is a nearly insurmountable challenge. In fact, I had a laundry list of injuries that suddenly made themselves known—mostly occupational from my style of piano-playing. All ignored as they developed. It turns out pianos hit back.

Hitting bottom takes all forms. It doesn't have to be a VH1 *Behind the Music* episode—you know that rockumentary TV series from the nineties, which was basically short documentaries of famous musical artists? Those were great! Each major musical artist's story would inevitably climax at that moment when the artist seemed to be on top of the world . . . and then . . . *addiction, debt, depression.* *Cue dramatic music and bad video effects.* It was always something. Without exception. But no matter how many times it's told, that story never gets old.

My hitting bottom didn't involve sleeping in my own piss in an alley (I don't *think*), or being taken away in handcuffs from a casino, or shooting holes in my girl's tires in my underwear while the neighbors called the cops. Nothing like that. That's not the way it works for most of us. But most everyone will hit bottom in some way—subtly or loudly, many times or just once—and that's why the sensational celebrity version of the story is always of interest. Hitting bottom is to acknowledge that the next lesson will not be cheap.

You don't actually need to have a demon you've run from your whole life to hit bottom. Demons can grow from a single cell in the petri dish of your soul while you're neglecting yourself for years on end. Demons can be of our own creation. Unforced-error demons. There's nothing romantic about any of that! It won't sell a rockumentary most of the time, but it's your life and you have to straighten it out. Eventually, as you address one issue you discover another, because everything is connected. Life. Love. Finances. Music. Even teeth.

· · ·

In 2010, my life was hitting bottom and I decided to finally say *uncle!* and submit myself to all the stuff that I'd been running from. I was going through my fourth divorce, the result of a personally devastating rebound that could've been avoided. If I didn't rethink it all, I was in danger of losing the respect of my family and friends, my health, and my mind, along with half of my earnings (again). I didn't know yet what drove this pattern of marriage and divorce, or my workaholism, the sleeplessness, or the dreaded gnawing anxiety I felt each morning before facing the day. But I knew it had real consequences. I had a spiritual toothache. And if my soul and artistry suffered too much more decay, not even Dr. McLeod would be able to help me. And I knew I had to turn the oil barge of patterns around and paddle ferociously to avert disaster.

I moved to Los Angeles in 2011 after the divorce was filed. I still had my recording studio and my place in Nashville, but the twins, who were now twelve, had been moved to L.A., and so that's where my heart would have to be. I went straight there, to space and silence, alone and shaking like a leaf. Sounds like a small deal, but I hadn't stopped moving in my adult life, save for the time I had pneumonia. I remember that first painfully quiet night in my new apartment in Santa Monica, sad and demoralized, sitting on some cardboard boxes, when, suddenly, I felt an unexpected tiny dash of optimism. Or maybe it was relief. I jotted this down in my new living room full of unpacked housewares and Saran-wrapped furniture. The opening lines to the song "So There":

> *A mattress and a stereo, just like I started*
> *And a note composed with thumbs and phone on unpacked boxes*

Los Angeles is the place to be for self-help, self-awareness, and self-everything, except maybe self-service. I had to rethink my old-fashioned stance on therapy, and all kinds of other show-biz whiny-ass self-discovery shit, because I had never been a big believer in turning a flashlight and microscope on myself. But there's a time and place for everything, and I had come to the right place at the right time. I needed to ignore all self-ridicule. I actually needed a hand. And asking for help can be scary for someone who has never let anyone near the black box.

If you detect a little Born Again™ vibe in all of this, then yeah, fine. It's an arduous process, rebooting your mind and soul. I did all the corny things you'd imagine you'd do upon moving to L.A.—old-fashioned jogging, yoga, Pilates, and, my favorite, Gyrotonic (look that up if you're bored). I had just learned Transcendental Meditation back in Nashville, prior to my decision to move to L.A., which I now consider a turning point. Meditation gave my mind space and just enough openness for some perspective—a little crack in the soul through which to drive some reason.

My neurologist friends, many of whom I've made through my interest in music therapy, tell me that new thinking requires new material pathways to be formed in your brain. You have to work to dig these new neuro highways every day, despite the old ruts and the grip that your old habits have on you. Old-fashioned plasticity. It's one day at a time. The physical and mental can't be separated any more than the music and the life. My Folds' Hack Method™ for rehabilitating myself was a simple matter of taking lessons from what had always worked in my artistry. After years of taking from my life to make songs, it was time to do the reverse and let what I'd learned from songwriting now inform my life.

I feel another play coming on. Let's imagine a surreal classroom lit magically with some dry ice for effect. Younger iterations of myself seated, dressed in variations of Angus Young from AC/DC, with older me the teacher in front—pacing the room full-thespian *Dead Poets Society* style. Here we go.

What Music Can Teach Life: A Damn Short Play

BEARDED NOW ME: "Okay, kids, settle down. Little Ben, seated up front in the muddy shoes, what did you learn after school waiting around construction sites?"

CHILD ME: "I learned the value of taking time. Taking the time to discover what it is *I* want to create, and not letting what's around me lead too much!"

BEARDED NOW ME: "Very good, very good. Okay! Pubescent Ben. Yes, you back there with all the zits. What have you got for me?"

TEENAGE ME: "As a musician you can only get so far without outside help, like a teacher or a mentor? Sir!"

BEARDED NOW ME: "That's exactly right. No man is an island. All right, you in the back, please wake up! Yes, you. Silly young man in the Bavarian getup, can you tell us something you've learned?"

YOUNG ADULT ME: "Always be present, because your actions affect others, and being on autopilot is being an existential chicken!"

[A few in the class chuckle. They think the word "chicken" is funny.]

BEARDED NOW ME: "Now, settle! Okay, my class of various-aged young Bens, there is one concept above all that has made your songs better. That bedrock we spoke about? What is that?"

ROOM FULL OF ME: "*SELF-HONESTY, SIR!*"

BEARDED NOW ME: "Right!" *[The classroom door opens slowly, interrupting the lesson.]* "Oh, wait, what do we have here? Sir, you're very late today!"

2008 ME: *[In suit and tie, sheepishly puts away cellphone and takes seat.]* "Sorry, sir. Meeting with my lawyer went late."

BEARDED NOW ME: "We're all telling what we learned. What's yours?"

2008 ME: "Uh . . . discovery?"

BEARDED NOW ME: "Well played! All the honesty in the world is great, but a life, like a song, needs to have a sense of *discovery*! People, can you see how all of these musical lessons, if they'd just sink in a little, might help you in your life, right? . . . All right, all you little shits, think about that as you go out into the world for the next forty years or so and fuck up a lot. Then write me a book about it. On my desk, 2019! Class dismissed—except you, 2008! We need to speak after class!"

All of those musically philosophical tidbits I worked so hard to learn for my musicianship actually did seem to apply to my life. Artistically, I knew not to always head for comfort. Maybe in other facets of my life I should try lurching toward things that made me terribly uncomfortable, that broke my habits and patterns? If it was a food I never wanted before—what the hell, I'd make myself try it. I'd never been social—ugh—so I'd do that too. I did stuff I wasn't coordinated at, even if it was just Pilates. I would say things aloud in therapy that were embarrassing and true, things I'd never said before. And I consciously attached those thoughts and feelings to all the physical therapy that felt equally awkward. Like an Alexander Technique session, for instance. Or basketball and volleyball. As I experienced how foreign and awkward an activity or physical movement could be, rather than fight it or avoid going into a weird physical position I would relax into it and laugh at myself. Who cares? It's like letting the water run brown and writing a few shitty verses.

I just let it all go. I embraced the cringe. I decided to associate new awkward thoughts with new awkward physical activities. Let's say I was afraid of telling friends "I love you." I'd chunk that with a yoga pose that I was equally self-conscious about—call it the "I love ya, man" pose. The pose didn't kill me, so neither would expressing the thought to which it was now connected.

As much as anything, I made myself slow down and experience some silence.

I also wrote for hours a day. About everything. It was a lot of god-awful embarrassing journaling. The reunion record I made in 2013 with Ben Folds Five, *The Sound of the Life of the Mind,* is basically the distilling of these thoughts into music with rhyme. "On Being Frank" is about having spent my life always needing to have a partner and suddenly deciding to take the steps to learn what it is I really want for myself, so that I can be a solid half of a partnership. The character in that song is an imaginary version of Frank Sinatra's tour manager, suffering from an identity crisis after Frank's death. The funny thing is that I ended up sitting next to this very man in real life in Las Vegas. I played him the song and he said it had a nice melody but he didn't think it sounded like him. Of course not; it was about me.

Home, for me, was always someone else, you know
And shadows always fall when the sun goes down

"Away When You Were Here" was about the death of my father—but not really, because he's still alive. It's another song on this album where I'm working out the cold harsh truth that there is only me, my decisions, and my own direction. No one else's stamp of approval can make things okay. That's up to us. Many lines came straight from my diary:

This morning I wake to be older than you were
Fresh white snow for miles—every footstep will be mine

The process of tending to myself, after years of refusal, was unbelievably time-consuming. Every day I woke up wanting to just abandon all of it and get back to work. *Avoid!* But I muscled through with a routine that started the minute I opened my eyes. The very carving out of time to do these things for myself was, for me, radical. And maybe that was all I needed to do. Just make the time. Maybe I could have done all of this stuff earlier along the way, in small doses, and avoided the crash I experienced, who knows? But here I am.

• • •

While taking the uncomfortable route and facing the scary stuff was foreign to me in my personal life, it was very familiar to my artistic self. The willingness to be brutally self-honest and to go somewhere unlit and awkward is the way I'd always written songs. That's not impulsiveness, as it turns out. That's courage. My bad impersonation of courage in my personal life was to jump off the deep end, belly flopping over and over again.

I dived into crazy shit regularly, not to discover something new, but to fill silence. The deep-end jumping became routine, and so did the punishment: "Thank you, sir, may I have another? Thank you, sir, may I have another?" That's not courage, *that's* running in a loop, like a scared child. And with each loop, the drama becomes less interesting. Loss of interest is, of course, a death blow to creativity.

So, I consider these years as ones of serious personal rehabilitation. I was still working and touring, but I took longer, and more frequent, breaks to stay healthy. And of course, like at any rehab, I was eventually discharged and began my transition back into the real world, knowing full well that I would need to keep an eye on my life and my choices every single day. I might relapse from time to time, but that was okay. As I got stronger personally, I had broader shoulders to rest my art upon. Soon, my artistic appetite began to return— and along with it, my interest. In fact, I became insatiably interested.

FOLLOWING INTEREST

I USED TO TELL PEOPLE THAT I FOLLOWED MY *INSTINCT* WHEN MAKING artistic and career decisions. But these days I am more likely to say that I follow my *interest*. The fine songwriter Dan Wilson once told me he thought interest is what makes the world go 'round, second only to the will to survive. It might seem like semantics, but these language cues make a difference to me. I'm compelled to turn corners and pages out of interest, not because of instinct.

Whenever I've announced, "I'm going with my *instincts* on this one," I've felt like I was throwing down a challenge against all advice, facts, or common sense.

The pundits said it couldn't be done, but Folds proved them all wrong! He has instinct!

That places too much pressure on my instinct. It's too results-oriented to feel artistic. I believe an artistic decision should be allowed to feel innocent, unburdened, and uncorrupted by considerations of outcome. Sure, I don't deny instinct itself exists, or that it drives many of our decisions. But I'd rather leave mine to do its subconscious work in the shadows beneath the slats of my ego. Not on display, with everyone placing bets on it.

I used to feel guilty when I strayed from the Script™. Mine, of course, has always been *tour-record-tour-record*. Yours may be *work-sleep-work-sleep, speak-travel-write-speak-travel-write,* or even *left-right-left-right*. Whatever your personal Script™, others become accustomed to, and dependent on, your following it. Veering off to follow interests can raise great concern. For instance, anyone whose livelihood might depend on my success might not want to see me taking too many unlucrative detours. Too many of those and lights out.

But I no longer feel guilt for following what glows, for going off-book. It turns out that it's actually my responsibility to identify and follow my interests. Being interested is why I still have a gig at all. Following my interests has resulted in rewarding but unpredictable gigs like *The Sing-Off,* an NBC prime-time singing show for a cappella groups. That came about because I was dillydallying around, recording university a cappella groups on their campuses, when I "should have been" touring or recording. Driving around with an engineer and mics and setting them up in cafeterias and dorm rooms didn't seem like a good way to spend my time, to some people I worked with. At least at the time. But my business partners chilled after I signed solid contracts with a major network TV show. Who'd have thunk? Not I. I was just interested in capturing live college singing, but, sure, I'll gladly take the opportunity and paycheck.

One standout detour of interest was taking a year to compose a concerto for piano and orchestra. I took a small commission and made the time because it was interesting. I agreed to a premiere performance of it with the NSO and the Nashville Ballet, which commissioned the piece. I did not expect that night to turn into six nights, and I've never otherwise sold eleven thousand tickets to premiere a new song or album. It turns out someone else was interested.

My manager these days, Mike, isn't even a music manager. I just found him interesting, so we joined forces eight years ago. He's not terribly concerned with the Script™. He could see how it was choking off my creativity. Mike's from a politics background, so he's quite happy to make time for me to travel to Washington, D.C., with Americans for the Arts to go to bat for arts funding, or to attend both the Republican and Democratic National Conventions for the same purpose. He books me on music-therapy panels or looks into letting scientists put me into a brain scanner while I improvise songs. These aren't terribly lucrative endeavors. But they seem to keep leading to better artistic places and better gigs. Like my role as Artistic Advisor to the National Symphony Orchestra. That isn't the sort of thing that normal music-biz managers would encourage. (To all those out there who think people who take government work are rolling in it: Uh. No.) It's not where the Script™ would have taken me. But surrounding myself with the people I find interesting, and who share the same interests, keeps my inner robot at bay.

When it comes to my method of working, and how I spend my time, I'll admit that I'm not terribly disciplined. But I *am* a hard worker and these are two different things. I'm fueled by obsession and hyperfocus more than by routine. The obvious downside to being undisciplined and obsessive is the very real risk that some things will go pear-shaped. I've taken some bad detours, as you've seen. For those like myself, it's often hard to know when perceived instinct is actually just some corrupted impulse. Like the impulse egging me on to have another tequila. Hey, *that's* not instinct! Or the one telling me to forgo sleep to spend another four hours robotically scrolling through eBay for a certain RCA speaker made in 1958. But the upside of my lack of discipline is that I've given myself a hall pass to roam. Over fences, through open doors, creatively.

I still see myself as a class tourist, equally uneasy and at home in different neighborhoods. There is no one class to be, no one club to join, no one way to create, no universal behavior of an artist, and there's no such thing as cool. Any songwriter I've ever admired was probably kicked out of the Serious Songwriters' Club™ long ago, if such a thing exists. I hope I've been kicked out too. I'll settle for writing good songs.

Throughout my life, each time I've spotted something inspiring, a beautiful flicker, an idea, or a feeling I wanted to capture, there were always bullying voices—inside, and out—suggesting it was off-limits:

You can't sing if you're a real man.

You can't move middle-class living room furniture into a rock dive.

You can't put a serious abortion song next to an irreverent joke song.

You can't use more than three chords, because Dylan and Cobain didn't.

The word "microscope" in a ballad doesn't work.

Don't put too many names in songs.

Major chords are happy, and of course happiness is vapid—not cool, so stick with minor.

But why shouldn't I be allowed to sing a nasty cussing song one day, compose a piano concerto the next, and finish the week doing a ridiculous cameo as myself as a raving drunk on *You're the Worst*—all while writing a political song for the *Washington Post*? Do you know what Charles Ives, one of the great celebrated American composers of the twentieth century, did in his spare time? He overhauled the insurance industry and laid the foundation for the modern practice of estate planning. Is that *cool*? Or is that *whack*? It's cool in retrospect, but what would the *Pitchfork* of 1918 have thought? I doubt there's much indie-cred for a songwriter who works at State Farm. But I say, follow your interests and let your art speak for itself. Business is based on creativity too.

Beware of little things that can erode our creativity as we grow up. One after another. One at a time, small choices eliminated incrementally. Flickers slowly dimmed. It never ends. You have to tune those voices out because your interests, those creative flickers, are truly miraculous. They are what drive us to keep seeing what's around the next corner. Chase 'em. Life is short. After you've put food on the table, if you're so lucky, then what? You follow your interests, that's what.

I believe deep in my bones that every person is inherently creative. But I also think our creativity has to be recognized, encouraged, cultivated, protected, and sometimes even put on life support. It can't live without oxygen. But it comes back, if you want it to, like your appetite after an illness. Like the lightning bugs when darkness falls again.

So then. What flickers do *you* see? What beauty glows for you that might have gone unnoticed by others?

Remain just innocent enough to keep dreaming. There's always some motherfucker who would like to fact-check your dreams and convince you there are no flickers, only the Script™, whatever that might be for you. Too often that fact-checking motherfucker is *you*. It's your own voice, whispering to yourself and to others that you're crazy for seeing glowing insects.

And maybe you are. Until you bottle and share them.

Okay. That's it. Fuck it, I'm done.

THE END.

2017 Paper Airplanes Request tour

ACKNOWLEDGMENTS

Robert and Darren; Louis; Gracie; Eli; Scotty; Dean and Peggy; Chuck, Tate and Carr; Philippa; Richard and Maria; Eric and Aaron; Jimmy; Manager Mike, Mary Nell and MaryKathryn; Leo and Gwen; Michael and Jenny; Alan and Annette; Aunt Ro; Sam, Ryan, Chad C, Andrew and Jared; Joe, Leslie, Gena and Sharon; yMusic, Bob and Kelly; M.M. Pudding Jeff; Practical Nick and Amanda; Regina and Jack; Amanda F.P. and Neil; Sara B, Josh the Larynx; British Matt; Jack and Nataly; Jason and Olivia; Neurologicals Dan and Heather; Bill and Liz; Divine Neil; Adelaidian Scott, Kerri, Jett and Scott; DeAnn and ELS; Joachim and Lisa; Paul V and Jason; Piano Boy Bill; Elton and David; Al and Suzanne; Millard; the late Masterful Paul B; Ben G and the late Polly A; Jonathan, Jeffrey, Jessica and Paradigm; Rob C and Laura at Coda; Victor, Denise at Citrin Cooperman; Marsha and Marlene for putting me on stages for years; (Barely) Legal Ken; P.R. Kenny; Travelin' Ruth and Late Checkout Lisa; Deborah, Gary, Nigel, Justin, and the NSO and Kennedy Center; Literary Laura; and of course Sara, Elana, and Ballantine. Needless to say, there are many more who made, and make, a difference. So love and thanks to the important names between the cracks.

ACKNOWLEDGMENTS

Robert and Darren; Louis; Gracie; Eli; Scotty; Dean and Peggy; Chuck, Tate and Carr; Philippa; Richard and Maria; Eric and Aaron; Jimmy; Manager Mike, Mary Nell and MaryKathryn; Leo and Gwen; Michael and Jenny; Alan and Annette; Aunt Ro; Sam, Ryan, Chad C, Andrew and Jared; Joe, Leslie, Gena and Sharon; yMusic, Bob and Kelly; M.M. Pudding Jeff; Practical Nick and Amanda; Regina and Jack; Amanda F.P. and Neil; Sara B, Josh the Larynx; British Matt; Jack and Nataly; Jason and Olivia; Neurologicals Dan and Heather; Bill and Liz; Divine Neil; Adelaidian Scott, Kerri, Jett and Scott; DeAnn and ELS; Joachim and Lisa; Paul V and Jason; Piano Boy Bill; Elton and David; Al and Suzanne; Millard; the late Masterful Paul B; Ben G and the late Polly A; Jonathan, Jeffrey, Jessica and Paradigm; Rob C and Laura at Coda; Victor, Denise at Citrin Cooperman; Marsha and Marlene for putting me on stages for years; (Barely) Legal Ken; P.R. Kenny; Travelin' Ruth and Late Checkout Lisa; Deborah, Gary, Nigel, Justin, and the NSO and Kennedy Center; Literary Laura; and of course Sara, Elana, and Ballantine. Needless to say, there are many more who made, and make, a difference. So love and thanks to the important names between the cracks.

ABOUT THE AUTHOR

BEN FOLDS is an American musician who has created an enormous body of genre-bending music that includes pop albums with Ben Folds Five, multiple solo albums, and collaborative records with artists ranging from Sara Bareilles to Regina Spektor to William Shatner. His last album, which included his "Concerto for Piano and Orchestra," was number one on both the *Billboard* classical and classical crossover charts. Folds, who also composes for film and TV, was a judge for five seasons on NBC's acclaimed a cappella show *The Sing-Off.* In 2017, he was named the first ever artistic advisor to the National Symphony Orchestra at the Kennedy Center. An avid photographer, Folds is a member of the prestigious Sony Artisans of Imagery, has worked as a guest photo editor for *National Geographic,* and was featured in a documentary by the Kennedy Center for his photographic works. An outspoken champion for arts funding in our schools and communities, Folds serves on the Artists Committee of Americans for the Arts and on the Board of its Arts Action Fund. He also serves on the Board of the new Planet Word museum in Washington, D.C. *A Dream About Lightning Bugs* is his first book.

benfolds.com
patreon.com/benfolds
Facebook.com/BenFolds
Twitter: @benfolds
Instagram: @murkanpianist

ABOUT THE TYPE

This book was set in Fairfield, the first typeface from the hand of the distinguished American artist and engraver Rudolph Ruzicka (1883–1978). Ruzicka was born in Bohemia (in the present-day Czech Republic) and came to America in 1894. He set up his own shop, devoted to wood engraving and printing, in New York in 1913 after a varied career working as a wood engraver, in photoengraving and banknote printing plants, and as an art director and freelance artist. He designed and illustrated many books, and was the creator of a considerable list of individual prints—wood engravings, line engravings on copper, and aquatints.